D0202793

The Capture of Constantinople

THE MIDDLE AGES SERIES

Ruth Mazo Karras, General Editor
Edward Peters, Founding Editor

A complete list of books in the series is available from the publisher.

The Capture of Constantinople

The *Hystoria Constantinopolitana* of Gunther of Pairis

Edited and translated by
ALFRED J. ANDREA

PENN

University of Pennsylvania Press

Philadelphia

Printed in the United States of America on acid-free paper

10 9 8 7 6 5 4 3 2 1

Published by
University of Pennsylvania Press
Philadelphia, Pennsylvania 19104-6097

Library of Congress Cataloging-in-Publication Data

Gunther, von Pairis, ca. 1150–ca. 1210.
[Historia Constantinopolitana. English]
The capture of Constantinople : the Hystoria Constantinopolitana of Gunther of Pairis / edited and translated by Alfred J. Andrea.
p. cm. — (Middle Ages series)
Includes bibliographical references and index.
ISBN 0-8122-3356-5 (alk. paper)
1. Instanbul (Turkey)—History—Siege, 1203–1204. 2. Civilization, Medieval—8th century. 3. Byzantine Empire—History. I. Andrea, Alfred J., 1941– . II. Title. III. Series.
PA8330.G85H97 1997
949.61′8013—dc21 96-45687
CIP

This book is dedicated, with love, to my parents:
Alfred and Athena Filios Andrea.

Contents

Preface

The publication of this translation and study marks the end of a project begun well over a decade ago. I undertook this work with the naïve assumption that six to twelve months would suffice to prepare a suitable translation and a few appropriate words of commentary upon what then seemed to me to be a minor source for the Fourth Crusade. Happily, I was wrong. The complexity and sophistication of Gunther of Pairis's *Hystoria Constantinopolitana* have provided years of fascination and delight.

In the course of these labors I have benefited from the support of many institutions and the wise counsel of many friends. To the Alexander von Humboldt Stiftung of Bad Godesburg, Germany I owe the favor of an extended period of residence in Munich which enabled me to examine at leisure two extant manuscripts of the *Hystoria Constantinopolitana*. The American Philosophical Society awarded a grant-in-aid, enabling me to return to Europe to complete this archival research. The University of Vermont has given several stipends which helped me to continue research. The university also granted a year of sabbatical leave for the completion of the project. A generous grant from the Translations Program of the National Endowment for the Humanities made it possible for me to accept that leave by providing funds to supplement my sabbatical salary and also to assist in various stages of research and typescript preparation. The staffs of the manuscript divisions of the Universitätsbibliothek and the Bayerische Staatsbibliothek, both of Munich, Germany, and of the Bibliothèque de la Ville, Colmar, France, have helped make my work in their respective archives enjoyable as well as productive.

My colleagues, in both the Department of History and the European Studies Program of the University of Vermont, have been similarly supportive, even when I must have stretched their patience with my incessant lectures, papers, and seminars on Gunther. Their tolerant good humor and collegial encouragement have not gone unnoticed or unappreciated. Professors Z. Philip Ambrose and Pieter Wessling deserve special recognition for their kindness in discussing with me matters relating to their respective fields of expertise. Without the competent assistance of the interlibrary loan staffs of both the University of Vermont and the University of Puget Sound, I could never have completed this research. Professors Michael Curley of the University of Puget Sound and Francis R. Swietek of the University of Dallas, who read and commented upon early versions of this translation, deserve special thanks for their many kind suggestions and for having rescued me from several embarrassing errors. The late Professor Donald E. Queller of the University of Illinois at Urbana-Champaign, a dear friend and valued colleague, consistently showed generous support of my work, even though he and I amiably disagreed on some basic issues of interpretation. My friend Roswitha Dunlap helped guide me through the often convoluted passages of some especially opaque academic German prose. Virginia de Fede-Cove and Florence Phillippi ably typed early drafts of portions of this book, and Carolyn Perry, with her usual efficiency and sense of order, prepared a complete typescript, often working from nearly illegible manuscripts. After Francis Swietek made a number of important suggestions for the improvement of that draft, the staff of Second Foundation, Inc. of South Burlington, Vermont (now Ventech of Louisville, Kentucky) converted the typescript to computer files free of charge. This generous gift enabled me to revise the book substantially with a minimum of labor. Bridget M. Butler, Nancy Effron, and Amory Garmey patiently printed out numerous drafts of this book once I had learned the heady power of word processing.

I must not overlook the support given by my family. Without the many sacrifices and countless instances of support, both great and small, of my wife, Juanita, and son and daughter, Peter

Damian and Kristina Ladas, I would not have had the time and freedom to complete this task.

Acknowledgment of all these debts in no way relieves me of the obligation to repay friends, colleagues, and family with a measure of the kindness and generous aid that they have given me, neither does it lift from my shoulders the sole responsibility for all that has been printed on the pages that follow.

A.J.A.
Burlington, Vermont
The feast of St. Martin, 1995

Abbreviations

C	Untitled. MS 248 (formerly 434), fols. 33v, col. 1–47v, col. 1 (formerly 35v–49v). Colmar: Bibliothèque de la Ville.
DC	*Devastatio Constantinopolitana*.
FC^{1}	Queller, Donald E. *The Fourth Crusade: The Conquest of Constantinople, 1201–1204*. Philadelphia: University of Pennsylvania Press, 1977.
FC^{2}	Queller, Donald E. and Thomas F. Madden. *The Fourth Crusade: The Conquest of Constantinople, 1201–1204*. 2nd. ed. Philadelphia: University of Pennsylvania Press, 1996.
GeH	*Gesta episcoporum Halberstadensium*.
HC	*Hystoria Constantinopolitana*
HI	Robert, Monk of Reims, *Historia Iherosolimitana*.
HP	*Historia peregrinorum*.
I	*De expugnatione Urbis Constantinopolitane, Unde, inter alias reliquias, magna pars sancte Crucis in Alemanniam est allata*. MS 321, fols. 1r-23r. Munich: Universitätsbibliothek.
M	*Hystoria Constantinopolitana*. MS *lat*. 903, fols. 115r–148r. Munich: Bayerische Staatsbibliothek.
MGH, SS	*Monumenta Germaniae Historica. Scriptores*, 32 vols. Hanover and Leipzig: Hahn, 1826–1934.

MGH, Script. rer. Germ.	*Monumenta Germaniae Historica. Scriptores Rerum Germanicarum*. 63 vols. Hanover and Leipzig: Hahn,
PL	J.-P. Migne, *Patrologiae cursus completus, series latina*, 221 vols. Paris, 1844–1864.
Reg.	Papal Register
RHC. H. Occ.	*Recueil des historiens des croisades. Historiens occidentaux*, 5 vols. Paris, 1844–1895.
RHGH	*Receuil des historiens des Gaules et de la France*. 24 vols. Paris, 1844–1895.
RIS^{2}	*Rerum Italicarum scriptores*, 2nd. rev. ed., 34 vols. in 109 fasc. Città di Castello [Bologna from 1917], 1900–.

INTRODUCTION

1. GUNTHER OF PAIRIS: THE MAN AND HIS WORKS

Gunther (ca. 1150–1210?), a Cistercian monk of the Alsatian abbey of Pairis, composed four Latin works, whose merits and range illustrate his literary talent, his erudition, and his life's twists and turns. His initial creation, dating from about 1186, was the *Solimarius*. This composition, whose strange-sounding title is best translated as *The Conqueror of Jerusalem*, is a poetic recasting in epic form of segments of Robert of Reims's *Historia Iherosolimitana* (*The Jerusalemite History*), an early twelfth-century history of the First Crusade. Unfortunately, only 232 lines of the poem are known to have survived the ravages of time.[1] Gunther's second work, the *Ligurinus* (*The Conqueror of Liguria*),[2] appeared around 1186/1187. Like its predecessor, it is a versification in heroic dactylic hexameters of someone else's prose history, in this instance books two through four of the mid-twelfth-century prose history *The Deeds of the Emperor Frederick I* by Otto of Freising and Rahewin. Gunther's third composition was the *Hystoria Constantinopolitana* (*The Constantinopolitan History*),[3] a contemporary history of the Fourth Crusade that he essentially completed before the end of 1205. As we shall see, it differs radically from his two earlier pieces and deserves to be recognized as his most significant and original creation. His fourth and last known work, probably composed shortly before his death, is the *De oratione ieiunio et eleemosyna* (*On Prayer, Fasting, and Almsgiving*),[4] a treatise that shows the hand of an author steeped in the best theological scholarship of his day.

Unfortunately, Gunther of Pairis's extant works provide little in the way of solid biographical detail. Indeed, in only one of his four compositions, the *Hystoria Constantinopolitana* (hereafter *HC*), is the author even identified as Gunther, a monk of Pairis.[5] Nowhere does his name appear in the text of the *Ligurinus*. To discover its author's name we must turn to a note in the poem's first printed edition of 1507, which was based on a now-lost manuscript. Here the printer simply refers to the medieval author as Gunther.[6] In the *Ligurinus* itself the shadowy Gunther claims authorship of the earlier *Solimarius*;[7] otherwise, we would never know the name of the man who composed those poetic fragments. Likewise, a note accompanying the *De oratione* refers to the author as "the venerable Father Gunther of the Order of Saint Benedict."[8] Notwithstanding these vague ascriptions, if we accept Gunther of Pairis's authorship of all four works, as do most scholars,[9] we can discover scattered among them a few tantalizing clues that will help us to construct a sketchy biography of this undeservedly obscure poet, historian, and spiritual writer.[10]

Each of Gunther's four works marked an important stage in the pilgrimage of his life as he journeyed from the secular world of the schools and the imperial court of Germany to the spiritual world of Pairis's cloister; a close study of those compositions enables us to sketch the general outlines of that life. Moreover, of the four works, the *HC* is pivotal because it was written at a point of personal transformation when Gunther the monk of Pairis was slowly and even painfully casting off the old man and putting on the new.

Gunther tells us very little about his monastic conversion or about his life either outside or within Pairis, but he does provide some clues and bits of information. He is silent about his origins and early life, yet we may reasonably postulate the following. He was born about the middle of the twelfth century in the upper Rhine valley of southwest Germany, more than likely in the region around Basel. He probably belonged to a minor knightly family that was known for its loyalty to the imperial House of Hohenstaufen, yet he was never trained as a warrior. He exhibited bookish tendencies, which marked him early in life for a career in the Church; he was widely educated in classical letters, became a secular cleric, and probably was an ordained priest; he possibly served as a *scholasticus*, or master of studies, at a cathedral school. If so, the cathedral was probably located in his native Rhineland. He enjoyed a sufficiently high reputation as a scholar to come to the notice of the imperial court, which he came to serve; that service did not result in his preferment to any high office, and he might well have believed that he had been treated ungenerously by his Hohenstaufen masters.

In the *Ligurinus* Gunther identifies Conrad, fourth son of the Emperor Frederick I, as a former pupil and the person to whom he had dedicated the *Solimarius*.[11] We do not know when or for how long Gunther served as Conrad's tutor, whether he taught any of Frederick's other sons, or what, if any, his other court duties were. Since Conrad was born in 1168, Gunther was probably tutoring him around 1180/1181. It seems doubtful that Gunther was much more than thirty at this time, given that he probably lived into the second decade of the thirteenth century and also that he did not complete his first two poetic compositions until 1186/1187. These early works show the mature vigor of a poet who is young but polished, a man perhaps about thirty-five.

We cannot be certain of the place of Gunther's birth, but circumstantial evidence points to the upper Rhine valley, in the region centering on Basel. The abbey of Pairis was located within the diocesan boundaries of Basel, and it is not too difficult to imagine a world-weary Gunther seeking the solace of a refuge near the place of his boyhood. In the parochial world of twelfth-century Europe most monks entered neighborhood cloisters, in large part due to social, cultural, and linguistic considerations. Pairis was not a great abbey in any sense of the word, although it was comfortably endowed.[12] Some historians believe the monastery also enjoyed a local reputation for scholarship, but this does not seem likely.[13] What else would have made it attractive to Gunther, except that it was situated among his people? In chapter 2 of the *HC* Gunther provides what seems to be a deliberately whimsical etymological explanation for the origin of the name Pairis. According to him, it was derived from the Middle High German *Bar Îs* (*bare ice*), a reference to the region's cold desolation. This is a pun, but only if one utters the words according to the dialectical eccentricities of this upper Rhine region, where *B* is pronounced as *P*. Apparently Gunther was speaking his native Alsatian dialect at Pairis.

The region was securely Hohenstaufen, and it is likely that the obvious loyalty to the imperial family that Gunther exhibits in the *HC*, as well as in his two earlier works, was learned at his parents' knees. There is reason to believe that Gunther was the unwarlike, younger child of a minor knightly family. Through-out both the *Ligurinus* and the *HC* he betrays a pro-noble prejudice, accepting the values of this class and assuming that its members are intrinsically superior. Indeed, despite his distaste for Greeks, Gunther recognizes the special status of even their nobility. In chapter 20 of the *HC* he (mistakenly) informs his readers that after the capture of Constantinople the crusaders apportioned a small piece of territory to the former Emperor Alexius III "because, even though a nefarious man, he was still of royal blood." Also, according to Gunther, the crusaders executed the "parricide," Morciflo, for having murdered his lord, Alexius IV. But then Gunther says of this same Morciflo, "even though he was a nefarious man, he was still of high blood." So, he explains, the crusaders decided to kill him in a manner "which would be, while admittedly very pitiful, nevertheless not entirely disgraceful." Yet, even as he exhibits these chivalric prejudices, Gunther displays a total naïveté toward combat. His descriptions in chapters 7 and 18 of a bloodless assault on Zara and a restrained attack by pious soldiers on Constantinople are contradicted by the eyewitness accounts of persons who participated in the attacks. Gunther is more than misinformed. He shares the ingenuousness of those who have never seen the brutality that battle arouses. As is typical of such persons, Gunther glorifies the profession of arms and identifies with the soldier. Hence, at the end of the *Ligurinus* he speaks of himself as a soldier of words in the service of his emperor, and in the *De oratione* he calls himself and his brother monks claustral warriors.[14]

Not trained as a man-at-arms, Gunther was undoubtedly educated as a secular cleric. He was widely read in the Latin classics and had a superficial knowledge of Greek. This alone indicates a clerical background. At some time in his life Gunther was apparently ordained a priest. The *De oratione* refers to him as Father Gunther, and Gunther informs us that he had to suspend writing this tract because of ministerial duties involving the care of souls.[15] We do not know whether Gunther became a priest before or after he entered Pairis, but he had likely been a cathedral canon before his monastic conversion. At the end of chapter 25 of the *HC*, we read that the author is Master Gunther, a former *scholasticus*. In its technical sense, the title *scholasticus* refers to the cleric in charge of instruction in a cathedral school. It is possible, however, that the person who appended this afternote to the *HC* accorded Gunther the title solely because of his pre-monastic career as a tutor at the Hohenstaufen court. Whatever the case, it is possible that young Gunther served for a while in the cathedral chapter at Strassburg, but he does not appear to have ever been its master of studies. A catalogue dating from 1181 lists thirty-six of the cathedral's canons. The last person on that list, junior in rank to even the child canon Henry of Urselingen, is an otherwise unidentified "Gunther."[16] Whoever this Gunther was, possibly our Gunther,[17] he was obviously a minor functionary. He certainly could not have been Strassburg's *scholasticus* when this list was compiled, and it is unlikely that he served in this capacity at any other time. Between 1157 and 1203 the position appears to have been held in turn by only two men, Henry of Hasenburg and Morand.[18] If Gunther was a canon of Strassburg in 1181, he must have left the post in that same year or shortly thereafter in order to serve as Conrad's tutor. Following his departure from the Hohenstaufen court, Gunther might have gone on to another episcopal chapter, where he possibly rose to the rank of *scholasticus*. If he did become a cathedral master of studies (and we probably will never know much about these "lost years"), we have no way of knowing whether or not he owed this office to the influence of his former imperial employer.

Other than identifying his pupil, Gunther tells us nothing about his service at Frederick's court. His ignorance at the time of the *Solimarius*'s composition of Henry's marriage to Constance,[19] which took place on January 27, 1186, indicates that by late 1185 Gunther was no longer present at court. We do not know whether he had been relieved of his duties because of some dissatisfaction with his work or because it was thought that the teenaged Conrad had had enough schooling.

It appears that it was only after his release from court that Gunther completed the first of his works, the *Solimarius*. As already noted, the work's title means *The Conqueror of Jerusalem*, for Gunther followed the ancient Roman custom of bestowing on a successful general an honorific surname to commemorate his victory. In this case the "conqueror" was, presumably, the entire crusader army, and its title was derived from *Solima*, the last half of *Iherosolima*.[20] The extant verses plainly show that Gunther converted Robert the Monk's prose *Historia Iherosolimitana* into a poetic epic. Such endeavors were common among the poets of the twelfth century's classical renaissance, and Gunther's attempt was especially successful. A virtuoso piece of learned poetry, its lines were, almost without exception, pure Virgilian hexameter, and its vocabulary matched.

Gunther dedicated the epic to Prince Conrad, probably hoping it would win him a high office and, possibly, renewed favor at court. His uncertainty over the *Solimarius*'s reception, which he later displayed in the *Ligurinus*,[21] seems eloquent proof that the Hohenstaufens were not impressed.

Five months after sending off this first epic,[22] that is in late 1186 or 1187,[23] Gunther completed a far more ambitious project, the *Ligurinus*, a composition he probably had begun while serving as Conrad's tutor. This poem, which he lavishly dedicated to Frederick and his five sons,[24] details, in 6577 lines of heroic dactylic hexameter, Barbarossa's exploits in Lombardy up until 1160. Gunther was determined to impress the Hohenstaufens this time, and the epic's magnitude and overall excellence proved equal to its grandiose dedication. Like its predecessor, with which it is expressly linked "as a sibling,"[25] the *Ligurinus* is a tour de force.[26] It is modeled on Lucan's first-century epic *De bello civili* (*On the Civil War*), and throughout the poem Gunther parades his knowledge of the works of such classical authors as Horace, Virgil, Ovid, Statius, and, what was rare for a medieval poet, Lucretius. Vivid descriptions of natural phenomena abound, reminding the reader not only of Lucan but also of the newly awakened interest in nature in twelfth-century Europe.

Gunther was aware of his accomplishment. Dropping the mask of feigned modesty that he had assumed earlier,[27] the poet proudly claims in the closing lines of the work to have singlehandedly awakened the literary art of the ancients that had lain slumbering in darkness for centuries and to have revived, through his poetry, the brilliance of the past.[28] More objective critics might disagree, but it would be rash to deny that Gunther was one of the twelfth-century renaissance's more self-conscious humanists.

The *Ligurinus*'s theme is Frederick's early attempts to impose imperial control over northern and central Italy, and Frederick is clearly the hero of the epic. Throughout the poem Gunther champions the imperial court's concept of the exalted power of the *sacrum imperium*—the holy empire. The emperor is lord of the world, and his every battle is righteous. Frederick is both Caesar and Charlemagne.[29] With deep Germanic pride, the poet celebrates Teutonic power over Italy and a now corrupt Rome.[30] Yet, although his politics were Ghibelline and his ethnic pride ran deep, Gunther was ever the loyal servant of the Church. That loyalty, however, did not preclude his pointing out areas of needed reformation.[31] When dealing with the papal schism of 1159 between Alexander III and Victor IV, Gunther departed from his prose source. The cleric Rahewin, who was writing at the height of the controversy, supported the claims of Victor, the imperial choice.[32] Gunther unequivocally disagreed: Alexander III was the legitimate pope, whose election was mandated by heaven, and Victor was a false pope.[33] Since Frederick had finally made his peace with Alexander in 1176/1177, Gunther undoubtedly believed it was acceptable to be explicitly pro-Alexander. Apparently he was mistaken.

At the close of the epic Gunther reminds Frederick that he is no less a soldier in the imperial service because he uses his tongue rather than a sword and asks to be rewarded accordingly for his unique poetic accomplishment.[34] There is no evidence that Gunther ever received imperial recognition for this poem, and there is reason to believe that his efforts went unrewarded.

Gunther wrote his poem at the wrong time.[35] Early in Barbarossa's reign, the imperial court, under the direction of Archchancellor Rainald of Dassel, had promoted the writing of official histories and Latin panegyrics extolling the emperor's virtues and marshaling support for his Grand Imperial Design.[36] As early as 1163, Rainald of Dassel had assigned the Archpoet of Cologne the task of composing an epic on the emperor's Italian expeditions—a task that the poet wisely declined, facetiously claiming it was beyond his powers.[37] Around 1165 an anonymous Italian, known only as the Master of Bergamo, composed the *Carmen de Frederico I imperatore* (*The Song of the Emperor Frederick I*)—3343 hexameters in five books.[38] Following the archchancellor's death in 1167, however, the imperial court largely abandoned its promotion of Latin historiography and epic poetry and turned, instead, to the new vernacular love poetry known as *minnesang*.[39] So Gunther was twenty years too late when he set out to compose what would be the best and longest of the Fredrican epics. Not only were there now fewer persons in authority at court who appreciated this sort of effort, but also historical circumstances had altered the atmosphere. Following the emperor's humiliating defeat at Legnano in 1176 and the subsequent negotiated peace with the Lombard cities, this poem's effusive praise of long-past and somewhat empty victories must have sounded hollow.[40]

Gunther probably hoped that Frederick's eldest son and coregent, Henry, would be his patron. With this hope in mind, Gunther in his dedication praised Henry's devotion to scholarship and promised to celebrate his exploits in a future work.[41] There is no evidence that Gunther ever wrote that promised poem. We may infer that the reason was that Henry did not respond favorably to the *Ligurinus*.

The years that immediately followed are obscure. As we have seen, it is possible Gunther served as a *scholasticus* at some Rhenish cathedral in the period between approximately 1187/1188 and the time of his entry into the monastery. If he wrote anything during those years, it is now lost. We do not know exactly when he became a monk, but it must have been early in the first decade of the thirteenth century and certainly before 1205. He chose Pairis in the valley of Orbey. Why Gunther became a monk is unknown. Some scholars have assumed that he fled the world because of some professional disappointment or disgrace,[42] but there is no hard evidence to support such a theory. In the *De oratione*, Gunther informs us that for a period of almost ten years he struggled with the call of the cloister, until finally he made his decision and left the world.[43] It is possible that, during this decade of what today's pop-psychologists would call a mid-life crisis, his inability to receive what he considered to be his due recognition, and the lack of a suitable office, preyed on his mind and became one of the factors that attracted him to the monastic life. But this explanation is only speculation. All we can assume is that his decision, when finally made, was that of a mature person, probably someone in his late forties or early fifties, who had given it years of thought and prayer.

Within two or three years of his arrival at Pairis, Gunther was composing the *HC*. Abbot Martin of Pairis returned from his crusade on June 24, 1205, and it certainly would have been high on his list of priorities to begin as quickly as possible to catalogue and authenticate the relics he had acquired at Constantinople. In all likelihood, Gunther essentially completed the *HC* before 1205 had ended and added chapter 25 as a postscript in late 1207 or early 1208.

The reasoning behind dating the first twenty-four chapters of the *HC* to 1205 revolves around three points. The first is obvious. The catalogue of relics in chapter 24 is dated 1205. One could conceivably argue that Gunther is simply quoting from an earlier document, perhaps even Philip of Swabia's now lost charter, which is mentioned in the following chapter. This does not seem likely, however. The catalogue is worded in such a manner that it clearly appears to be a list Gunther has personally drawn up and dated. Moreover, chapter 24 is not an addendum to the *HC* but an integral part of a highly structured and complex piece of literature. It is, as shall be demonstrated in section 3, the *HC*'s original conclusion, and it brings the work to its artistic climax. When seen in this light, the date of 1205 takes on added significance. Finally, it is only in chapter 25, the last chapter of the *HC* as we now have it, that Philip of Swabia is referred to as "unconquered King Philip" and "the most serene emperor." In all earlier appearances he is simply

"King Philip." These epithets indicate that this chapter, *but only this chapter*, was composed after Philip had made his peace with Innocent III in August of 1207, following Philip's momentary victory over Otto of Brunswick and before the Hohenstaufen's death on June 21, 1208. As will be argued in section 3, the *HC*'s structure, as well as the anticlimactic tone of chapter 25, point to the fact that the chapter was added at a later date either by a reluctant Gunther or by some other person.

Upon completion of the *HC*, Gunther undertook a new project. No later than five years after his entry into the abbey, and probably closer to the fourth year following his monastic conversion, Gunther began composing the *De oratione*. A few years later, in the seventh year of his residence at Pairis (1210?), Gunther struggled to complete this, his last work. He was now elderly, plagued by serious physical disabilities, and preparing himself for a death he believed imminent. His ill health dispensed him from the rigor of the *Rule*. Terrible headaches, which he had suffered ever since he first put on the monastic habit, made it impossible for him to function properly. He complained that he could not remember ever feeling well, except at meals and at sleep, for the entire period of his monastic career.[44] His complaints have the ring of a very sick man who, in his pain, exaggerated his history of delicate health and physical infirmity. The humor, which at times is quite whimsical, that pervades the *HC* seems to belie Gunther's contention that the past seven years of his life had been filled with ceaseless pain. Yet there can be no doubt that he had suffered. The apparent speed yet care with which he composed his earlier works indicates an intense, hard-driving perfectionist, who might well have suffered from hypertension, which occasionally is accompanied by symptomatic headaches. Gunther provides another clue to his medical problems. At some now unknown moment in the recent past he had experienced what he terms an unbearable illness—a painful disorder in his head that resulted in a severe speech impediment.[45] This was probably a cerebral stroke, which can be induced by hypertension.

The *De oratione* reveals not only an infirm Gunther but also a man who is more the monk than ever before. In the *HC*, as a recent convert, Gunther had attempted, with some success, to write a monastic history that celebrated his new home and, above all else, that justified the ways of God to humanity. Yet, while the product of a man attempting to become a monk, the *HC* still betrays an essential orientation toward Gunther's secular clerical past. Its poetry and philosophical overtones are more in tune with the spirit of Cologne and Chartres than of Cîteaux and Clairvaux. The *De oratione*, Gunther's only strictly prose composition, is essentially a devotional manual, and its short epilogue is an example of monastic confessional literature, a genre that took shape in the twelfth century. Even though Gunther continues to display his secular erudition, showing off his limited knowledge of Greek,[46] and citing Priscian, Porphyry, Juvenal, Horace, and Cicero,[47] patristic authorities are quite frequent, and biblical citations, noticeably rare in the *HC*, outnumber all other references. Throughout this tract Gunther displays a sincere spirituality, and his monastic conversion, which he mentions several times, appears to have become the defining moment in his life. His frank admission, in the closing lines of the work, of his weaknesses and inadequacies as a monk,[48] strikes the reader as the sentiment of a man who was seriously working at his monastic vocation and also preparing for death.

The first eleven books of this thirteen-book treatise deal in detail with various modes of prayer, books 9 and 10 being an analysis of the Lord's Prayer. Book 12 very superficially covers fasting, and almsgiving is treated in almost equal fashion in the last book. At the beginning of book 12 Gunther informs his reader that he has only taken up the task of writing again after a long hiatus and will only briefly deal with the last two topics. For almost two years he had been entrusted with a ministry that prevented his writing.[49] Following that, he suffered his "unbearable illness." Now, God willing, he was released from that duty which had been forced on him—it seems Gunther preferred books to the care of souls—and he would now put his infirmity to the test. He was still very weak, however, and scarcely able to dictate to his secretary.[50] It must have been painful for Gunther to complete these last two books, both of which are quite short.

In his epilogue Gunther expresses his hope in eternal salvation, despite the human frailties that he openly confesses. We do not know when Gunther died, nor do we know anything else about his life at Pairis. Apparently he lived out the remainder of his days as a simple monk and was buried in some now unknown grave.

2. WHY THE *HYSTORIA CONSTANTINOPOLITANA*?

It is easy to fathom why Gunther composed his two epic poems, and he provides us with reasonable motives for the *De oratione*. He undertook the latter, he informs us, because there were no other works on the subject, at least of which he was cognizant, and he wanted to be remembered by his brothers in fraternal love, win their approval, and earn their pious prayers.[51] His reasons for composing the *HC* are less obvious and more complex. The work appears to have been commissioned by Abbot Martin of Pairis, who served as Gunther's oral source and plays the role of hero in this demi-epic. Abbot Martin's ego certainly figured prominently in the commission and execution of this history, and the abbey of Pairis shared proportionately, if not equally, in the glory.

Pairis, a great-granddaughter of Morimond Abbey and one of the smaller daughters of the Alsatian house of Lucelle, was a minor monastery. As such, it was overshadowed by its older monastic siblings within in the family of Morimond, especially nearby Salem. Suddenly and unexpectedly Pairis had been greatly enriched by the relic booty that Martin had brought back with him from the Fourth Crusade. There arose a need to authenticate and catalogue the relics and to justify their translation. The *HC* served that triple purpose; major portions of it conform to the traditions of the relic translation genre, particularly that special subgroup written in defense of *furtum sacrum*—pious thievery. Although this type of thievery had a long and venerable history,[52] not everyone agreed that it was a legitimate enterprise. Certainly there was divided judgment on the way in which Abbot Martin had secured his sacred treasures.

Around 1209, Otto of St. Blasien, the continuator of Otto of Freising and Rahewin's *Gesta*, commented favorably:

> Thus the riches of Greece were carried to many western lands, particularly the ornaments of that temple which the Emperor Justinian constructed some time ago to the honor of *Hagia Sophia*, noted for its great quantity of gold, along with relics of innumerable saints, in which this city surpassed the entire East. To a large extent this [treasure] was carried off to Venice, and other regions and cities were enriched by these relics and treasures to a great degree. Moreover, a certain Cistercian abbot by the name of Martin, from the monastery of Pairis, which is located in Alsace, went on this expedition, participated in the storming of Constantinople, and thereafter carried back to his homeland a very large portion of the Living Cross and other relics of Our Lord, along with many relics of the saints, ornamented with gold, silver, and precious stones. Through these he greatly ennobled all of Germany, along with Alsace. And thus the severe Judge, God Almighty, avenged the injuries done his pilgrims. . . . The Lord God of vengeance repaid the proud with retribution, but he did not forget mercy in his anger, because he effected this scourging of the sons of pestilence not through pagans but through Christians. No doubt this was made necessary by the merits of the saints, so that their magnificent relics would not be polluted by pagan hands. Rather, through this deserved translation to another, they would be venerated with honor by Christians.[53]

If we compare Otto's words with the *HC*'s subtitle and chapters 1, 11, 19, and 24, it is clear that Otto borrowed these arguments as well as some phrases from the *HC*. So, Gunther's apologetic history had at least one reader who found its thesis compelling.

The early thirteenth-century Praemonstratensian canon Burchard of Ursperg also seems to have been aware of Gunther's defense of Abbot Martin's actions, but he was less certain of the propriety of stealing relics. Although Burchard did not unequivocally condemn Martin or the other crusaders,[54] he displayed his reservations when he wrote:

Also a certain abbot of the Cistercian Order from the place called Pairis, located in the Vosges forest, carried many relics back to his monastery, which are still kept there. Whether they were stolen, let him who reads decide. Or can the lord pope clearly justify such thievery made on a Christian people, just as the thievery of the people of Israel in Egypt was justified by divine authority?[55]

The lord pope was similarly ambivalent. Although Pope Innocent rejoiced in 1204 that, "He, who has dominion over the Kingdom of Man, . . . has transferred the empire of Constantinople from the proud to the humble, from the disobedient to the devout, from schismatics to Catholics,"[56] he condemned the Venetian and crusader despoilment of Greek churches.[57] Even the crusader leaders, shortly before the final assault on Constantinople, had expressly commanded all members of the army to swear solemnly, on sacred relics, that they would not break into any churches or monasteries.[58] Moreover, all the crusaders had been forced to bind themselves, under penalty of excommunication and even death, to hand over all spoils for redistribution according to rank.[59] However, as the scandalized Geoffrey de Villehardouin reported:

Then each man began to bring in and collect the booty. Some contributed fairly, others poorly, for covetousness, which is the root of all evil, was not idle. Rather, the covetous began at this point to hold some things back, and our Lord began to love them the less. Ah God, how loyally they had comported themselves up to this point! And the Lord God had been well disposed to them, so that in all their affairs he had favored them and raised them above every other people. Oft time the good are injured by the evil.[60]

To Geoffrey's mind, the crusaders' subsequent reverses were due to the sinful covetousness of these hoarders. The morality of Martin's actions, therefore, was sufficiently ambiguous to warrant a defense.

One of the time-honored justifications of *furtum sacrum* was the argument that the very saint whose relics had been piously pilfered had directed the theft, in order to assure the relics' proper veneration and to protect them from possible desecration.[61] Since the foremost relic that Martin had brought back with him was a trace of the Precious Blood, it was only fitting, in Gunther's poetic words, that: "Christ wished to enrich you with the wrongdoers' spoils,/ Lest some other conquering people despoil them."[62] Moreover, Gunther left no doubt in his reader's mind that these Greeks, although still Christian brethren,[63] were a schismatic, heretical,[64] and sacrilegious breed of profane people,[65] who no longer deserved to possess such holy objects. So Gunther continually assures his audience that Divine Providence foreordained all the events of the Fourth Crusade, and that it was God himself who had given the relics to his holy servant.[66] Gunther even credits the Greek priest whom Martin had robbed with the wisdom to perceive that it was better for this pious abbot to carry off the relics in devotion than to hazard their being desecrated by less holy hands.[67]

Closely connected with the theme of heavenly direction was the *topos* that relic thefts were justified by the thief's holiness and noble motives.[68] Here, again, Gunther conformed to hagiographical models and constantly affirmed his abbot's personal sanctity and nobility of purpose.[69] A third traditional justification was that the newly stolen relics sanctified the community to which they were transported.[70] Gunther also made this argument in several places.[71]

No translation story would be complete without touches of the prophetic and the miraculous. The authenticity and power of the relics had to be demonstrated beyond all possible doubt, and visions and miracles provided indisputable proof. Chapter 22, where Martin's companion is treated to a vision of angels venerating these spoils and calling upon God to protect the good abbot and where Martin narrates his own dream of a promised safe voyage home, certainly provides the prophetic element, especially since Gunther had already emphasized in chapter 15 the prophetic qualities of dreams and visions. Chapter 23 proves the validity of these visions, when pirates and highwaymen are miraculously inhibited from attacking Martin and his sacred cargo as he makes his homeward journey.

Finally, after the circumstances of the translation have been recorded, the act justified, and the relics proven authentic, the author must clearly catalogue them, so that there is a permanent public record. Gunther does this in chapter 24, taking care to note in the following chapter their confirmation and protection under imperial charter.

The purposes behind the *HC* did not stop here. Abbot Martin needed more than just a defense of his pious pilferage. Martin apparently had a reputation for being lax in his observance of monastic discipline. In September 1206 the Chapter General of the Cistercian Order commissioned the abbot of Morimond to investigate charges of irregularity at Pairis, to make the necessary corrections, and to report back to the Chapter General of 1207. Martin was accused of having admitted a novice who ate three daily meals, instead of the single meal permitted during winter (September 14 to Easter) and the two meals allowed during the longer summer days; with keeping peacocks in the cloister; and with using his personal chambers as a hospice and infirmary[72]—presumably so he and his guests could eat less coarse bread and meat, which would normally be forbidden to the abbot's table. The charge of keeping peacocks was already proven to the Chapter's satisfaction. And the Chapter laid a light penance on the abbot of Lucelle for having failed, when he had learned of that departure from good order at this daughter abbey, to correct it.[73] This was not the first time that Martin had been found guilty of an irregularity, assuming he was already abbot in 1196. In that year the unnamed abbot of Pairis received three days light penance, one of which was a fast of bread and water, for not having made a required annual visitation.[74]

At almost every turn the *HC* extols Martin's monastic virtues and endeavors to show that he was always scrupulous in conforming to the highest standards of his vocation. Gunther takes special pains to portray his abbot as obedient, humble, shy,[75] and abstemious, with no concern for worldly possessions or pleasures[76] and an abiding fidelity to his pope, profession, Order, and brethren at Pairis.[77] He is a living saint in the model of his holy namesake, St. Martin of Tours. In particular, he is modeled after St. Martin as interpreted by Bernard of Clairvaux, who emphasized Martin's heroic obedience to God, his meekness, humility, patience, and compassion, and the richness of his humanity.[78]

This apologetic tone has convinced several scholars that Gunther must have embarked on the project after September of 1206.[79] This does not necessarily follow. The charges of 1206 might well have been anticipated. Gunther's zealous defense of Martin's conduct has the ring of protesting too much, especially on certain apparently sensitive issues.

Admittedly, Abbot Martin's scruples before Zara and his priestly ministrations to the plague victims of Acre, if true, indicate that he possessed a number of admirable, even heroic, qualities. Even so, he appears to have been less than the perfect paragon of Cistercian simplicity. The fact that Gunther assures his readers that the good abbot's quarters both on board ship and in Constantinople were properly monastic,[80] and that when Martin returned to Pairis he did so "with the great humility of piety," even though he traveled in a grand style,[81] suggests that Martin was a man of some ego who enjoyed many of the comforts and trappings of this world—such as the visual joys of peacocks—and who, to his chagrin, had a reputation for such eccentricities. Gunther might well have been simply attempting to prove the contrary to the abbot's general reputation, rather than responding to any specific indictments brought by the Order.

We do not know the outcome of the investigation by the abbot of Morimond or what penance, if any, was imposed on Martin. The extant records of later Chapters General cite no other instances of alleged irregularities on Martin's part, and Martin sinks into historical obscurity. In fact, we know nothing else about his subsequent life.[82]

Abbot Martin seems to have felt the need for defense on other, allied fronts, as well. Martin might well have believed himself vulnerable to the charges that he had illicitly or imprudently joined the crusader ranks, that he had conducted himself throughout these several years with very unmonastic independence, and that, while on crusade, he had consistently shirked his duties, seeking easy rather than heroic courses of action.

It is likely that Martin saw the crusade as a way to avoid the embarrassing and dangerous situation of having to choose between obedience to the papacy and loyalty to Philip of Swabia and the House of Hohenstaufen. Innocent and his papal legate to Germany, Guido, cardinal-bishop of Palestrina, had been pressing high-ranking clerics such as Martin to abandon their powerful neighbor and to support Philip's rival for the throne, Otto of Brunswick. Martin apparently wished to alienate neither the pope nor Philip and probably saw the crusade as a welcome opportunity to leave Germany until matters cooled down.[83] If this was Martin's strategy, it worked. Otto's fortunes slipped badly while Martin was absent from Germany, and when the abbot returned to Europe in the late spring of 1205 Pope Innocent was considerably less intractable on the issue.[84] Even so, Philip would not be reconciled with the papacy until August of 1207. This meant that throughout the latter half of 1205—the period when Gunther was composing the *HC*'s original twenty-four chapters—Innocent still officially supported Otto. It is in this light that we should appreciate Gunther's skill as he walked the tightrope of loyalty to both Philip of Swabia and Innocent III.

We see Gunther strike this balance most clearly in chapter 24, where he dates the relic catalogue by reference to the reigns of both King Philip and Pope Innocent. Indeed, throughout the first twenty-four chapters Gunther consistently accords Philip the title "king,"[85] even though the pope then recognized Otto as legitimate king of Germany. Equally noteworthy is the fact that the *HC* refers to Philip as "most serene emperor" only in chapter 25, written after the Hohenstaufen had made his peace with the papacy. Gunther (and, by extension, Martin) denied the pope any right to intervene in German dynastic and royal affairs but fully recognized the pope's authority to bestow the crown of empire.[86] Chapters 2, 4, and 9 affirm Abbot Martin's loyalty to and respect for the spiritual authority of the Holy See, and chapter 7 contains an extravagant encomium on Pope Innocent's virtues. Significantly, chapter 25 picks up the oxymoron "mature youth" that Gunther applies to the pope in chapter 7 and employs it to flatter "Emperor" Philip, who at this point, by virtue of his apparent victory over Otto, is accorded the title "unconquered king."[87]

We will never know for certain why Martin assumed the Cross, and we certainly cannot accept the *HC*'s explanation at face value. Gunther makes it appear to have been a simple case of obedience to higher authority. In chapter 2 he states that Martin had received a direct papal order to assume the crusader's Cross and to preach the crusade publicly. There is, however, no solid evidence to support this claim.

In chapter 4 Gunther asserts that, even though he had a papal mandate, Martin, out of reverence for his monastic profession, traveled to Cîteaux, where he received the permission and blessing of the abbot of Cîteaux, as well as the blessing of a number of other eminent abbots of the Order. This, we may assume, took place during the meeting of the Chapter General of September 1201, for it was during that convocation that several Cistercian abbots received permission from the Order to embark on the forthcoming crusade. Yet nowhere do we find Martin listed among these men.

Statute 37 of the Chapter General of 1201 states:

> At the command of the supreme pontiff and in response to the entreaties of the marquis of . . . [Montferrat] . . . and the counts of Flanders and Blois, permission is extended to the abbots of [Vaux-de-] Cernay, Perseigne, Loos, and Cercanceaux to depart signed with the Cross.[88]

The English Cistercian historian Ralph, abbot of Coggeshall from 1207 to 1218, identifies five abbots who were given permission in 1201 to go on crusade. According to Ralph, Fulk of Neuilly, the primary preacher of the crusade,[89] appeared at the Chapter General with a letter from the pope naming three Cistercians who would join his company on the crusade: the abbots of la Columba, Perseigne, and Vaux-de-Cernay.[90] In one manuscript the designation "la Columba" is struck out and someone, of roughly the same period, has correctly penned in "Cercanceaux."[91] In addition, Ralph notes that several lay lords in attendance prevailed on the Chapter to allow additional abbots to join their respective retinues. The abbot of Loos was allowed to accompany Count Baldwin of Flanders, and Boniface de Montferrat pleaded successfully for "a certain Cistercian abbot of his region, namely the abbot of *Lucelane*."[92] We know that the Cistercian who traveled with Boniface on the crusade was Peter, abbot of Locedio. Locedio, a convent located in Italy's Piedmont,[93] was within the territory ruled by the marquis and had been founded by Boniface's family.[94] The reason the abbot of Locedio is not mentioned in Statute 37, quoted above, most likely has some connection with the broken text, which only partially identifies Boniface, marquis of Montferrat. Abbot Peter also seems to have suffered from another of Ralph of Coggeshall's slips of the pen. While Locedio was written in a variety of ways in medieval Latin, never was it written as *Lucelane*.[95] This Latin placename can only refer to Lucelle (Lützel), the mother abbey of Pairis.[96] Lucelle was not located anywhere near the marquis's lands, and its abbot definitely did not go on the Fourth Crusade. Could Ralph's error have been caused by some vague knowledge that there had been an abbot, somehow connected with Lucelle, who received the Order's permission to go on the crusade, even though he did not have a papal mandate to do so? There is no known extant copy of the papal letter that Fulk carried to Cîteaux in 1201. So we cannot say with certainty whether or not Martin's name appeared in that document, but it appears unlikely.

Gunther claims, of course, that Martin received his papal commission well before he went to Cîteaux. The evidence does not support that claim. In addition to Gunther's questionable testimony, there are two independent sources that have been used to link Martin with some sort of papal order to participate in the crusade. However, close analysis of each shows that one has absolutely no connection whatsoever with Martin, and the other is hearsay and ambiguous hearsay at that.

Our first piece of apparent supporting evidence is a directive from the chancery of Innocent III to a variety of clerics in Germany, England, Ireland, and Sicily, ordering them to preach a crusade and collect alms for the projected expedition. Because most of the recipients were Cistercians, Angel Manrique printed the letter, which he dated to the third year of Innocent's pontificate (between February 22, 1200 and February 21, 1201), and listed what he claimed were all of the recipients and their respective assigned regions.[97] Among them he included "M. abbot of Pairis," who was to preach "throughout Germany."

Elizabeth A. R. Brown and Francis Swietek have both accepted Manrique's version of the letter and the list of recipients as authentic Fourth Crusade documents, although both also agree that in no way does the letter command or even give permission to any preacher to become a crusader himself. They conclude that Gunther later misrepresented this letter as a papal commission to his abbot to travel on the crusade.[98] Curiously both accept the letter as genuine despite the fact that Brown could not find it listed in any standard calendar of Innocent's letters.[99] Moreover, there are a number of disquieting errors and inconsistencies in the document as recorded and dated by Manrique. Two of the clerics on the list, Walter, archdeacon of London, and "the former bishop of Halberstadt," could not have received a commission to preach the Fourth Crusade. Master Walter did not become archdeacon of London until 1212 or 1213,[100] and the only former bishop of Halberstadt functioning in the early thirteenth century was Conrad of Krosigk, who did not step down from that office until 1208.[101] Not only did the papal chancery lack the power of prescience, it also was not given to making sloppy mistakes. It is scarcely imaginable that it would have noted that the abbot of Pairis was commissioned to preach throughout Germany when, as we learn from Gunther, Martin preached only in his immediate area of Alsace.[102] Still, the letter is not a forgery. Manrique copied a genuine papal document, but he gravely misdated and misquoted it.

The actual letter, *Pium et sanctum*, was issued between April and mid-May of 1213 and concerned the Fifth Crusade, not the Fourth.[103] When we read the letter and its list of recipients, we find the entire cast of Cistercian monks listed by Manrique, with the exception of the abbots of Rievaulx and Pairis. Rievaulx need not concern us here, but Pairis does. It seems obvious that Manrique, who knew and used the *HC*, cavalierly added Martin of Pairis's name to what he claimed was a literal transcription of a chancery note. He probably honestly misdated the letter and then ingenuously filled in Martin's name, believing that he was correct in supplying what history had accidentally misplaced.

So there is no extant official record of any papal commission for Martin. Still, it seems likely that the abbot of Pairis did receive papal orders to preach the crusade and to collect alms. He then parlayed that simple task into an adventure by exaggerating his duties. Echoes of that exaggeration seem to have been picked up by a contemporary historian in distant Saxony.

Our second source for Abbot Martin's putative papal commission is by an author known only as the Anonymous of Halberstadt.[104] This short work is similar in many respects to the *HC*. Composed in late 1208 or early 1209 and incorporated as an integral part of the *Deeds of the Bishops of Halberstadt* (*GeH*), it is a secondhand description of the crusade, based upon the eyewitness account of Conrad of Krosigk, bishop of Halberstadt (r. 1201–1208), who, like Martin, brought back a wealth of relics from Constantinople. The work served, therefore, many of the same purposes as the *HC*.[105]

According to this source, Bishop Conrad heard of the plan to divert the army to Zara while he was still in Venice. Troubled, he told the papal legate, Peter Capuano, of his reservations. The legate advised him that the pope preferred to overlook this transgression, rather than allow the army to break up, and that the bishop should not, under any circumstances, desert the army. Consequently, Conrad "bound himself to the army, as also did four abbots of the Cistercian Order whom the pope specially chose to lead the crusaders by word and example."[106] Who were these four "papally commissioned" abbots? There were only four Cistercian abbots with the army in Venice at that moment: Guy of Vaux-de-Cernay; Simon of Loos; the unnamed abbot of Cercanceaux; and Martin, who had recently arrived with the Alsatian cohort.[107] Obviously Bishop Conrad thought that each had been given a special papal appointment. When we compare the Halberstadt account with chapter 6 of the *HC* we find some interesting parallels. According to Gunther, Martin, similarly shocked at the planned diversion to Zara, also approached the cardinal legate and asked for dispensation from his vow and permission to return to Pairis. Not only did Capuano refuse the request, he added to Martin's burdens by making him responsible for all the Germans in the army and "also charged him and several other religious who were present to stay with their comrades through every peril and to restrain them, insofar as it was possible, from shedding Christian blood." This does not prove, however, that the Anonymous of Halberstadt was correct in his implication that Innocent III had earlier given each of these Cistercians a commission to accompany the army as a chaplain. At best the Anonymous provides only secondhand, hearsay evidence. The pattern of distortion and half truths that runs throughout the *HC* makes it quite conceivable that as early as 1202 Martin was misrepresenting himself and his role in the crusade. Conrad of Halberstadt cannot be faulted for having reported to his chronicler what he had accepted, in good faith, as the truth. Even Geoffrey de Villehardouin, who was far from gullible, reports that at some unspecified moment after the army had learned of Alexius V's murder of Alexius IV: "All the clergy, including those who had an apostolic mandate, agreed and pointed out to the barons and the pilgrims that 'the battle is right and just.'"[108] It seems likely that, although he never mentions Martin by name in his account, Villehardouin thought of the abbot as one of those papally mandated clerics.

It was in Martin's best interest to twist the truth and present himself as the obedient papal agent. The Order of Cîteaux had been decidedly lukewarm toward the Fourth Crusade, at least in its early stages. When Fulk of Neuilly initially requested the Order to provide preaching associates, the Chapter General of 1198 rebuffed him on the ground that public preaching was not part of the Cistercian ministry.[109] The Order relented three years later "at the command of the supreme pontiff"[110] and, as we have seen, gave permission to several abbots to go on crusade. However, as late as September 1203 a minority of abbots tried unsuccessfully at the Chapter General to have all crusading monks recalled to their monasteries.[111] At least some Cistercians were disquieted by the phenomenon of wandering monks. If, as seems likely, Martin had secured permission from the Chapter General of 1201 to go on crusade by misrepresenting his papal commission, it was necessary for him to continue the lie throughout his crusade and well after his return from overseas. We might well marvel at the abbot's *sang-froid* and wonder if his claims were ever challenged.

One area in which the *HC*'s account of Martin's actions can be challenged is in its portrayal of the abbot as a humble exemplar of monastic obedience and humility who, because of those qualities, had positions of great responsibility laid upon him and who comported himself heroically in the performance of his duties. In chapter 2 Martin receives his papal orders. In chapter 4 he is called to ever greater responsibilities when the people of Basel prevail on him to lead their contingent, as well as serving as its chaplain. In this same chapter Martin also exhibits his scrupulous obedience to his Order and his monastic vocation. Despite his papal commission, he still travels to Cîteaux, where he gains the blessing and permission of a number of leading abbots of the Order, including the abbot of Cîteaux. At Zara Martin has new duties laid upon him when the papal legate places all the Germans in the army under Martin's care and instructs him to try to restrain the army from shedding Christian blood. After the transgression at Zara he is elected by the army to be one of its representatives to go to Rome and to beg papal indulgence.[112] By this time Martin is greatly troubled by developments in the crusade army and, after accomplishing his mission in Rome, seeks papal permission to return to the quiet of his cloister. The pope refuses to release Martin from his sacred vow and informs him that he cannot return to Pairis until he has first reached the Holy Land.[113] Upon completion of a successful mission to Rome, his duty to the army fulfilled, Martin now entrusts the letter of papal absolution to his fellow envoys and joins the papal legate Peter Capuano in sailing directly to Syria.[114] His vow, as both he and the pope understand it, has been to reach the Holy Land, not to sail to either Alexandria or Constantinople, as the army intends. So, even in leaving the army he is acting out of conscience and conforming strictly to papal direction. Abbot Martin eventually travels to Constantinople, of course, but only as a result of his deference to the needs and entreaties of others who choose him to serve as a legate of the kingdom of Jerusalem at Acre.[115] At every turn Martin appears to assume positions of great responsibility, not because he sought them but because they were legitimately laid upon his obedient and competent shoulders. But was this the case?

Gunther obviously exaggerated and distorted Martin's role. We know from other sources that the abbot was not in charge of the legation sent to Rome from Zara. In fact, he had not been chosen as one of the army's four envoys and was probably only tagging along as self-appointed representative of the German faction, hoping he could gain papal release from his vow and disassociate himself from a crusade that was turning out quite differently from what he had envisioned.[116] Why this particular lie or, if one wishes to be charitable, artful fabrication? One motive suggests itself. The Order of Cîteaux was extremely unenthusiastic about its members presenting themselves before the papal curia, lest their actions reflect badly on the Order.[117] According to a statute of 1157, in time of crisis a Cistercian could go to Rome, but only with the prior consent of the abbot of Cîteaux and at least two of the abbots of Cîteaux's four elder daughters.[118] The Chapter General of 1201, the very meeting that Martin had attended prior to leaving on the crusade, had prescribed the punishments to be meted out to those who flaunted this rule.[119] In 1203, the very year in which Abbot Martin was at the papal court presumably on a mission on behalf of the army, the Chapter General ordained that no member of the Order was to go to Rome as a petitioner for any lay person, save by permission of the abbot of Cîteaux or the license of the abbots of at least two of Cîteaux's four elder daughters. Those who failed to observe this rule were to be punished by perpetual banishment to another house within the Order.[120] The best defense that Gunther could offer on Abbot Martin's behalf was that the responsibilities laid on the abbot by the pope, by the papal legate, and by crusaders sworn to the Cross compelled Martin to act as he did.

A desire to deflect criticism partially inspired this web of misrepresentation, but Martin's ego was an equally important factor. Consider chapter 6. Its prose portion implies that Capuano gave Martin secular control over all the Germans in the crusade army, and the verse that follows unambiguously states that the churchman had now become: "a comrade, or better, leader and prince of the German cohort." This is sheer puffery and nonsense. Cardinal Peter appears from all other accounts, such as the already cited Anonymous of Halberstadt, to have viewed the clerics traveling with the army as persons with only spiritual functions. Although clerics had led armed contingents in earlier crusades, it is beyond belief that a seasoned diplomat would have placed an untrained non-combatant in charge of an army, when there were sufficient professional warriors of suitable rank and experience available. It is even less likely that these soldiers would have meekly surrendered their prerogative of electing their own leader.

What are we to make of all of this? Did the vain and conscience-plagued Abbot Martin simply misinform gullible Gunther? This might well have been the case, but it appears that there was more behind these misrepresentations than simply the vanity of one man and the naïveté of another. Gunther, who repeatedly stressed the factual accuracy of his history, appears to have been involved in a conspiracy, spinning a tale that made the often banal, arbitrary, independent, and self-seeking actions of Martin appear as instances of praiseworthy devotion to duty, heroic exploits, and personally salvific, God-directed actions. As Francis Swietek has convincingly argued, there is a coherent pattern of distortion and omission in the *HC*'s portrayal of the abbot's actions, which cannot be simply explained as the product of Martin's selective memory and ability to shade the truth.[121] It is far more plausible to conclude that the *HC*'s gifted author played an active role in distorting facts to serve both artistic and apologetical ends.

Martin was not the *HC*'s only defendant nor was the abbot its only recipient of fame through partisan history. It also offered a defense of the entire crusade army and, by extension, all Latin Christendom. Moreover, it served to glorify the abbey of Pairis and gave Gunther an opportunity to display his literary-intellectual skills and the depth of his new monastic vocation.

Modern historians have too often misrepresented the Fourth Crusade as a purely secular venture.[122] Although commercial and other worldly interests were important factors in the unfolding of these historical events, as even contemporaries such as Gunther and Innocent III acknowledged,[123] they played a subsidiary role. The Fourth Crusade was primarily a religious expression for the Venetian merchant as well as for the simple French knight. Doubtlessly most participants looked upon this crusade as a sacramental experience, in retrospect as well as in anticipation.[124] Yet, paradoxically, this religious enthusiasm and orientation raised some disturbing doubts and occasioned many persons to look ambivalently on the Fourth Crusade. A crusader was primarily a pilgrim sworn to visit and help liberate the Holy Land. The Fourth Crusade captured Constantinople, degenerated into a series of land-grabbing enterprises, and never reached Palestine. Crusaders were either warriors sworn to fight "infidel" Muslims, or they were noncombatants, such as clerics, dedicated to assisting these warriors of Christ. In the case of crusade clerics, it was assumed that they would serve lay pilgrims by offering the sacraments and prudent spiritual counsel. The army of the Fourth Crusade attacked Latin Christians at Zara and Greek Christians at Corfu[125] and in Constantinople. At Zara the crusade clergy uncanonically absolved the army,[126] and at Constantinople it "commanded the pilgrims . . . not to be afraid of attacking the Greeks, for they were the enemies of God."[127] It was popularly believed that participation in a crusade assured remission of one's sins. The army was excommunicated for its action at Zara[128] and was possibly excommunicated a second time for what it did at Constantinople.[129] Surely the Fourth Crusade needed to be defended, its events justified, and its hidden meanings made manifest.

The crusade's two secular historians were aware of this need, and both Geoffrey de Villehardouin and Robert de Clari offered essentially feudal justifications and explanations. To be sure, their accounts mention the moral support and spiritual advice rendered by the army's clergy;[130] both men also argue that the crusaders' actions at Constantinople were partly motivated by a desire to heal the schism between the churches of Rome and Constantinople.[131] Villehardouin, whose history is generally interpreted as an attempt to present the events of the crusade as a series of connected, unforeseen accidents,[132] goes as far as to mention, on seven separate occasions, his belief that the crusader actions and successes, even the conquest of Zara, were divinely guided.[133] Yet Villehardouin's remarks are little more than asides and pious clichés; he makes no attempt to demonstrate systematically how the crusade was the handiwork of the Almighty. Albeit believers in Providence and conventionally devout, both men were essentially feudal soldiers, leading them to interpret the crusaders' actions and the expedition's outcome from the perspective of contemporary military values. Grand strategy, tactical expediency, and logistical demands; duty, honor, and all the other rules of honorable soldierly conduct: Such were their points of reference and understanding. The honor of the house of Montferrat;[134] the need to honor their own commitments,[135] to punish those who had proven false, and to defend the oppressed;[136] the strategic necessity to sail elsewhere other than directly to the Holy Land in order to conquer Islam;[137] the need to provision[138] and reinforce[139] themselves and to keep the army together[140]: All were circumstances that combined to force the crusaders into duties that they dared not shirk. The fact that they had won their trials by combat was proof positive of the wisdom and righteousness of their actions.

On his part, Gunther did not totally ignore secular factors. Even though he recognized that the crusaders had vowed to go to the Holy Land,[141] he acknowledged the strategic wisdom of their plan to strike first at Alexandria,[142] and he also seemed to agree that by assuring a friendly Constantinople, the passage through Greece to Syria would be secured.[143] Like Villehardouin, he saw the expedition to Zara as necessary to keep the army from breaking up, and those who shrank from this unhappy task as weakening the army through their defections.[144] At the same time, unlike Villehardouin and Clari, Gunther blamed Venetian perfidy, commercial greed, and imperial motives for the diversions to both Zara and Constantinople.[145] Crusader penury also figured into his account. One reason the army decided to sail to the Greek empire was Prince Alexius's promise of three hundred thousand marks of silver.[146] Not only were they cheated out of this money, thereby acquiring a valid reason to seek retribution, they also had wasted their precious, limited resources in traveling to Byzantium and now faced a desperate crisis.[147] Encamped outside Constantinople, it was the Latin army that was besieged and attacked, not the Greeks.[148] Outnumbered but not outfought, the crusaders struggled for their very survival. As a result, they waged a just war because they fought defensively.[149] Their generosity and sense of fair play, as well as Greek deceit, had placed them in this precarious situation. Moved by feudal and emotional ties to Philip of Swabia, they had listened to the young Greek prince whose father had been deposed as emperor.[150] Convinced of the righteousness of Prince Alexius's cause, they sailed to Constantinople.[151] If the young man had been allowed to live, they would not have been forced to attack the city for a second time.[152] But Latin guilelessness and Greek deceit, especially the treachery of Morciflo, combined to precipitate the crisis from which they could not retreat.[153] Yet, in overcoming these numerous adversities, the crusaders never forgot who they were: As Christian soldiers, they comported themselves with restraint. As befit men fighting a just war, they took no pleasure in the awful deeds they were forced to commit, and they refrained from excess.[154]

However, all of these defenses of crusader conduct were only tangential to the *HC*'s thesis and avowed purpose. Gunther's primary goal was not to justify human conduct but to make the ways of God known to His people. A single theological theme runs throughout this history and unifies its apparently disparate elements: Although the events of the Fourth Crusade shocked many, all were the handiwork of Divine Providence. All the incidents that occurred during that crusade, including those that seemed totally fortuitous and even those that appeared to be impious, had to be interpreted in this light and judged by divine standards.[155] This view of history was not new. It had been a cliché for centuries, and Gunther was not the first to apply the argument to the Fourth Crusade. Shortly after his coronation on May 16, 1204, the new

Latin emperor, Baldwin of Flanders, dispatched an encyclical letter to the West defending and trumpeting the crusader actions at Constantinople. In its opening lines, the letter proclaimed:

> His wonders follow ever upon His wonders in our regard, so that even the infidels should not doubt that the hand of the Lord is at work in all these matters, since nothing of what we had earlier hoped for or foreseen came about, but then in the end the Lord gave us new help, when it seemed that human wisdom failed.[156]

As we have already seen, Pope Innocent also publicly proclaimed God's agency in these affairs.[157] Yet, if not the first to express this belief, Gunther was certainly the only analyst of the Fourth Crusade to elevate the theme from a simple pious sentiment to a highly developed idea. He alone, of all of his contemporaries, had the intellectual confidence and training that allowed him to dare to develop his understanding of the higher purposes that underlay these events in a logical, systematic manner. And that Divine Plan needed revealing, because not everyone in the West was as sanguine as Emperor Baldwin or the pope about God's role in the crusader capture of Constantinople. Arnold of Lübeck, for example, writing possibly as late as 1209, still reserved judgment, when he noted:

> To be sure, great deeds, both remarkable and worth the telling, were done there by the Latins, but whether or not they were the deeds of God or men, a worthy ending has not yet made manifest.[158]

On a far less grand scale, Gunther also attempted to honor and glorify his home abbey. Pairis was not a major house, but it came from noble stock, being the great-granddaughter of Morimond, one of Cîteaux's four "elder daughters." It seems likely that Gunther wanted to demonstrate that in Abbot Martin's exploits, the monastery had shown itself to be a fitting heir of the proud crusading traditions of the Cistercian Order and, more particularly, of the family of Morimond.

In theory monks, whose vocations are predicated upon the

ideal of "sacred stability," should not go on pilgrimages, especially those that have a military overtone. If the cloister is a spiritual Jerusalem, what need is there to visit the earthly Jerusalem? Certainly St. Bernard realized the intrinsic conflict between crusading and the monastic life and was opposed to monks' going on the very crusade that he preached.[159] Throughout the twelfth and thirteenth centuries there was general agreement at the highest legal and administrative levels of the Church that monks should be discouraged from crusading and could not assume a valid crusade vow without the explicit consent of their superiors.[160] However, there was no way that monks could be totally excluded from crusading, and the best that could be realized was to control and limit their crusade activities. While this was largely achieved, there was plenty of leeway for Cistercian participation, despite deep opposition from within the Order toward the notion of crusader monks.

From its origins, the Order of Cîteaux contained within itself the creative tension of contradictory principles: the stability and original simplicity of the Rule of Saint Benedict, to which the Cistercians desired to return, and the dynamism of the early desert elders of Egypt, from whom the Cistercians equally drew inspiration. Some Cistercians expressed their propensity toward spiritual adventurousness in pilgrimage and crusade activities. As early as 1124 Arnold, first abbot of Morimond, tired of his duties and their resultant frustrations. In the company of a handful of monks he abandoned his abbey and announced his intention to establish a house in the Holy Land. His untimely death and, possibly, St. Bernard's eloquent opposition prevented the project's immediate fruition,[161] but there were other Cistercians to follow Arnold's dream. In 1157 several monks of Morimond founded Belmont in Syria as the abbey's twenty-second daughter house.[162] Yet, well before then, several Cistercian bishops had participated in the Second Crusade, a pilgrimage called by a Cistercian pope and preached by the abbot of Clairvaux. Godfrey, bishop of Langres and former prior of Clairvaux, traveled with Louis VII.[163] Otto, bishop of Freising and former abbot of Morimond, accompanied his half-brother, Emperor Conrad III, and commanded a portion of the German army.[164]

Following St. Bernard's death in the mid-twelfth century, the tempo of Cistercian involvement in the crusades accelerated.[165] Henry de Marcy, former abbot of Clairvaux and cardinal bishop of Albano, was one of the prime movers behind the Third Crusade,[166] while Gerard, archbishop of Ravenna, and Baldwin of Ford, archbishop of Canterbury, also preached the Cross.[167] Baldwin, moreover, took the Cross himself,[168] and led a group of English crusaders from Marseilles to Syria. Once in the Holy Land, the elderly Baldwin participated in an offensive against Saladin and, according to Ralph of Coggeshall, personally commanded troops in the campaign. Several days later he died.[169] Henry of Horburg, bishop of Basel and former monk of Cîteaux and Lucelle, also died on this crusade, a victim of disease.[170] A third Cistercian to give his life was Archbishop Gerard of Ravenna, who sailed from Venice at the head of a large group of crusaders. He led a mixed force of Italians and Germans to the siege of Acre, where he apparently fell while leading his troops in an assault upon the city.[171] Cistercian bishops were not the only members of the Order to assist in this undertaking. Garnier de Rochefort, abbot of Clairvaux, preached the crusade in France,[172] and four of his fellow abbots traveled with the armies, including two future Fourth Crusade participants: Simon of Loos and Guy of Vaux-de-Cernay.[173] Unknown numbers of lower- ranking Cistercians also made the trek eastward. There was an inevitable but surprisingly mild reaction within the Order over all of this involvement.[174] The very tepidity of this reaction could only give a further stamp of legitimacy to the Cistercian crusade tradition, despite the vocal faction within the Order that favored an uncompromising policy of non-participation in the crusades.

Many might question the propriety of a monk's joining or even preaching a crusade, but few would deny that crusade historiography was an appropriate monastic activity. Otto, bishop of Freising, the Cistercian Order's first great historian, had only dealt briefly with the Second Crusade in his *Deeds of Frederick I*. As he explained, the crusade's dismal outcome was known to all, and his purpose was to write a joyous history, not a tragedy.[175] The Third Crusade could hardly be termed a rousing success, at least from the German perspective. However, around 1200 a Swabian-German cleric from the area around Lake Constance composed a history of the German role in that recent expedition. The work, known as the *Historia peregrinorum* (*The Pilgrim History*, hereafter *HP*),[176] was written for an unknown patron who was clearly connected with the House of Hohenstaufen. It was essentially an unoriginal creation, showing great dependence on a slightly earlier history of Frederick's crusade by Ansbert. Although most of its quotations and allusions are biblical, the *HP* also contains occasional echoes of the works of Horace, Persius, Lucan, Virgil, Ovid, Martial, Claudian, and Silius. However, these citations seem more the product of a *florilegium*, or collection of quotations, than evidence of the author's intimate knowledge of classical Latin literature. Even so, there was some obvious attempt at writing history in a "literary" style, and this fact momentarily led the nineteenth-century scholar Albert Pannenborg to conclude that Gunther of Pairis was the author. Criticism forced him to abandon that thesis,[177] and today the author of the *HP* remains a mystery.[178] Anton Chroust argues that this anonymous historian was possibly a monk of Salem.[179] The *HP*'s manuscript tradition points clearly in that direction. If Chroust is correct,[180] not only was the author a Cistercian, he was a member of the monastic families of Morimond and Lucelle.

If the *HP* was a product of Salem, as seems likely, then Gunther knew of it. The cultural, geographic, and ecclesiastical ties between Pairis and Salem were too close for a man of Gunther's interests not to be aware of this text. It is similarly difficult to believe that Gunther did not look upon the *HP* as an inviting challenge. With his background and proven talent, he could easily help Pairis outdo its larger sibling, at least in this particular form of crusade participation.

In poetic and bookish ways, bards and historians participate in the deeds they commemorate. Certainly Gunther believed that celebrating crusade exploits meant sharing in the merit of those who had preached, marched, and fought. Less than two decades earlier he had claimed equality with the soldiers who served Barbarossa.[181] Now he would prove the depth of his monastic vocation. His treatment of Abbot Martin's crusade would equally win for Gunther the status of *miles Christi*—soldier of Christ.

As an imperial courtier and schoolman, Gunther had utilized an essentially secular genre, the Virgilian epic, when he composed the *Solimarius* and the *Ligurinus* and had viewed the military and even crusade exploits that he wrote about from a scholastic perspective. As a monk, it was now appropriate that he not only look at the crusade with new eyes but that he adopt a form more appropriate to the traditions of monastic crusade historiography. He chose prosimetry, and that choice tells us quite a bit about how Gunther viewed his subject and his purpose. Prosimetry, or the juxtaposing of prose and poetry, was not a new genre in crusade historiography. Two earlier monastic historians, Robert the Monk of Reims[182] and Guibert of Nogent,[183] had interspersed their crusade histories with poems, as had Ralph of Caen, a layperson.[184] It is possible that Gunther never read Guibert or Ralph, but he certainly knew Robert the Monk's work very well. When Magister Gunther had earlier used Robert's *Historia Iherosolimitana* as the source for his *Solimarius*, he had chosen to tell the story in pre-Christian epic form. Now, instead of composing an epic sequel entitled *Constantinopolitanus*, Brother Gunther chose to write a Christian crusade history entitled *Hystoria Constantinopolitana*.

3. THE *HYSTORIA CONSTANTINOPOLITANA* AS HISTORY

History was not an independent art or area of systematic study during the Middle Ages, nor was it recognized as a profession. It served as a minor auxiliary to both grammar and rhetoric, and history writing was considered an amateur literary pursuit. To be sure, history was a special form of literature, because historians, even those who patently lied, claimed to deal with fact rather than fiction. Yet medieval historians and their audiences did not share the modern fixation with exhaustive, systematic research nor did they generally concern themselves with epistemological questions concerning the merits of various modes of investigation, analysis, and interpretation. Because history was neither a profession nor an organized academic discipline, there were no rules governing method, form, or content. As far as medieval devotees of history were concerned, what distinguished historians from one another was the manner in which they told their stories. Gunther certainly expected to be judged from this perspective and, if we are to understand and appreciate what he accomplished, we must not draw any modern dichotomy between the *HC*'s literary structure and its historical theme.

Not only are structure and theme inextricably intertwined in the *HC*, both are highly sophisticated, indeed extraordinarily so. In one of the more significant studies in the field of medieval historiography, Nancy F. Partner argues that twelfth-century historical accounts were paratactic and discursive. That is, they were essentially shapeless by ancient and modern standards, without clear structure and theme. A paratactic narrative is a string of substantially equal elements with no discernible attempt to develop disconnected episodes into coherent patterns, either by ranking them in order of importance or by linking them temporally or causally. Parataxis, which naturally lends itself to ornamental amplification, free association, and complex digressions, appealed emotionally and aesthetically to a twelfth-century audience.[185] Partner further states that, although histories of the time were filled with miracles, portents, and other wonders, very few twelfth-century historians undertook to write contemporary Christian history, which she defines as "[making] systematically known their own understanding of any higher purpose informing recent history."[186] Her insights and conclusions are essentially valid, but each fails when tested against the *HC*. Gunther was an exceptional medieval historian, inasmuch as he imposed a highly ordered and logical structure on his narrative and possessed sufficient intellectual and spiritual confidence to write Christian history.

In both structure and theme the *HC* imitates and depicts a

world that is consonant with the highest ideals and aspirations of twelfth-century humanism. It is an ordered world whose order is intelligible to human reason. It is a world governed by a loving and merciful God. It is a world in which humans enjoy dignity in spite of their weaknesses and frailties, and a world in which humans are raised to positions of dignity because they are used by this loving God for His purposes. It is, moreover, a world whose history is dynamic and progressive, which sees itself not as alienated from its classical past but transcending it. What is more, far from being a jumble of one disconnected event after another, the *HC* is a tightly organized and rather spare piece of history. Each element is subordinated to the work's overarching theme: All the deeds mentioned in this history were done under the direction of God in order to effect an historically significant change in the course of human events and to offer His servants an opportunity to cooperate in the salvation of their souls. Each element in this history is also subordinated to an underlying tone of irony that runs throughout the work. This is not the bitter irony of Edward Gibbon or of Voltaire, and it is certainly not the masked irony of a heretic. It is the irony of an orthodox believer who perceives and takes comfort in the fact that humanity proposes, but ultimately God disposes. Throughout this history Gunther constantly juxtaposes human motives, human causation, human weakness and blindness with divine direction, power, and omniscience. Although the joke is on humanity, including the human hero of this account, Abbot Martin, it is a warm and gentle joke. For Gunther perceives and argues that Martin and his fellow Christian crusaders have contributed to their salvation by unwittingly acting as God's agents. Significantly, although Gunther claims that all of these deeds were accomplished through divine aid and direction, he does not see this divine guidance as a compromising force vis-à-vis human free will. While he ironically juxtaposes human frailty and selfishness with divine omnipotence and perfection, he clearly delineates, as he understands them, the human motives and the chain of temporal events that drove the crusaders along their path. He faults the Venetians for their economic greed in diverting the crusade in the first place; he accepts the causality of the series of historical events that led the crusaders to attack Constantinople, and he provides tangible historical explanations for each of Martin's choices and actions. So, even as he serves as a divinely guided agent of God, the human remains a responsible moral person, and his dignity and merit are thereby the greater. For Gunther, sacred and secular history can and do coexist; while secular history is subordinate and ultimately guided and defined by sacred history, it does proceed along its natural historical course. Yet, at significant points in time these two histories intersect. The events of April 1204 constitute for Gunther one of those miraculous moments of confluence between the sacred and the secular. As a result, human history reached a new plateau.

Gunther's vision was grand, and his art was equally impressive. As already noted, Gunther probably chose to employ prosimetry in part because it was a form that Robert the Monk of Reims had employed. The fact is, Robert had not done so very successfully. His poetic excursions were sporadic, and his verses were little more than ditties that served no structural purpose.

At best they were occasional ornaments. This probably troubled Gunther's artistic sense, especially since Robert claimed to be rewriting an earlier, anonymous crusade account because:

> Since the creation of the world, what has been done, except for the mystery of the salvific Cross, that is more wondrous than what has happened in modern times in this journey of our Jerusalem pilgrims? The more one carefully reflects on it, the more fully he is awe struck in the wide recesses of his mind. For this was not a human work, it was divine. For this reason it should be memorialized in a literary style for the equal edification of both the present generation and posterity, so that, through this, Christian hope in God might be made more firm and His praise might be excited to greater expressiveness in their souls.[187]

Robert never consistently or fully developed the metahistorical theme he established in his prologue. Nor, it must have seemed to Gunther, had Robert's literary skills done full justice to the grandeur of the First Crusade. That might have been one of the reasons a younger Gunther had recast the *Historia Iherosolimitana* into the *Solimarius*. Now, two decades later, Gunther was faced with celebrating and explaining an equally wondrous crusade. He had to have felt that prosimetrum would be the only proper medium for composing not an academic revision of someone else's history, as he had done before, but a true Christian analysis of God's recent intervention in human affairs. He hoped, in the bargain, to beat Robert at his own game and was not disappointed. From the opening lines of chapter 1, which echo and parody Robert's prologue, to the last lines of chapter 24, the *HC* presents a tightly organized and logically developed Christian history.

Twelfth-century Christian historiography could not be separated from Christian metaphysics. By mid-century the school of Chartres had made prosimetry a major vehicle for expressing its brand of Christian Neo-Platonism. The leader of this movement was Master Bernard Silvestris of Tours, who, between 1143 and 1148, in a work known variously as *De mundi universitate* (*On the Totality of the World*) and the *Cosmographia*, presented Christian Europe with a Neo-Platonic interpretation of the workings of the cosmos in a prosimetrical dialogue between *Natura* and *Noys*, or the Divine Mind.[188] Alan of Lille continued this tradition in his *De planctu naturae* (*Nature's Complaint*) of about 1160–1170.[189] Borrowing heavily from Macrobius's late fourth-century *Commentary on Cicero's Dream of Scipio*,[190] the Chartrians had equated *Noys* (in Greek, *Nous*) with

> the consummate and profound reason of God, whom his prime substance brought forth of itself, a second self, not in time, but out of that eternal state in which it abides unmoved, . . . the knowledge and judgment of the divine will in the disposition of things.[191]

The Chartrian marriage of Neo-Platonic metaphysics and prosimetry[192] was undoubtedly a major reason why Gunther chose to employ this particular literary medium.[193] Indeed, Chartres's particular brand of Christian Neo-Platonism provides a key for unlocking the *HC*'s structural and thematic mysteries.

An even more important key is Boethius's *Consolation of Phi-

losophy, itself a prosimetrical masterpiece of seventy-eight sections of alternating poetry and prose.[194] It is difficult to exaggerate the influence of the *Consolation of Philosophy* on pre-modern Europe's intelligentsia.[195] More manuscripts of this early sixth-century treatise survive than of virtually any other medieval text. The *Consolation* is a work of moral philosophy whose purpose is to teach how the vicissitudes of worldly fortune must be understood in the context of Providence's universal order. Lady Philosophy instructs her pupil Boethius that:

> It is no wonder . . . that a situation should seem random and confused when its principle of order is not understood. But, although you do not know why things are as they are, still you cannot doubt that in a world ruled by a good Governor all things do happen justly. . . . Therefore, even though things may seem confused and discordant to you, because you cannot discern the order that governs them, nevertheless everything is governed by its own proper order directing all things toward the good.[196]

This message is the heart and soul of the *HC* and even forms its skeleton: Despite the apparent confusion and randomness of human events, the universe does follow the laws of a divinely mandated moral order.

That order is often obscure to humans blinded by the vicissitudes of human fortune, especially when it seems that too often the good suffer and the evil prosper. One of Boethius's most important contributions to the literary-intellectual baggage of medieval Europe was his creation of the image of the wheel of Fortune. Lady Philosophy, speaking for Fortune, explains this phenomenon in the following manner:

> Here is the source of my power, the game I always play: I spin my wheel and find pleasure in raising the low to a high place and lowering those who were on top. Go up, if you like, but only on condition that you will not feel abused when my sport requires your fall.[197]

Compare this with Gunther's poetic excursus on the vagaries of fortune:

> Now it is clear by what has been laid bare that fickle fortune by such
> sport

Treats human affairs as though they were vile and vain.
Nothing remains or has endured; quickly it is acquired and quickly it passes away—
The vainglory of sufficient earthly prosperity.
Him, whom the wheel of fortune carried to the foyer of heaven,
It hurls headlong back. Sometimes it impoverishes; sometimes it enriches.
Him, who first was poor, it leads aloft from the depths.
Him, stuffed with wealth, it returns to poverty from riches.[198]

The parallels do not end here. In the *Consolation* Boethius and the reader move from ignorance to enlightenment. Under the instruction of Lady Philosophy both learn that only in God can one find perfect goodness and happiness. Moreover, ultimately good does triumph, and evil is punished. In a similar manner, Martin, the crusaders, and the *HC*'s readers slowly discover the providential design that has brought the army to Constantinople. That army proves to be the divine instrument for the punishment of evil. For both Boethius and Gunther, however, providential order and divine foreknowledge in no way negate human free will or relieve people of their moral responsibilities. The choices made by mortals, in the exercise of their freedom, provide the mainspring of action in both the *Consolation of Philosophy* and the *HC*.

The most striking parallelism between the two compositions can be seen in chapter 12 of the *HC*, where Gunther expounds on the manner in which the Divine Mind governs the cosmos. Here, in what is the structural and thematic fulcrum of his history, Gunther writes:

Therefore, all things that are created or happen in time proceed along a fixed path and an immutable course in accordance with that so secret and unfathomable Idea within the Divine Mind, which comprehends the Forms of all things and from which neither the number of grains of sand, nor of drops of water in the sea, nor of leaves in the forest can hide.

Almost seven hundred years earlier, Boethius expressed the same idea in this manner:

The generation of all things, and the whole course of mutable natures and of whatever is in any way subject to change, take their causes, order, and forms from the unchanging mind of God. This divine mind established the manifold rules by which all things are governed.[199]

St. Augustine of Hippo and Boethius between them laid the basis for a tradition of European historical thought that lasted over a thousand years. Augustine's *City of God* defined the pattern of salvation history; Boethius's *Consolation of Philosophy* established a scheme of Christian secular history.[200] Whereas Augustine focused on the journey of the individual soul to God as the most important phenomenon in history and concerned himself very little with the rise and fall of earthly fortunes, Boethius attempted to explain the vagaries of mundane existence within the context of a Christian understanding of Providence. The fact that Boethius presented his message as a *prosimetrum* was not lost on those who followed in his footsteps.

In addition to a Boethian heritage that had imbued it with Christian loftiness, prosimetry also offered Gunther stylistic flexibility. Each of the *HC*'s twenty-five prose chapters is followed by anywhere from seventeen to thirty-four lines of poetry, with most poems measuring twenty. In all, the work contains 537 metrical lines. Unquestionably the poems are decorative, but they also have important structural functions. They annotate the prose by serving as lyrical conclusions, didactic summaries, and moral commentaries upon preceding chapters. In fact, Gunther relegated most of his moral judgments to the poems. At times they supply additional information, and on occasion they anticipate events to be developed in some later chapter. This strategy enabled Gunther to use the poems as convenient repositories for interesting but unessential materials, which would otherwise clutter up and detract from the deliberate spareness of his prose. The poems also serve as transitions, tying chapters together and giving the entire history an organic unity. Above all else, they frame the action of each prose chapter. The chapters are so clearly delineated that they easily lend themselves to architectonic arrangement. In the hands of a master they become literary building blocks for the construction of an impressive edifice.

While the poems ably serve the prose and add greatly to its

impact, they cannot stand on their own; yet stylistically they are impressive. Unlike Gunther's earlier poetry, which closely followed the conventions of Virgil's epic style, the *HC* freely employs the popular rhyme patterns of the day. And, like Boethius's *Consolation of Philosophy*, the *HC*'s poetry is a medley of styles that show the influence of many poets, both ancient and contemporary. At its best, Gunther's poetry is more than imitative. It is rich in imagery and in the various figures of speech or "colors" so popular among twelfth-century poets and theoreticians of poetic style. More significant than his use of decoration and wordplay is the manner in which Gunther controls the sound and rhythm of his poetry to produce some startling effects—effects that bring to mind the music of both church and court in twelfth-century Europe. Two examples must suffice.

Poem 5 is nothing less than the poetical apotheosis of Abbot Martin. Its opening line reads: *Promeruit memorem Martinus uterque favorem*. Note not only the centrality of Martin's name but also the preponderance of the sound *M*. This melodic refrain continues into the next line, but by line three it begins slowly to give way to a new sound, that of *C*. There is a rough equilibrium between *M* and *C* sounds in lines six through ten, but from line eleven onward *C* totally dominates. What does all of this mean? We must look to the poem's message—Abbot Martin's present holiness and future sanctity. What Gunther has done is to demonstrate through sound the process of Martin's growth in Christ—*Martinus crescit in Christo*.

Poem 20 stands at the opposite end of creation's spectrum, being one of the *HC*'s several poetic curses. Here Gunther achieves a staccato effect through his symphony of meter, rhyme scheme, and a continuous series of short phrases and sentences, heavy with dissyllabic words. Consider the impact of the poem's opening lines:

Nunc age, cece, vola! Neque dignus es hac nece sola;
Sed cruce fune mola; nunc age, cece, vola!
Dignus es igne mori, rapido cibus esse calori,
Certa lege fori dignus es igne mori.[201]

Clearly Gunther is striving to approximate the flight and fear of Morciflo, and here we can hear the hurried cadence of running feet and a pounding heart. But flight ends in capture, and in these short, angry bursts of words Gunther is also jabbing at and tormenting this hated object of his curse, much as one would torment a caged prisoner. All in all, the poet has successfully communicated the emotions he wishes his audience to share.

Gunther did not simply want his audience to feel; he demanded that it think. Poem 20, a curse, and poem 7, a panegyric, share the same meter and have largely the same eccentric rhyme pattern. In fact, they are the only two poems to employ this particular rhyme scheme. Poem 7 is a glowing tribute to Pope Innocent III who, Gunther claims, is innocent in life as well as in name. Poem 20 curses Morciflo, the usurper of the throne of Constantinople, in whom Gunther finds every vice and whom he characterizes as the "dregs of humanity." The message created by this contrast is obvious.[202] Many other echoes and parallels exist among the poems, and virtually all of them provide antiphonal harmony through a juxtaposition of moods and themes. Poem 5, analyzed above, anticipates the action of the second half of the *HC*: when Martin will serve as one of Christ's agents at Constantinople. Here Gunther foreshadows chapter 19, the structural counterpart to chapter 5, where Martin, the ever loyal servant of Christ, is favored with holy relics. These tokens of divine favor will bring this modest man deserved fame on earth and serve as tokens of his future salvation—themes introduced in poem 5.

As interesting and as structurally important as the poems are, they are subordinate to the prose. It is in the prose that we find Gunther at his thought provoking best.

What is most impressive about the prose is its tone of sophisticated irony. Parallelisms, word and phrase echoes, and oxymorons abound, and each of these rhetorical devices underscores a single message: Things are not as they often appear. Thus the doge can be blind but foresighted; both Innocent and Philip of Swabia can be young in years but respectively old in wisdom and mature in the fear of God. Martin can bring back to Pairis holy plunder, which he has obtained through sacred sacrilege. When in chapter 9 Abbot Martin tries to gain papal dispensation from his crusade vow, because he does not wish to go to Constantinople, he presses his case *omni precum molimine* (with every manner of prayer). The irony cannot be lost on the reader, who only one chapter earlier read that Philip of Swabia had made his case to the army to go to Constantinople *omni precum molimine*. Yes, nothing is quite as it appears. But while the phenomenal world might appear unordered and contradictory to the human mind, there is basic divine order and harmony in the cosmos. Just as Gunther's rhetoric skillfully imitates the confusion of life's apparent contradictions, so the overall structure of these prose chapters is a pale imitation of the order and balance that the Divine Mind has imposed on creation.

In order to perceive the *HC*'s structure, one must realize that originally it consisted of only twenty-four chapters. In chapter 19 Gunther tells us that his list of the relics carried home by Martin appears at the end of the work.[203] We find that list in chapter 24. Indeed, both the prose and poetry of chapter 24 have the ring of finality; themes introduced in the first chapter are now concluded. Chapter 25 simply limps along as a weak anticlimax. As noted in section 1, this discordant epilogue was surely tacked on at a later date, probably in 1207 or 1208 and probably at Abbot Martin's insistence, in order to make public King Philip's charter confirming the abbey's possession of the relics and to insure against the charter's loss.

With twenty-four chapters forming the body of the *HC*, the twelfth chapter becomes its theological fulcrum and historiographical turning point. The first half of the chapter, at first glance, seems to be an aimless digression. Here, borrowing heavily from Boethius and the Neo-Platonic writings of Macrobius and Bernard Silvestris, Gunther describes the manner in which the Divine Mind (*Noys*) governs all creation. This is, of course, anything but a digression, for here we see the theological foundation of the entire work. Lest the reader miss the point, Gunther explicitly notes: "We have to believe that it followed from the uncontrovertible Providence of God that our army . . . by a change of plans declared war against this great city." The chapter then ends with a brief description of the army's arrival at Constantinople and Alexius III's flight from the city. Chapter 24 completes both the historical action and the theological argument. Here Gunther catalogues the sacred spoils that Divine Providence had transferred to the West through Martin, and he reminds his reader of the various events in this history that could only have been effected by God's will.

It is not just chapters 12 and 24 that balance one another; each chapter has its structural and thematic counterpart. The result is that balanced motifs and scenes combine to create a work whose structure illustrates and becomes one with its message. The schematic pattern that unites the *HC*'s original twenty-four chapters into a coherent whole can be illustrated by a simple diagram:

	12	
11		13
10		14
9		15
8		16
7		17
6		18
5		19
4		20
3		21
2		22
1		23
	24	

In this schema, each chapter thematically balances its counterpart by either foreshadowing or completing the action of its paired "twin." In turn, the twelve pairs of chapters unite to create a harmonious single work, in which the underlying connections that tie each and every event narrated in this history become manifest to the reader. In essence, chapters 1 through 11 could be subtitled "humanity proposes," whereas chapters 13 through 23 could be subtitled "God disposes."

Let us look at each of these twelve pairs in some detail in order to understand better the artistic mastery of Gunther and the message that he expected his reader to derive from this work.[204]

Chapter 1 presents a straightforward argument: God chooses the humble and lowly as agents, thereby exalting them when they perform His great deeds. Gunther also notes that all the exploits recorded in this history were accomplished under the guidance of God and are, therefore, righteous. Consonant with the humility of God's agent, Abbot Martin, Gunther promises that he will narrate his story in a humble and plain style. The accompanying poem conveys several themes. First, the poet assures us that the gift of the Cross is forever renewed. At the same time he juxtaposes the moods of fear and joy when he writes: "Our hearts, albeit trembling, sparkle at the sight.// Although they narrow in fear, our eyes light up with joy." Within this poem light appears twice as a metaphor. Now consider chapter 23, its counterpart. The stamp of divine approval is put on Martin's pious pilferage by the miraculous manner in which he is protected on his homeward journey. He arrives home "in grand style but with the great humility of piety." In the accompanying poem joy and fear are juxtaposed when the poet writes: "Now, in safety, you can, with carefree heart,// Be free from fear and breathe quietly." The metaphor of light dispersing darkness appears twice, and the reader is assured that the Cross of Christ has brought Martin home safely.

Chapters 2 and 22 play on the theme that God leads and teaches Martin who rightly trusts in Providence. In chapter 2 the crusade begins on a wondrous note, insofar as both Fulk and Martin are from Paris/Pairis and bear the toponym *Parisiensis*. Other subthemes include the fact of the early poverty of Pairis and its contemporary wealth, despite the land's cold desolation. Gunther also notes that Martin is regarded by the laity of Alsace as lovable, but he was universally believed, by those who knew him, to be physically unequal to the tasks laid upon him by the pope. Nevertheless, the crusade is launched in Basel by a large crowd at the Münster. In the poem Martin prays. Anticipating the crusade, he is confident of success. In chapter 22 Martin is happily received in Acre by the Germans who are especially fond of him. His friend and countryman Werner does not believe it likely that Martin's relics can be safely brought back to Germany. Martin rejects an abbey on Mt. Carmel, despite its richness, in order to bring the relics back to Pairis, thereby enriching it. Then Martin embarks for home, attended by a great crowd, and his homeward journey begins on a wondrous note with his visions. In the poem Martin prays. He anticipates his journey home and is confident that the relics are guarantees of a safe voyage.

In chapter 3 God speaks through His prophet, Martin. Every incident in the life of Christ that Martin mentions in his sermon has a corresponding relic in chapter 24. Without realizing it, Martin is foretelling his own success. Martin also holds out the promise of earthly treasures for his audience (in chapter 21 Martin will return with heavenly treasures). In his sermon Martin speaks of the recent loss of the Holy Cross. Little does he know that he will bring a portion of the Cross home to Alsace. After giving his sermon, Martin assumes the crusade vow. In the poem Gunther presents the theme of visiting the Holy Land as a crusader. Martin is obedient to the pope and becomes a soldier. In chapter 21 God speaks through the prophetic images on the column. Without realizing it, Constantinople harbors images of its own chastisement. In this same chapter, Martin begins his return voyage to the Holy Land, which he had vowed to reach. The poem focuses on the theme of returning to the Holy Land, thereby illustrating Martin's obedience to his colleagues in Acre. Consequently, this "unwarlike man" completes his duties.

In chapter 4 Martin is chosen to lead the army from Basel. The crusaders put their affairs in order, and like a good Cistercian, Martin insists on going to Cîteaux to receive permission to go on crusade. Fearlessly and happily, Martin faces the beginning of his journey. In the poem the crusaders from Basel are lighthearted;

led by Christ, their reward is guaranteed. Chapter 20 not only completes the action of chapter 4, it also provides an interesting contrast with the God-directed crusaders from Basel. In this chapter Baldwin is elected "king" of Constantinople, and the crusaders put the affairs of the new empire in order. Like a good Cistercian, Martin turns down a bishopric and insists on returning home to Pairis. Meanwhile, fearfully and unhappily, Morciflo comes to a sad end. The poem is a curse on Morciflo, whose damnation is merited.

The most interesting and certainly the most important balancing act is that of chapters 5 and 19. In chapter 5 Gunther compares Martin of Pairis's sanctity with that of his namesake, St. Martin of Tours. Although the comparison seems intentionally strained and, thereby, humorous, Gunther has a serious point to make: We should not be deceived by appearances. Just as Martin of Tours was a man of God even as he served as a soldier, so this monk turned crusader remains a man of God and potentially a divine agent even though he rides at the head of a troop. In the light of what will happen in chapter 19, it is necessary for Gunther to establish that his abbot is a virtuous man. Chapter 19 is undoubtedly the most humorous and ironic chapter in the entire history, because it deals with Martin's theft of relics. Martin is a comic figure in a wildly funny scene, and the comedy is intentional, but it is divine comedy and sacred irony. Gunther's point clearly is that this apparent impiety—the looting of a church—is the act of a holy man performing God's work. Appearances are truly deceiving at first glance in both chapters, but in chapter 19 Gunther assures us that this monk/soldier/thief is neither a soldier nor a robber. He is "a man . . . of totally spiritual life," and his thievery is "sacred sacrilege."

A few other parallels between chapters 5 and 19 are worth noting. The crusaders depart Basel (called the royal city in chapter 2) with Abbot Martin in command, and during their journey the countryside willingly supports the crusader army. Gunther also informs us that Abbot Martin will beggar himself and, consequently, return home "poor in spirit . . . but wealthy in and 'full of' the riches of a heavenly treasure." The poem strikes the theme that God's truth prevails and "the fame of virtuous men grows beyond death." In chapter 19 the crusaders sack Constantinople (called the royal city). Relics and money had been brought to a certain church from the surrounding countryside. Therefore, these country folk unwittingly and unwillingly support the crusaders who would plunder this wealth. Abbot Martin conducts a "personal military exploit" by stealing relics and is enriched thereby. Indeed, he is "overstuffed" with relics. Martin, the priest/soldier is "girded for action" and uses the folds of his habit to carry off the sacred spoils—a subtle play on the legend of St. Martin's cloak mentioned in chapter 5. In the poem we learn that pagan antiquity's lies stand in stark contrast to Christian truth: "Let poetic deception cease."

In chapter 6 the pilgrims plan to assault Egypt, an impoverished land. Here Gunther also informs his readers of the injuries the Zarans have committed against Venice and the Venetians' planned revenge. In the face of that plan, many fear that capturing a Christian city will entail visiting slaughter and arson on those Christians. Consequently, Martin is charged with preventing the spilling of Christian blood at Zara. Another theme is the poverty of the crusaders at Venice. In the light of these events and themes, the poem strikes a tone of fear, uncertainty, and near despair. In chapter 18 the pilgrims seize Constantinople, a fabulously wealthy city. Here we also learn of the injuries that the Greek citizens of Constantinople had committed against the city's Latin inhabitants and of the Latins' revenge. In the course of its assault on the city, the army refrains from slaughtering the Greeks because of the admonishments of Martin and the other clerics. Even so, almost two thousand Greeks die, and fire destroys almost one-third of the city. As a consequence of its successful assault, everyone in the crusader army is suddenly wealthy. In the light of this success, the poem strikes a note of triumph.

Chapter 7 focuses on the capture of Zara. The scene opens with a sea exploit, as the crusaders sail through the Adriatic. Upon arrival at Zara, the crusaders attack the city slowly and reluctantly, choosing to frighten the Zarans rather than kill them. In this battle, the crusaders are "engaged against Christians for Christ's honor." The theme of the poem is straightforward: The crusaders deserve forgiveness. Chapter 17 focuses on the capture of Constantinople. The scene opens with a sea exploit, as the crusaders repel Greek naval attacks. The crusaders attack eagerly and with élan. They frighten and fight the Christian Greeks "for the honor of God." The theme of this poem is equally straightforward: The crusaders deserve praise and spoils.

The scene of chapter 8 is Rome. Here the reader learns certain facts that illustrate the contemporary degeneracy of Constantinople, namely the deposition of Isaac, the Greeks' religious error, and their rebelliousness toward the Roman Church. Despite his desire to see the city in the hands of pious Catholics, Constantinople seems impregnable to the pope. The poem deals with Martin's quandary as he contemplates disaster. The scene of chapter 16 is Constantinople—the Second Rome. Here the reader learns certain facts that illustrate the orthodox foundations of Constantinople, namely the close and proper relationship between Constantine and Pope Sylvester and their respective roles in the creation of Constantinople. Despite the crusaders' desire to force their will upon the city, Constantinople seems impregnable. The poem deals with the crusaders' quandary as they contemplate disaster.

Chapter 9 sees Martin at Acre, a city that serves as a bulwark of Christianity in the Holy Land (chapter 3) but which now appears to be in dire straits. Chapter 15 sees the army at Constantinople, a schismatic and heretical city (chapter 8) that appears impregnable.

Chapter 10 opens with the contagion of pestilence, a theme carried over from the previous chapter. Here we also learn of the deceit of the Muslims, who break the truce with the Latin kingdom. We see, in the face of that deceit, the desperate yet brave resolve and quick response of the Latins at Acre—"that little enclave in the Holy Land." We also learn of Conrad of Schwarzenberg's ingenuous truthfulness, and the willingness of the army at

Constantinople to fight a hopeless battle. The poem catches our attention by proclaiming, "Learn of the marvels," (*accipe mira*), as it announces the coming story of Greek treachery, cowardice, and shame and the punishment that a small group of Latins will visit upon them. Chapter 14 opens with the contagion of parricide, a theme carried over from the previous chapter. Here we also learn of the deceit of Morciflo, who plots to destroy the crusader army. We see first the ingenuous guilelessness of the army and the desperate yet brave resolve and quick response of the Latins at Constantinople—"few and impoverished, in the midst of enemies." The poem catches our attention by proclaiming, "Learn of . . . wondrous phenomena" (*accipe . . . miraque rerum*), as it trumpets the story of crusader heroism and manliness and the fact that a small group of Latins will punish the perfidious Greeks.

In chapter 11 Alexius (IV) comes to camp and gains the support of the army, which decides to install him on his rightful throne, and concord reigns between the Greek prince and the crusaders. On one level, the imperfect plane of human cupidity, the Venetians and crusaders desire the promised wealth of Constantinople. On a higher level, the perfect plane of God's Will, Divine Goodness intends to bring the schismatic Greeks back to concord with the Church and to enrich the Latin pilgrims with the wealth of Constantinople. In chapter 13 Alexius III flees the city, and Alexius IV, the rightful king, successfully wins over the citizens of Constantinople. However, discord ensues between the Greeks and Latins, because the Greeks fear they are losing their wealth to the Latins. Alexius loses the support of the Greeks and is deposed and murdered by Morciflo.

We have already seen the core antiphonal relationship between chapters 12 and 24, but a few other parallels are worthy of note. In chapter 12 Gunther informs us that God the First Form, "comprehends the Forms of all things" and directs "all things . . . along a fixed path." After this proclamation, Gunther notes the army's arrival at Constantinople. In the poem a curse is delivered on Alexius III. According to Gunther, Alexius is defeated and shameless, and he who has faithlessly enriched himself with Greek *rega-*

lia is forced to flee in a cowardly fashion. This man, who has subverted his realm and overturned its laws, is so base that no one may rightfully speak his despised name. Chapter 24 proclaims: "Blessed be God! He alone effects wondrous miracles." There follows a catalogue of the relics taken at Constantinople and transferred under God's direction to Pairis. Gunther wants us to see these relics as concrete images of the eternal Forms that he introduced in chapter 12. Here we also find a repetition and summary in prose and poetry of the thesis of the *HC* as set out in chapters 1 and 12: None of this was chance; everything was accomplished under God's direction. In poem 24,which employs the same rhyme scheme and metrical form as poem 12 but which is twice its length, Gunther delivers an encomium on Abbot Martin, who, unlike Alexius III, merits the honor of being remembered. Martin has enriched his people and has bravely and faithfully come through every trial victorious: "The man of religion was enriched with . . . sacred wares . . . the rich plunder of piety." From the *HC*'s opening lines, Gunther has prepares his reader for this moment of epiphany when suddenly Abbot Martin's role in the unfolding of God's holy plan is fully revealed.

This schematic structure is impressive, but equally impressive is the historical message it serves. Gunther was not content to claim simply that the events of the Fourth Crusade were directed by God; he attempted to define their place and importance in the flow of human history. As this synopsis indicates, in chapter 8 Gunther outlines the lamentable state of affairs in Constantinople on the eve of the Fourth Crusade. In chapter 16, its counterbalance, he traces the history of Constantine's foundation of the city, as the result of a divinely inspired vision. The argument of this latter chapter is that, by constructing Constantinople upon the decaying ruins of Greek Byzantium, Constantine gave new Christian life to the ancient world. In poem 18 Gunther returns to this theme. The very spoils of plundered Troy, he states, had eventually passed into the possession of Constantinople. Now these same riches of antiquity were being carried off by Latin Christians. Why? Chapter 11 supplies the answer: The Greeks are no longer worthy. The inevitable, but only implied, conclusion is that European Roman Christendom had, by divine judgment, meritoriously come into full inheritance of the entire antique world, and human history, at that moment, had reached a new stage of evolution. Indeed, on three separate occasions Gunther emphasizes the historical uniqueness of what happened at Constantinople. In the verse to chapter 1 he claims that, although Christ unfolds old truths anew to every generation, in this present age He has effected something the like of which has never before been seen and never will be seen again. Poem 14 again reminds us that these events are unprecedented, and poem 19 claims that the events of the Fourth Crusade are greater by far than the conquest of Troy. They are greater because, as Gunther reminds us continuously throughout the work, they were not the happenstances of chance. They were divinely directed. True to the model of Boethius's *Consolation of Philosophy*, Gunther turns even fickle Fortune's wheel into a metaphor for God's inscrutable historical plan.[205]

Peter Burke has argued that medieval historical thought differed from that of post-Petrarchan Europe in several major ways, chief of which was its lack of a sense of anachronism—a notion that the past was essentially different from the present.[206] This was not true of Gunther, who had a sense of history that led him to believe that his age had transcended antiquity. What is also true is that, unlike the humanist historians of the *Quattrocento* and *Cinquecento*, Gunther had no nostalgia for the past or any desire to find refuge in it. At the same time, he felt an affinity with the classical past rather than a sense of estrangement from it. The paradox is more apparent than real. While Gunther perceived meaningful differences between his own age and that of antiquity, what struck him the most was the ordered process of historical development and, therefore, continuity from the antique past to the present. This process was rational and could be comprehended, even though its full meaning transcended human understanding. Above all else, it was an historical dynamic in which humans played dignified and responsible roles even as they were directed by a divine plan that could not be frustrated.

Such, in brief, is the argument, thesis, and structure of the *HC*, a carefully constructed work that illustrates a triple faith. It shows us a faith in the ultimate friendly composition of the universe and a faith in the beneficent direction of human history. It also reveals a faith in the ability of the human mind to perceive, albeit dimly, and to explain, admittedly inadequately, the beneficence of that divinely controlled cosmos and the dynamic role accorded God's historical agents. As such, it is an expression of the highest ideals of twelfth-century Christian humanism.

This grand view of human history carried with it a price, inasmuch as Gunther twisted certain historical phenomena to fit his metahistorical mold. His apologetic purposes also compromised the *HC*'s worth as a factual source. Errors abound in the work, and, were we to use it uncritically, we would be misled on many points. No historian today would be as naïve as the seventeenth-century savant Angel Manrique, who accepted at face value Gunther's claim that he wrote only the truth,[207] but there is still a wide spectrum of disagreement among scholars concerning the value of this history and its trustworthiness as a source. At one pole is Anna Maria Nada Patrone, who has mistakenly characterized the *HC* as one of the best eyewitness accounts of the crusade;[208] at the other is Francis Swietek, who sees the *HC* as "an intriguing and sophisticated text of quite limited value to historical researchers."[209] Most historians would probably align themselves with Donald Queller, who describes the *HC* as flawed but valuable.[210] How flawed and how valuable remain to be established.

The *HC* has severely limited value for anyone concentrating exclusively on the political and military aspects of the Fourth Crusade, but that fact is not surprising. Both Gunther and Martin were clerics and, more specifically, monks. Each had, at best, only a meager understanding of and interest in military grand strategy and battlefield tactics. Martin had not been involved in the high councils of the barons and the Venetians nor had he directly participated in the assaults on Zara and Constantinople. His memories of these battles could not have been more than hazy impressions. Martin's imperfect recollections combined with Gunther's artistic, apologetic, and theological purposes result in an account heavy with factual errors.

Gunther lays the whole blame for the diversion to Zara on Venetian "deception and perfidy," failing to mention the essential reason for this incident—the crusaders' inability to pay Venice in full for the ships and supplies for which they had contracted.[211] He wrongly informs us that the voyage to Zara was speedy and incorrectly reports that the Venetians razed the city shortly after its capitulation in November 1202.[212] He also mistakenly states that Alexius arrived at Zara while the army was still encamped there and that the young prince won the army over to his cause at that point.[213] Gunther appears ignorant of the fact that the army stopped at Corfu on its way to Constantinople, and he seems equally unaware of the crisis there, when it seemed that the crusade would disintegrate because of the fierce opposition of a majority of the crusaders to the diversion to Constantinople. Indeed, he states that the voyage from Zara to Constantinople was nonstop[214]—a sailing impossibility in the early thirteenth century. He misleads his reader when he writes that Alexius III was defeated in a single, short battle outside the walls of the imperial city.[215] He likewise fails to note that Isaac II was restored to the throne and ruled as co-emperor with his son, Alexius IV; in fact, Gunther tells us nothing about Isaac, save that he had been deposed and, as a result, the young Alexius had been cheated out of his patrimony.[216] Gunther does not mention any of the hostilities that eventually erupted between Alexius IV and his crusader patrons, and he ascribes the young Greek's murder by Morciflo solely to the fact that Alexius refused to turn against his Latin friends.[217] Gunther's accounts of the assaults of 1204 are even more inaccurate. He wildly exaggerates the naval threat that the Byzantine fleet presented to the army[218] and the tactical advantage that crossbows gave the Latins.[219] He totally neglects to mention the many skirmishes between the Greeks and the army during February and March and the costly set back that the crusaders suffered on April 9 when they unsuccessfully tried to carry portions of both the land and sea walls. Gunther's account leads to the false conclusion that the crusaders captured the city in a single, fairly quick assault, in which they lost only one soldier.[220] This catalogue of errors, inaccuracies, and distortions could be multiplied several times over,[221] but it is unnecessary here. The notes that accompany the present translation indicate where Gunther's story is contradicted by other evidence.

Are we then to dismiss the *HC* as a work whose "pattern of suppression and distortion . . . renders the text profoundly suspect as an historical source?"[222] Such a judgment goes a bit too far and fails to take into account the *HC*'s special perspective and purposes. Consider chapter 8. Because of Gunther's clerical interests and Abbot Martin's good fortune to be at the papal court in March 1203, we have a valuable insight into Innocent III's attitude and policy toward the diversion to Constantinople. Through Gunther and Martin we enter into a papal consistory where Innocent freely expresses his distaste for the Greeks but also gives good reasons why he cannot support this plan to sail to Constantinople: He fears the Byzantine fleet, and he shrinks from shedding Greek Christian blood. To forestall what he fears will be a disaster, the pope is willing to compromise, and he allows the crusaders to forage along the Greek coast. The papal register for Innocent's sixth pontifical year has preserved the letter in which he authorized the army to commandeer supplies from the Greeks.[223] With such corroboration, Gunther's account becomes an especially valuable piece of evidence that must be seriously studied by anyone interested in the pope's role in the Fourth Crusade.[224] Chapter 6 provides equally interesting evidence. Alone of all our Western sources, Gunther mentions why the crusaders originally planned to sail against Egypt rather than to Syria: A treaty between the Christians of Outremer and the Muslims was still in effect, and Egypt was especially vulnerable, having recently suffered a debilitating famine. External evidence from Levantine sources supports Gunther on both points.[225] Gunther also informs us of how Cardinal Peter Capuano worked to keep the army from breaking up over the Zaran affair. In this instance the *GeH* offers corroboration.[226] Supported in these and other instances, the *HC* is clearly not a worthless source for even the strictly political-military events of the crusade. However, its value far exceeds its being simply an adjunct to the accounts of Clari and Villehardouin.

As a clerical history, the *HC* provides important insights for historians specializing in medieval religious culture. At one level Gunther's history gives us a glimpse of how one early thirteenth-century man—Abbot Martin—perceived and attempted to conform to the religious ideals of his society. Martin was a decent yet flawed man, who lacked the heroic sanctity of St. Bernard and the greatness of Innocent III, but who, by virtue of his mediocrity, better represented the general culture of his age.

The crusade sermon in chapter 3, although surely crafted by Gunther,[227] in all likelihood contains the basic elements of the sermon that Martin delivered in Basel. As such, it reveals the major motives of the rank and file crusader: a conviction that he was called to this duty by Christ who needed his help; a belief that the Holy Land possessed a special sanctity—the sanctity of a relic—which had to be defended against the defilement of the unbeliever; and the hope that God would reward him for this holy work with both salvation and earthly prosperity.[228] We must understand this expectation of a sure reward at the expense of those whom God judges unworthy, if we wish to understand Abbot Martin's desire at Constantinople not to "remain empty-handed while everyone else got rich."[229] To refuse these heaven-endowed rewards would be tantamount to denying the will of God.

Martin's journey to Acre to fulfill his crusade vow tells us quite a bit about how crusaders perceived their vows and their relationship to the armies with which they traveled. Crusaders were, above all else, persons engaged in a pilgrimage. Their vows were personal obligations to visit and defend the Holy Land. The armed contingents that they joined were essentially logistical conveniences, and we must not impose modern concepts of military unity and discipline upon these crusade "armies." For this reason the pilgrim-crusader's overriding loyalty was to the vow and his perception of what actions were consonant with that vow.[230] We see this clearly in Abbot Martin's very different reactions to the attacks on Zara and Constantinople.

Martin's actions at Constantinople and Gunther's commentaries on the Greeks provide insight into the status of Greco-Latin Christian relations in the early thirteenth century. Some students of the schism between the churches of Rome and Constantinople have already looked at Gunther in this regard; others have overlooked him.[231]

Gunther also manages to tell us a fair amount about some of his own values and beliefs. We see that Gunther had a certain mistrust of those who bought and sold for profit. In chapters 6 and 11 his only explanation for Venice's going respectively to Zara and Constantinople was greed and protection of its mercantile interests.[232] This learned churchman also shared at least one of the beliefs of the lowest elements of Christian society, although in his case it appears to have been based on reason as well as faith. We should not doubt that Gunther accepted the reality of the visions, dreams, and other portents that he related and which played such important roles in his story.[233] If, indeed, the phenomena of this world are nothing more than hazy shadows of the eternal Forms created by Divine Providence, then Gunther reasonably expected this loving and merciful God to send his people occasional supernatural signs to guide them in their participation in the workings of the Divine Will in human history.[234]

In summary, the *HC* is a valuable historical source when appreciated for what it is and understood for what it is not. It merits continued, careful study by historians, especially those concerned with medieval mentalities.

4. A NOTE ON THE TRANSLATION

Three known manuscripts of the *HC* exist: MS 321, fols. 1r–23r (hereafter I) in the Munich University library; MS 248 (formerly 434), fols 33v–47v (hereafter C) in the municipal library of Colmar, France; and MS lat. 903, fols. 115r–148r (hereafter M) in the Bavarian State Library in Munich.[235] In 1875 Paul Riant produced the first complete modern edition of the *HC* based on a collation of the three extant manuscripts.[236] Two years later he reprinted that edition in the first volume of *Exuviae sacrae Constantinopolitanae* (*The Holy Relics of Constantinople*),[237] his compendium of Latin sources dealing with relics stolen from Constantinople in the wake of the Fourth Crusade.

The first to try his hand at rendering the *HC* into a modern language was Theodor Renaud. Assuming the pseudonym Theodor Vulpinus, he published in 1889 a German translation under the auspices of the Vogesen Club, a German patriotic association of Alsace-Lorraine.[238] His translation, however, was flawed and the work had limited circulation. In 1901 Dana C. Munro helped popularize Abbot Martin of Pairis's exploits in Constantinople by translating into English portions of chapters 19 and 24 of the *HC* for an undergraduate anthology of Fourth Crusade sources.[239] The excerpt from chapter 19, which details Martin's pious theft of relics, became a minor classic, especially after Charles Homer Haskins quoted it in *The Renaissance of the Twelfth Century*.[240] Haskins's book, popular for well over half a century, has been read by tens of thousands of American students. Because of the account's humor and broad irony, several generations of university-trained people have remembered the good abbot's adventures, even though they might have forgotten his name and the source of the story. Recently Louise and Jonathan Riley-Smith published their own translation of this famous scene from the *HC*, as well as a translation of the crusade sermon that Gunther puts into Abbot Martin's mouth in chapter 3.[241] The only successful translation to date of the entire *HC* was published in 1956 by Erwin Assmann.[242] His German rendition of the work was well done and finally provided Gunther with a wider audience in his native land.

All of these translations shared a problem, inasmuch as they were based on Riant's edition, which contains quite a few transcriptional errors, despite attempts by Riant and several of his early reviewers to correct some obvious misreadings.[243] Realizing the flaws in the text established by Riant, I prepared my own edition of the *HC* after traveling to the libraries where the three manuscripts reside. Study of the manuscripts led me to conclude that M, an early fifteenth-century copy, is closest to the now lost manuscript composed at Pairis in the early thirteenth century. At the same time, M, as is true of C and I, clearly contains errors. Any new edition of the *HC* would necessitate one's having to collate all three texts, often deciding among variant readings. In several places one would have to reconstruct the original words from three clearly erroneous transcriptions. The resultant edition that I fashioned served as the Latin text for my translation. Before I could submit this new edition to a publisher, Peter Orth's own, quite excellent edition of the *HC* appeared in print, rendering my edition of the Latin text moot—at least as far as publication was concerned. I checked my already-completed translation against the text that Orth established, and discovered that he and I agree on almost all points. In several places, however, I accepted his readings and emendations of the received text as superior to my own and amended my translation accordingly. In the almost equally rare instances where I disagreed with his judgment, I followed my own edition, indicating my reasoning in the notes that accompany the present translation. Anyone who wishes to check that translation should, therefore, use Orth's edition. It is now and will be perhaps for all time the standard edition of the *HC*.

THE CAPTURE OF CONSTANTINOPLE

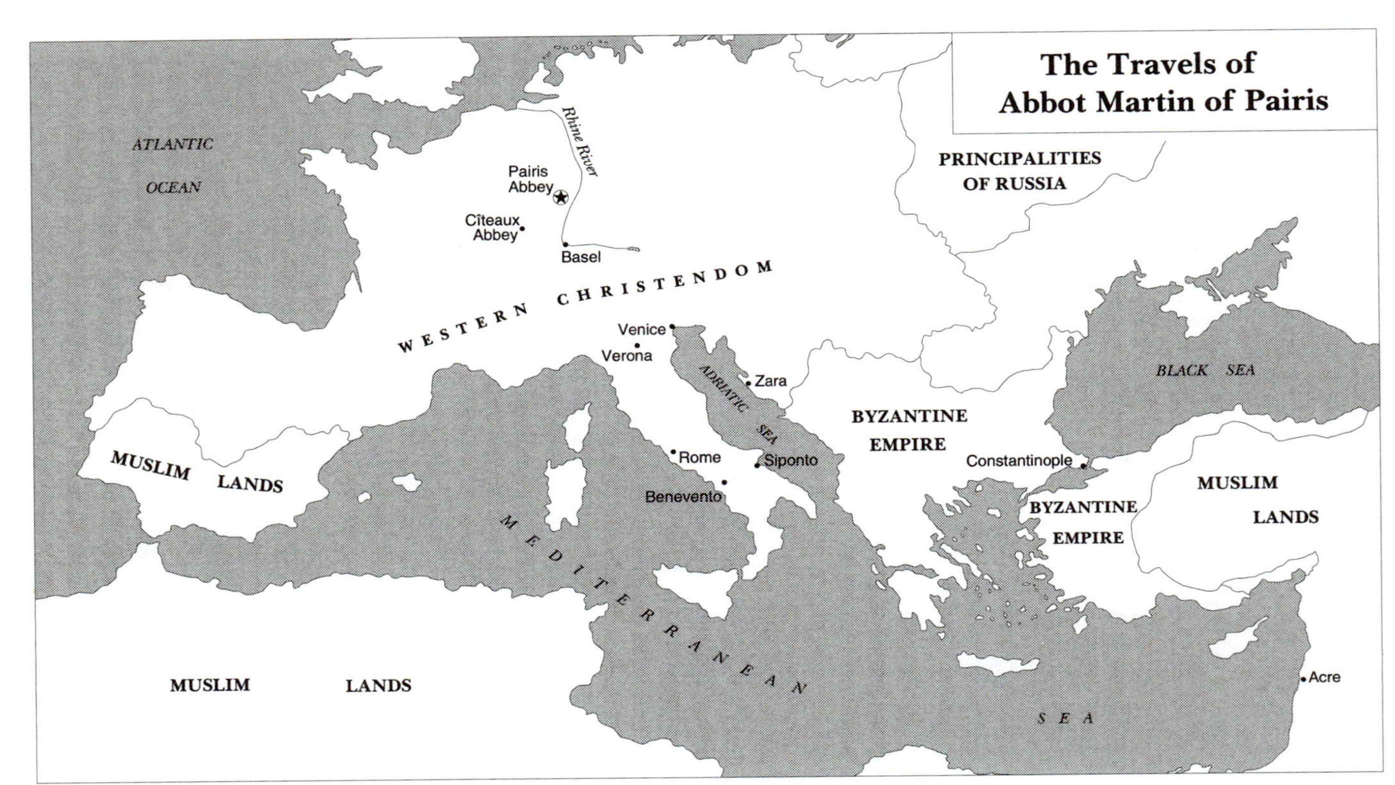
The Travels of
Abbot Martin of Pairis
ATLANTIC
OCEAN
Rhine River
Pairis
Abbey
Cîteaux
Abbey
Basel
PRINCIPALITIES
OF RUSSIA
WESTERN CHRISTENDOM
Venice
Verona
Zara
ADRIATIC SEA
BLACK SEA
BYZANTINE
EMPIRE
Constantinople
Rome
Siponto
Benevento
MUSLIM LANDS
MUSLIM
LANDS
BYZANTINE
EMPIRE
MEDITERRANEAN
SEA
MUSLIM LANDS
Acre

Hystoria Constantinopolitana: The Capture of the City of Constantinople from which, among other relics, a large part of the Holy Cross was translated to Alsace[1]

1. All manifestations of divine power excite such intensive wonder that unextraordinary phenomena should not be judged divine. Still, we are particularly in the habit of marveling at those great and difficult deeds which that divine power deigns to display through simple persons—persons who humbly in their own sight are the least of humanity and are deemed unequal to such tasks by others. For this reason, it is more marvelous that the people of the children of Israel were delivered from the tyranny of Pharaoh and out of the iron furnace of Egyptian slavery through Moses, a humble man who, holding no office,[2] tended the sheep of his father-in-law Jethro, than if this people had been freed through some very powerful king in mighty battle and by thousands of soldiers. So also it is with greater astonishment that we acknowledge the world received the faith of Christ through unsophisticated people—poor fishermen and unlettered persons—than if the religion of this Christian faith had been taught and established by the authority of Augustus Caesar, the learning of Plato, or the eloquence of Demosthenes or Cicero.[3] Certainly, the less God's works are joined to human ability, the more the majesty of divine power shines forth within them.[4]

For this reason, it seemed acceptable for me to relate, although in a low and plain style and in straightforward discourse,[5] certain truly great and difficult deeds that the Lord has deigned to effect in our time through a certain rather modest and humble man to the praise and glory of His name, the pious memory[6] of this particular man, the perpetual felicity of our present place, and, most assuredly, the honor and delight of the entire German people or, more truly and importantly, for the consolation and protection of the whole Western Church. The pages of this story of ours will contain absolutely nothing false or doubtful.[7] Rather, they will adhere to the true and strict sequence of events, just as this man, about whom we are about to say much, rather humbly and bashfully[8] narrated the pure and simple story to us. We do not dare write about the praise and commendation of which this man is worthy lest he, who attributes everything to God and seeks to ascribe nothing to himself, be offended by his praises. Nevertheless, neither will we be able to keep entirely silent altogether, lest we do a clear injustice to God, the author of all these deeds, who is accustomed to exalt his humble people. Therefore we will be careful to balance our pen between the two, so that the mighty works of God, which were accomplished through him,[9] might not lie concealed, and so that this man might remain undisturbed in his humility.

Therefore, whoever is inspired to pick up this, our little book, or to read it, let him also zealously bring sagacity and diligence of mind to the things treated herein, which are meant to be minutely examined. For he will find here momentous, well-known events which would never have taken place or happened without divine direction. We also want the reader to be forewarned that even if things done by our own people appear impious, he must not doubt that they were, nevertheless, effected by the Divine Will, which is always and everywhere just.[10]

Let every man hear the joys I proclaim, and how great their
  number,
And may my labor add to the glory and praise of God!
Rich gifts of God, tokens of heavenly victory
Brought to this spot; by right do I call them "joys."
You did it; you made possible what was done,
And you order it written; glory to you, Christ.
You often rekindle revered memories of the Cross,
And repeat, at any time, the old with the new;
The things which happened by your pleasure are forever
  made new.
Lest darkness hide them, you order them illuminated.
Our age produces what no other time had yielded—
Such things have never been nor ever will be.[11]
Happy, indeed, are those to whom it has been given to see
  these things,

Which we see unblemished and unclouded.
Our hearts, albeit trembling, sparkle at the sight.
Although they narrow in fear, our eyes light up with joy.
I wish to write about great events, but only on the path of truth.
What I recall with certainty, I follow without artifice.[12]
May His Majesty, Witness of Truth, smile on this work,
And may He grant it be done undisguisedly who granted those deeds be done.

2. Accordingly, at the time, when that famous French preacher, Fulk of Paris,[13] was stirring up all the people of France[14] and all of Flanders, Normandy, and Brittany, as well as other provinces, with his sermons to rescue the Holy Land and that special city, Jerusalem, which had been occupied by the heathen for some time,[15] there lived in Upper Germany[16] a certain man, Martin by name, abbot of a Cistercian monastery, itself called Paris,[17] which is located in the diocese of Basel. Anyway, at its very inception this undertaking seems to have already had a certain miraculous tone, since both he who was already preaching the word of the Cross publicly and this other man, who would very shortly become its preacher—both of these men, I say—just as they were equals in their ministry,[18] so both were identified by the same place-name "Paris": one, in fact, after the city in which he had been born in the flesh;[19] the other after the monastery over which he presided, as we have mentioned, as spiritual father. Indeed, each place is called Paris—that is the aforementioned cloister (spoken of a short while ago) and that famous French city. Whereas this name, to be sure, has its own etymological origin in French,[20] in German it seems to have the following connection and root: The first monks, who were sent to inhabit this region from the monastery of Lucelle,[21] discovered here nothing other than a cold wasteland and "bare ice."[22] Now, however, through the grace of God, who exalts and raises up his paupers, the church is crowded, enriched with possessions and estates,[23] adorned with buildings and, what is more important than all of this, devoted night and day to divine services.

The abbot, therefore, of whom we speak, was certainly mature in mind but merry in countenance, a prudent counsellor, a genial friend, a popular preacher, and gentle and humble among his brethren. As a result, he enjoyed extraordinary authority among laypeople, no matter who they might be, and was regarded by both clerics and laity as lovable and easy to deal with. This was the man who received from the supreme pontiff Innocent, who then was presiding over the Holy Roman Church as the third to bear this name,[24] a mandate that he assume the sign of the Cross without delay and that he preach this same Cross publicly to others in these parts. Furthermore, he obeyed both papal commands and, with energetic self-confidence, seized upon the medium of preaching. This amazed everyone, because he was thought to have a weak constitution and was universally considered unequal to such a task.

Consequently, he delivered a sermon to the clergy and laity of his own city, which is called Basel after the Greek word for "royal."[25] Here a large multitude of both orders,[26] stimulated by current rumors, had gathered in the crowded church of the Blessed Virgin Mary.[27] In fact, they had heard for quite a while how other regions round about were being summoned to this army of Christ at well-attended sermons. However, no one had, as yet, spoken a word about this undertaking in these parts.[28]

Consequently, large numbers of the people of this area, prepared in their hearts to enlist in Christ's camp, were hungrily anticipating an exhortation of this sort. Accordingly, everyone stood still, with ears pricked and eyes fastened on him, anticipating avidly whatever he might teach or enjoin on them in this matter and whatever of God's goodness he might promise to the submissive.[29]

He sees a large crowd of laity assemble;
Equally a crowd of clergy fills the holy place.
Now with the harvest almost assured, he rejoices in
 anticipation.
His heart pours out benedictions, and silently he offers pious
 prayers

That the Lord do what He knows to be necessary.
Quite calmly and appropriately he casts his eyes about.
He perceives that all are ready and eager to hear,
Their ears pricked, thirsting with burning zeal.
He sees so many strong and fresh assistants.
His face is a mask, but secretly his heart rejoices.
And now eliciting from his soul sure presages of the future,
And nurturing great hopes and the joys of a pure heart,
He feels his whole being afire with celestial devotion,
And he yearns to place these men under God's command.
In his soul he calls upon Him, whom they will have as their leader.
Then with gentle voice he follows the Teacher,
Who skillfully loosens the throats of the mute,
Who teaches the untutored the rewards[30] of divine summons.
Joyfully, thankfully, secure in his trust in Christ,
He is reported[31] to have spoken in these or similar words:

3. "Heed my word to you,[32] my lords and brothers; heed my word to you! Indeed, not my word, but Christ's. Christ himself is the author of this sermon; I am his fragile instrument. Today Christ addresses you in his words through my mouth. It is he who grieves before you over his wounds.

"Christ has been expelled from his holy place—his seat of power. He has been exiled from that city which he consecrated to himself with his own blood. Oh, the pain! The land where once the holy prophets foretold the incarnation of the Son of God, where, moreover, he was born and where, as a child, he deigned to be presented in the temple, where he personally preached and taught moral perfection and frequently worked wonders, where, while eating with his disciples, he instituted the sacrament of his holy body and blood, where he suffered and died and was buried, where he arose from the dead after three days, where before the eyes of his disciples he was assumed into heaven and ten days later poured the Holy Spirit forth on those disciples in the form of tongues of fire—this land is now dominated by the barbarism of a heathen people. Oh, the misery, the sorrow, the utter calamity! The Holy Land, which Christ impressed with his footprints, in which he cured the lame, caused the blind to see, cleansed lepers, raised the dead—that land, I say—has been given over into the hands of the impious. Its churches have been destroyed, its shrine[33] polluted, its royal throne and dignity transferred to the gentiles. That most sacred and venerable Cross of wood, which was drenched with the blood of Christ, is locked and hidden away by persons to whom the word of the Cross is foolishness, so that no Christian might know what was done with it or where to look for it.[34] Virtually all of our people who used to inhabit that frontier have been eliminated, either by the enemy's sword or an already prolonged captivity. A few, who have been able to escape that destruction, find shelter in Acre[35] or in other more secure places, where they suffer repeated attacks from the barbarians. Such is Christ's plight, which forces him today to appeal to you through my mouth.

"And so now, true warriors, hasten to help Christ. Enlist in his Christian army. Rush to join the happy ranks. Today I commit you to the cause of Christ. I give him into your hands, so to speak, so that you might labor to restore him to his patrimony, from which he has been so unmercifully expelled.[36]

"Lest you be frightened by the fact that presently the heathens' savagery against our people has greatly increased in its fury, I want you to remember the accomplishments of our predecessors. At the time when that famous expedition led by the noble Duke Godfrey and other French and German princes was made,[37] that infidel people, then as now, had occupied that land, having killed or captured all Christians. They had held in secure and fearless dominion for forty years the holy city of Jerusalem, Tyre, Sidon, Antioch itself, and other fortified cities, in fact all territory right up to Constantinople.[38] Yet, by God's will, all of these places were recovered by that army in the briefest span of time, as in a flash. Nicaea, Iconium, Antioch, Tripoli, and other cities were taken by storm. Also, the very capital of the kingdom, Jerusalem, was restored to our people. Now, however, although godless people again hold by force that special seat of power and a major portion of the land, nevertheless Acre is ours, Antioch is ours, and certain other strongly fortified centers are still ours. With the aid of these garrisons, through our soldiery, and by God's favor, we will, my renowned warriors, be able to restore to our control even that splendid seat of power, along with everything else.

"However, if you ask what guaranteed payment you should expect from God for such a great labor, I promise you absolutely that whoever takes the sign of the Cross and makes a sincere confession will be totally absolved of every sin, and when he quits his present life, no matter where, when, or by what happenstance, he will receive life eternal. Now I shall not even mention that the land to which you are headed is by far richer and more fertile than this land, and it is easily possible that likewise many from your ranks will acquire a greater prosperity even in material goods there than they will have remembered enjoying back here. Now, brothers, look at how great a guarantee comes with this pilgrimage. Here, in the matter of the kingdom of heaven, there is an unconditional pledge; in the matter of temporal prosperity, a better than average hope.

"I, myself, vow to join in both the journey and the labor and, insofar as it is God's will, I hope to share in all your successes and trials. Now therefore, brothers, take the triumphal sign of the Cross in a spirit of joy, so that, by faithfully serving the cause of Him who was crucified, you will earn sumptuous and eternal pay for brief and trivial work."

By the time the reverend man had finished speaking, those present were totally spent.[39] You could see tears flowing copiously on his face as well as from the eyes of everyone else. You could hear groans, and sobs, and sighs, and all manner of similar signs which gave indication of internal remorse.

And so we have carefully reported this sermon of the aforementioned abbot, because we will quote nothing from any other exhortation of his, even though later he frequently and vigorously encouraged both these and other persons. Therefore, on the basis of this example of his zeal, one should infer how ardent he should be believed to have been even on other occasions.

Then, when with compressed lips, the wise man fell silent,
The mob roared on every side, stung by a sweet pain;
They hurry to assume cruciform tokens[40] and divine service,
To enlist in the ranks of the Leader who leads us to the stars, by way of the Cross;
Breast and back are graced by that happy sign,
Indeed a double destiny, but each in its proper place.
Not without mystery whenever this is perceived,
There was an established reason, which now we reveal:
He who bears the Cross in front indicates he does not wish to return;
He who bears it on the back is seen as one hoping to return.
This is its ancient meaning, known to few today,
And the passage of time has hidden it from the hearts of many.
Hence, long ago, when this was known,
It was the custom to be marked front or back with the token of the Cross, for this reason.[41]
Then this honorable task is given Christ's servant:
That he simultaneously lead the people as duke, count, and father.
It was by order of the supreme pontiff
That he had accepted this quite difficult and burdensome responsibility.[42]
Yet he took quiet joy in the labor assigned him
Rather than in the honor conferred on him.

4. Finally the man of God gave into their entreaties, and he who, as we have already said, had already received from the supreme pontiff the care of souls, also took at their request the office of caring for their bodies.[43] Then he exhorted and bolstered them up in Christ, in whose army they had enlisted. He set a definite date when, having put their private affairs in order, all would assemble in readiness with him at that same place, and there they would take up with him the path of holy pilgrimage. Moreover, he attentively counseled those returning home to be chaste and pure in the intervening period and to act as soldiers worthy of Christ, who loves all purity. On his part, accompanied by a worthy retinue, he traveled about to the principal and heavily populated centers of the entire region, stopping frequently to preach, and he converted many to that same army of Christ. He also made sure to enjoin them to assemble, if they could, at the established time in the aforementioned place with the others, with whom they would set out together. Those, however, who were not able to disengage from their affairs because of the shortness of time, were to follow the others as quickly as possible.

Moreover, it now being close to departure time, Martin, even though armed with the authority of a papal commission, wished, nevertheless, to show reverence for his holy profession. He went to Cîteaux, the home of the entire Order, where he received permission and blessing for the pilgrimage from the very abbot of that place, as well as from certain other important abbots. He then returned to his own monastery, where he also commended himself to the prayers of his brothers and, with reciprocal charity, committed them to God's grace.

He went to Basel, where already a large mass of enlistees had gathered, who greeted him enthusiastically. After also delivering an exhortatory sermon there, he commended himself and his companions to the Blessed Virgin, humbly begging that she intercede for this new army before her son. After bidding farewell to the clergy and laity of the same city, by whom he was well loved, he set off, with a happy countenance and a fearless mind, along with his companions on the labor of the holy journey. From this we can surmise that the man of God already had in his soul a sense of some sort of greatness and, in fact, by reason of a certain prescience of mind, anticipated those things which God would effect through him.[44]

Then together and equally, captain with raw army,
Quickly, soberly, uniform in expression and step,
They begin the march, in number almost twelve hundred,[45]
With no distinction among the ranks, neither swaggerers nor
laggards,

They do nothing light and nothing lightly;
Astride a spirited horse Martin rides at the head, his face serene.
The entire cohort follows; some enjoy the use of reins,
Others, for lack of such transportation, march on foot;
Yet no one complains that he lacks another's fortune.
No matter who, his fortune proves to be good, sweet, and agreeable;
No one in this battle formation has a mournful face or heart;
Songs of joy resound in the name of Christ.
For You were the reason for the journey, Christ, Leader and Way;
You, Piety itself, gave to a pious people pious vows,
Whose fulfillment they faithfully begin today.
Good hope, which warms hearts, gives vigor to limbs,
Drives sluggishness from the body and sorrow from the heart;
Insofar as they dedicate themselves to holy wars, this people imbibes a love of war,
And turning fear to hope and labor to a sure reward,
The armed camp is on the move, scorning a sense of sorrow.

5. In this manner the army of crusaders departed from the city of Basel. Leaving the others behind,[46] it took that road which leads to Verona through the narrow curves of the valley of Trent,[47] but with less trouble and greater directness. What is more, the reputation preceding them was so great and their fame so widespread that not only the people through whose lands they marched but also, in fact, those living in villages and towns came out in troops, and sustained them with great support and friendship, offering needed food at fair prices.

They especially marveled at Martin, because a man in a religious habit and of totally spiritual life was leading a host of armed soldiers[48] and giving himself so energetically to the duty of so great a task. And for this reason they constantly repeated his name among themselves and, because of a certain resemblance, kept calling him the other Martin, after Martin of Tours, who is practically first and foremost in the catalogue of holy confessors. And really, if we examine the situation closely, certain similarities (I ought not to say many) do parallel one another in each man. First, of course, as has been written about Martin of Tours, while serving in armed military service, he kept himself so saintly and pure that even then he was regarded as not so much a soldier as a monk;[49] and so also this true monk[50] (more correctly, this father of monks), while leading an armed contingent, so conducted himself in the midst of war-like men that, insofar as the labor of the journey and the cares of the office which had been given him permitted, in no way did he inwardly relax from the rigor of his profession.[51] In the second place, just as Martin of Tours had such great compassion for the poor that in very biting cold he divided his woolen cape, of which he had but one, with a naked pauper,[52] so also this man distributed to his indigent associates large amounts of his possessions, both from goods he had brought with him and from those which afterward, by God's will, he obtained in large quantity, to the point that in two days he generously disbursed one hundred and twenty marks for such purposes, and on the third day seventy marks of silver.[53] The third point is that Martin of Tours, called out of a monastery and made a bishop, still continued always to comport himself with the humility of poverty,[54] so also this man, as we learned from an unimpeachable source, although he could have obtained either a bishopric or any other ecclesiastical dignities he might desire, as several people urged,[55] and even a large fortune in gold and silver,[56] still turned these offers down, out of love for the Order and his monastery, which God through him and he, through God's grace, intended to reward in a very sacred way. And when his pilgrimage was completed, he returned to his brethren poor in spirit, to be sure, but wealthy in and full of[57] the riches of a heavenly treasury. There are also other, perhaps many other, parallels that can be discovered in both Martins, pertaining equally to one as to the other. Yet, we probably should not give the less discerning reader the appearance either of being overly disparaging toward the most holy confessor[58] or of praising excessively the virtuous man about whom we speak. For this reason, it is fitting that we pay homage to both within the proper limits of honor: one, of course, as a most sanctified soul who already enjoys the company of angels; the other, to be sure, as a prudent man, still in the flesh, and who now enjoys high esteem before God and humanity and later, through the grace of God, will be more filled with grace in the eyes of both. But we do not believe that we should fail to mention that because this Martin was born into the world on the sacred birthday of St. Martin,[59] he was consequently named Martin.

Each Martin earned remembrance and acclaim.
Granted this Martin[60] is perhaps the lesser,
Yet each is sufficiently celebrated and deservedly so for his
admirable deeds.
And in my judgment each is dear to God.
One lived for God, God loves him and blessed him.
Agreed, through him God achieved great things.
Although this man may be the lesser, so also, as I believe,
When he has left his body, he will be great.
The fame of virtuous men grows beyond death,
Even as due honor already befalls all good men;
This man also, when his bodily life is over,
Will grow full of endless personal honor.
He will grow and multiply a hundred times a hundred.[61]
He will be greater in name than ever before.
Now humble, modest, no lover of personal praise,
For fear of broadcasting his reputation, he is shy in spirit.
Now he deserves the fame of a poor and modest man;
When his troubles are over, he will pass happily to heaven.
We beg you, Christ, do deliver this man of peace
Into the bosom of Abraham, the abode of delight.

6. Consequently, when the armed pilgrims and their leader arrived at Verona,[62] they were joyously received by the citizens of the city and by another exceedingly large body of crusaders which, coming from the various corners of the world, had preceded them there. And, in fact, the bishop of this city[63] piously and respectfully took Martin into his home and for almost eight weeks[64] kindly paid his expenses and showed him deference. Following this they departed and headed for Venice.

They had decided to board vessels here and sail in a direct assault against Alexandria, an Egyptian city. They chose this destination because at this time a truce between our people and the barbarians was in effect in the regions beyond the sea. Our people could not violate what they had pledged in good faith.[65] Moreover, the crusade army contained quite a few persons of renown and power, both lay and clerical, among whom Baldwin, count of Flanders,[66] and Boniface, marquis of Montferrat,[67] were regarded as first in authority, power, and wisdom. All of these men had unanimously agreed to strike at Alexandria and besiege it aggressively, thereby putting to the test not so much the fortunes of war as the power of divine might. In any case, if they did so, they could reasonably hope to gain possession of this rich city and most of Egypt with a minimum of effort, because almost the entire population of the land had either perished, the victim of famine, or was barely eking out a poor living. This was plainly due to the land's infertility. As is reported, the Nile had already for the past five years withheld its fructifying waters which normally irrigate the soil.[68]

This quite commendable plan of our princes was, however, frustrated by the deception and perfidy of the Venetians who, in their capacity as lords of the ships and princes of the Adriatic Sea, refused them further transit unless they first joined the Venetians in an attack on the heavily trafficked Dalmatian city of Zara, which rightfully belonged to Hungary.[69] For the Venetians claimed that this city had always opposed their interests, to the extent that citizens of Zara often launched piratical assaults, plundering their ships when they were laden with merchandise.[70] In any case, this proposition seemed both beastly and impious to our God-fearing princes,[71] because Zara was a Christian city belonging to the king of Hungary, who had himself assumed the Cross and, according to tradition, enjoyed papal protection of his person and possessions.[72] Therefore, even in the face of importunate pressure, our people stubbornly continued to say no. As a result, a good deal of time passed in dissentious argument. They clearly considered this affair utterly detestable and unlawful for Christians—soldiers of the Cross of Christ—to visit the fury of slaughter, rapine, and arson upon fellow Christians (for such things usually happen when cities are captured by assault).

And for this reason, many poor persons who had brought little with them, and had consumed it, had nothing more for the journey; they left the army and, retracing their footsteps, returned home. Moreover, some of the powerful and rich, not so much suffering from want as frightened to the point of terror at the thought of committing an outrage, reluctantly and almost unwillingly, turned around and headed back.[73] Some traveled to Rome, where they were barely able to obtain license from the supreme pontiff to return home, on the condition that they at least fulfill their pilgrimage vow within a few years. The retreat of these pilgrims not only weakened our army by reason of their defection, it also dampened the deep fervor which many persons had had who were hurriedly preparing to follow along from Germany and other regions. The result was that they stayed rooted in their homes.

On the other hand, at that moment a certain cardinal, namely Peter Capuano, was dispatched to our army.[74] The supreme pontiff had directed him to settle the aforementioned controversy and to deal with the Venetians, so that they might quickly provide passage to Alexandria for this auspicious invasion, that is, for Christ's army. Because he was unable to force anything out of the Venetians, save on the condition that our people meet the established terms, it seemed to them more pardonable and less blameworthy to secure the greater good through means of the lesser evil, rather than to leave their crusade vow unfulfilled and, retracing their steps homeward, to carry back with them infamy along with sin.[75] Consequently, they pledged to do what the Venetians so insistently demanded, receiving, nonetheless, a solemn guarantee from the Venetians that they would, under arms, escort and carry our people all the way to Alexandria.

When our Martin saw not only the business of the Cross tied up in delays but also our entire army being forced to shed Christian blood, he did not know where to turn or what to do. He was totally terror-stricken, and from many choices, all of which displeased him, he opted for the one which, in that particular situation, seemed best. He, therefore, approached the aforementioned cardinal and humbly pleaded, with the insistence of every manner of prayer, that he allow him to return to the solitary quiet of claustral life, dispensed from his pilgrimage vow. Cardinal Peter, however, absolutely forbade him to return home under any circumstance until first he had completed his pilgrimage; moreover, he laid an even greater burden on him. By the authority of the supreme pontiff, he placed under Martin's care all the Germans—those whom he had personally led there, those whom he had found there, and those who might later join the army.[76] He also charged him and several other religious who were present to stay with their comrades through every peril and to restrain them, insofar as it was possible, from shedding Christian blood.[77]

How Martin groaned, when leave was now denied him.
Who could imagine it, who would believe it, if I tried to
relate it?
He stands wavering; a man of devout mind, he stands with
breaking heart.
Pained in his breast, he has no wish for such things and, like
one constrained,
He fears for himself and his comrades. He fears even more
For himself and his people lest he be party to wicked
slaughter.
Yet he submits and suffers to yield to his vows;
He pledges to go on; barely the better course, but his heart is
not in it.
He becomes a comrade or, better, leader and prince of the
German cohort,
Strong in might and no longer so in moderation.
No wonder! Absolutely every man who might be German,
By divine authority, Capuano ordered to submit to him,
Both him whom he had discovered there, whose name,
perhaps was unknown to him,

And him whom earlier he had confirmed in his crusade vow.
Then with a far greater force than before,
They prepare to set sail and to be given to the sea and the course of the wind.
Presently they plow through calm sea and heaving waves;
They surrender ship to oars, their vessels to sails,
So a pious folk, doing what it does not will, what it believes profitless
In its pious mind, although not at all wavering, obeys unwillingly.

7. Therefore, the fleet sailed through the Adriatic Sea, which is also called the Dalmatian Sea. The former name is, in fact, derived either from the city of Adria[78] or, as the fables have it, from Adriagne, the daughter of Minos;[79] the latter, certainly, is derived from Dalmatia, against which it washes. With rapid progress[80] but slow and somber minds, our soldiers reached the opposite shore. To insure that they would not be detained too long by this odious and personally detestable business, they besieged the aforementioned city with a great show of ferocity and noise and after three days[81] they stormed it with more menace than aggression. Without slaughter or bloodshed,[82] they forced its capitulation. Directly upon the city's surrender to its conquerors, the Venetians, out of pitiless hatred, razed it to its foundations.[83]

Upon completion of this, because our people had incurred the sentence of excommunication by laying hands on possessions of the king of Hungary (possessions that he had committed to the protection of St. Peter and the supreme pontiff by assuming the Cross), our people decided to send delegates to that same supreme pontiff, in the hope that he would mercifully consider the fact that they had sinned under duress and would absolve them from sentence of excommunication. Since they sought qualified persons of ability to travel in this delegation, Abbot Martin was elected[84] and along with him the bishop of Soissons,[85] a man of great sanctity and sweet eloquence, and a third was Master John of Paris, a Frenchman of superior erudition and courteous tongue.[86]

Through their personal representation a favorable case could be more fully argued before the supreme pontiff.

When the three men arrived and were allowed to plead the case which they had faithfully carried, they humbly begged the lord pope's merciful forgiveness, since our soldiers had sinned under duress and had been engaged against Christians for Christ's honor, and begged that he lift the sentence of excommunication, after a careful review of the case. Indeed, he thought the matter over and, convinced partly by the excuse that necessity was an extenuating factor, partly by our army's humble entreaty, and partly by the courtesy and ability of the delegates, he kindly assented to grant the requested indulgence. And he ordered absolution in written form sent to our army.[87] For he was a man of great discretion and courtesy; indeed, young in years[88] but aged in prudence, mature in intellect, well-suited to the righteousness of his character, a noble by birth, distinguished in bearing, a lover of virtue and justice yet an enemy to wickedness and malice, so much so that it was not by chance but by merit that he was called Innocent.

He, whom such great grace filled, was worthy of his name;[89]
What fortune had given him he was worthy of in name.
Ignorant himself of evil, he gloried in such a name
And in his vital office, ignorant himself of evil.
Pope and father of fathers, showplace of sweet virtue,
Friend of religious brethren, pope and father of fathers.
A man without deceit, unadulterated, the clergy gloried in his fatherhood;
He was a true pastor, a man without deceit, unadulterated.
Inclined to every good, he gave himself to the service of good,
Generous in giving, inclined to every good.
A loving prelate, both venerable and high-minded,
Pope and parent, a man without blemish, and a hater of evil,
A man without crime, noble in birth, calm of mind,
A man filled with faith, a man filled with love of God, a man also filled with hope

In his heavenly Leader, a lover of His uncommon Cross.
Where he was able, he was a zealous servant of the Cross.
The holy father himself thought it pardonable,
Because he noted that a pious host had done it in pious fervor;
He accepted and approved that which was necessary; when justice
Was done, this holy case compelled the way of forgiveness.

8. Moreover, it happened that, while our delegates were still engaged at the papal court, a rumor made the rounds, namely that a youth, Alexius, had come to the encampment—a Greek by birth, indeed, the son of Isaac, king of Constantinople.[90] He was sent there by Philip, king of Germany,[91] and accompanied by envoys and letters, through which Philip urgently requested the army to try to restore the aforementioned youth to his kingdom.[92]

The sequence of events in this affair is as follows (if it is possible to narrate in an orderly fashion events that happened in such a cruel and unordered way). While this Isaac, whom we have mentioned, was reigning among the Greeks, his brother Alexius,[93] paternal uncle of the younger Alexius,[94] whom we have also just mentioned, followed the advice of some evil persons, and most especially of a certain relative of his, to be sure a nobleman but a scoundrel, who was called by these people Morciflo (that is, "blossom of the heart"),[95] and he dethroned his own brother Isaac, seizing the kingdom himself.[96] He placed Alexius, Isaac's son and his own nephew, the person whom we are now discussing, into prison under close guard. Yet, when the opportunity was found, he secretly escaped and traveled quickly and surreptitiously to Germany.[97] Arriving in the kingdom of King Philip, who was married to his sister,[98] he mournfully complained to him about his and his father's misfortunes and the cruelty of his uncle. Philip received the young man quite decently, entertained him with great affection for a good length of time, and provided generously and freely for his expenses and needs.

When Philip heard, however, that our army, had taken Zara

and was encamped along the frontiers of Greece, he sent the oft-mentioned youth to the army's leaders. Accompanying him were delegates from Philip with the message that, were it possible, they should endeavor to reinstate him in his father's kingdom. Moreover, Philip laid this matter self-confidently and rather imperiously on the Germans, since they patently were subject to his jurisdiction. He reminded the marquis, his kinsman, of the relationship that existed between them.[99] He energetically entreated the Flemings, French, Venetians, and men from other regions with every manner of prayer, guaranteeing that if, with their help, Alexius recovered his throne, the road through both Germany and all of Greece would be perpetually open and safe for every pilgrim. He also supported this same youth's absolute promise: If he were reinstated by their troops, Alexius would give them, as a group, three hundred thousand marks of silver.[100]

All these arguments combined to produce a single result. The greater part of our army had already begun to lean in favor of the young man. Yet a few, who were more concerned with the success of the Cross, steadfastly dissented, arguing the position, which seemed plausible, that in no way could the aforementioned youth be reinstated without violence and bloodshed. For it seemed to them foolish and wrong for a small band of pilgrims, who had no place to retreat, to forsake their intended holy pilgrimage and to declare war, with its certain danger, on such a city, so fortified and populous, in order to accommodate a stranger. This war could not be concluded without a good deal of carnage on one side and, possibly, on both.

Yet on this matter (that is, the restoration of the young man), we will be silent for the time being; we will take up the succeeding events in their own time.

As I had begun to narrate, following the dissemination of that rumor in Rome, the lord pope, along with all of his clergy, our delegates, and quite a few other persons, became exceedingly frightened, fearing that the evil one[101] in his envy might, by this incident, either contrive the annihilation of our entire army or, at least, impede the business of the Cross. To be sure, the supreme pontiff had for a considerable time hated that city,[102] as had his predecessors, since already for so long it had been in rebellion against the Roman Church[103] and had differed from the Catholic faith in certain articles of faith, such as the question of the procession of the Holy Spirit, who the Greeks deny proceeds from the Son,[104] and in the liturgy of the sacrifice of the mass, since they, by custom, use fermented bread.[105] And for this reason, when the supreme pontiff sent a cardinal to them for their admonishment and instruction, they hanged him in the air, with his feet facing up and his head down, until, united in martyrdom with St. Peter,[106] he breathed forth his soul.[107] Therefore, the pope hated that city, as we said, and hoped, if it were possible, for it to be captured without bloodshed by a Catholic people, as long as he did not have to fear the destruction of our army. Yet he did not expect our people to accomplish this. As he stated, this very city possessed a fishing fleet which alone was larger than the crusaders' entire navy. Indeed, it had sixteen hundred fishing boats, each of which, throughout the entire year, paid into the royal treasury every fourteen days a gold coin—called customarily *perpera*[108] or farthings. That is, one is equal to a quarter of a mark.[109] They also possessed vessels in countless numbers[110] and a very secure harbor. It was the advice and decision of the supreme pontiff, who was exceedingly worried about the business of the Cross, that our people should sail directly to Alexandria. He furthermore permitted them to take, in moderation, half a year's supply of free food (that is, without paying for it) from those maritime regions of Romania[111] against which this sea washes.[112] Because he feared that this plan of his would be altered and the progress of the Cross impeded by earthly entanglements, both he and everyone else were rightly upset by the recent rumors.

Then also Martin, pious abbot, pilgrim,
Before the supreme pontiff, with the zeal of friendly
  discourse,
And the diligence of prayers, labors so that the prelate
Might act favorably toward him in this and direct him home.

It had begun to torture the abbot that he should have
seen
Such impiety; that in his presence there should have sunk
To sad ruin a proud city that worships Christ;
That the holy cause of the Cross, forestalled by vain pursuits,
Might yield no fruit or be delayed for a while;
That on the army of Christ the burden of the kings of the
Greek city
(A burden so massive its elements could scarcely be borne)
Would be placed, and under it the entire folk would labor,
Or perhaps collapse, if fortune so surrender itself.
Or, if fortune showed itself favorable, that worthless city
Still would have to be captured by our men in the face of
massive carnage,
Only after first revenging itself bitterly. Thus victory
Would have to be accompanied[113] by fearful losses and almost
a double catastrophe.
So the prudent man, in the silence of his heart, thrashed these
things out,
And afraid of possible future calamities
And seeing no guarantees, he rightfully wanted to return
home.

9. Consequently, the abbot pressed forward with every manner of prayer and, bringing up all these reasons we have mentioned, as well as others, begged permission to return home. Yet the pope utterly refused to allow him to return home without first reaching the Holy Land, which he had vowed to seek. Therefore, Martin left the papal court in the company of his associates, having received a pontifical blessing, along with a letter of absolution for delivery to our army.

He headed for Benevento, where he found Peter Capuano (whom we mentioned above), who was desirous of sailing directly to Acre. Martin joined him and sent the pontifical letters on to the encamped army through his associates.[114] He also sent through these men a message of explanation and farewell to the German contingent which he had formerly commanded.[115] This was done on the fourth of April.[116] From there they took ship at Siponto.[117] Following a lengthy and distressing journey, they reached the port of Acre on the twenty-fifth of April,[118] where they were received by everyone in a most festive manner.

There were quite a few Germans among these people, including certain nobles and other men of influence, who had formerly known and admired Martin back in Germany, and they greeted him with great reverence. In fact, by authority of the supreme pontiff, Capuano committed to his care all the Germans—those now there and those expected to arrive later.

That summer, during those days which, because of the wickedness of the heat, we call "dog days," a very serious epidemic broke out, and the human mortality rate was so great that more than two thousand corpses are said to have been buried on one day. Moreover, the plague attacked so swiftly and unexpectedly that whoever began to feel ill could, most certainly, expect to be dead within three days.[119] As a result, many persons seized by the quick-killing illness were not able to settle their affairs and called the abbot, handing over to him all of their possessions for disposition. He could either keep them in his possession or distribute them among their indigent comrades, retaining a portion for himself as it pleased him. Martin personally executed this task so faithfully that within two days, as was said a short while ago, he paid out one hundred and twenty marks in expenditures of this sort, and on the third day seventy marks.[120] He also redeemed, without any recompense but rather in a spirit of generosity, the weapons of certain brave men which, in their poverty, they had pawned. Furthermore, he rushed around to the stricken with pious speed, kindly giving counsel as well as providing for expenses. He advised them that with a sincere confession and a certain hope in eternity, they need have no fear of this brief and transitory death, following which they would immediately receive life everlasting. He also manfully exhorted the healthy that this brief and transient calamity should not throw them into terror, but they should be prepared in their resolute souls for either eventuality, either to continue living this life for the honor of God or, following their comrades, happily to acquire eternal life by a short cut.

In the face of evil fortune, Martin conducted himself
With such solicitude. He weighed himself down with such a burden.
Whoever looked into his face saw nothing
Within or without, save signs of sure pain,
And barely a comrade, he suffers through compassion the evils of comrades.
He believed his lot to be whatever anyone suffered.
Unconcerned with himself, like a man without sin, pure,
Like a father and a servant, he was concerned for the salvation of all.
He stood by all. He loved them like a brother.
Pulled from every which way in his various acts of piety,
He made rounds to the sick, humble and famous alike.
He proves himself a physician in counsel, a friend in deeds;
He instructs the ignorant, as if they were his brothers and dear ones.
Let no one be burdened by sins he purely confesses.
Let them not conceal anything within from the Lord; let them lay bare their hearts.
He reminds each victim it is time to give everything away
To the strong and healthy, lest wealth,
Which was not first spent for the Lord, be totally worthless after death.
And he encourages the dejected, so that the vile plague does not terrify them,
And they might be ready to suffer death with peace of mind.

10. The pestilence pervaded that city and its environs for quite a while. As a result, a majority of Acre's citizens and the pilgrims pausing there were carried off by the corruption of the contagion. For example, of the sixteen persons dwelling in the abbot's hospice, four barely escaped death. All the others fell victim to the peril. But even those who survived, as if they had accepted the answer of death, awaited it every single moment, languid and drawn.

In addition, another misfortune occurred, inasmuch as the peace treaty, which had been confirmed by oath between us and the barbarians, was broken through their deceit and wickedness when they captured and pillaged two of our people's ships, plundering everything that was carried on them. However, our people quickly and vigorously repaid this injury. Seizing on the sea six of their great ships, filled with grain, trade goods, and other commodities, they took them and all they contained as prize.[121] Thus, through God's power and their own, they manfully wreaked vengeance on their deceit. Now that the war was renewed, the enemy's mad fury pressed in upon our people more vigorously than usual, both because of fewer numbers and because those who did remain were reputed to be as impotent and feeble as if they were at death's door. For this reason, it occurred to those who were considered influential among them to send delegates to our[122] pilgrim encampment, which they had learned was situated in Greece, so that they might render timely assistance to the city of Acre and that little enclave in the Holy Land which, thus far, our people had held on to by dint of considerable labor and danger, or else know that it could now be scarcely defended any longer. At their request, also, Abbot Martin undertook this embassy,[123] along with another man, namely Conrad, advocate[124] of Schwarzenberg.[125] The abbot gives witness that his integrity was so great that whenever he recalled having told a falsehood, be it in jest, in earnest, or by accident, it was his custom to seek forgiveness in secret. From this it is quite clear that he who was so careful in minor matters, in those things which almost all others consider negligible, was never negligent in greater matters.

Therefore, on the third day before the feast of St. Martin,[126] the two aforementioned men embarked, and on the feast of the Circumcision of the Lord[127] they reached the shores near Constantinople, where then our army was not very happily spending its time, because it had come to a moment of great crisis while entangled in foreign affairs.[128] Anyway, it just has to be believed that God so ordained it that this city, which by reason of its magnitude and might had already been a rebel against the Roman See for so long, was returned to the unity of the Church through our power[129] and by an unforeseen victory. Consequently, when the delegates from Christ's army across the sea came to them, they were reverently and kindly received by all, and especially by those Germans whom the abbot used to lead.

However, upon revealing the reason for their visit, they received at least a great deal of sympathy but perceived there was absolutely no hope for advice or aid from our people, inasmuch as they seemed unable to help[130] themselves adequately. For they were at such a point of extreme adversity that they were not secure in the city's environs, on account of the enormous mass of hostile Greek people, nor were they able to disengage from there without substantial effort and danger, because of the Greeks' innumerable ships, with which, our people believed, the Greeks would pursue and attack them quite fiercely should they flee. So there happened what rarely comes to pass. Our people planned to besiege the very city from which they dared not flee.

To achieve a clear picture of this affair, it is worth the effort to pick up that story which, we recall, we momentarily interrupted above.[131] If any one carefully pays attention to it, he will be able to perceive God's secret judgments and the hidden causes behind these fortuitous events.

Here, come on; take a breath. Reader, learn of the marvels
That, by reason of their ominous nature, we recount with
    righteous anger.
Learn, note mentally, the things we write, as they are well
    known;
Learn of the accursed deed,[132] far removed from piety.
Marvel at the mad race, a profane race.
And what I sing is true; do not believe it vain.
It is all too true that it originated not among the base
    commons

But among the foremost nobility of rich estate.
Greece, the scum of scum—a people impious to Greek kings,
Whom it is wont to butcher or blind.[133]
An evil city, full of deceit and unworthy of the sun's light.
Constantinople: A hardworking folk—but only for flim-flam;
A people ignorant of government, happily subject to no law;
Citizens of sacrilege, a people impious to its own king;
An idle, cowardly rabble, an unfaithful burden to its kings;
A people in whom evil deceit has found a comfortable
home.
Yet unquestionably in the course of events it will pay for its
crimes,
And within a few days it will atone for its impious deeds,
And, conquered by a brave yet tiny band,
This vile people will suffer its fate, because of the ignominious
death of a youth.

11. Now the series of events that had led our people to this constraining crisis can be condensed as follows. When the royal youth Alexius (as was mentioned above)[134] came to the encampment accompanied by messengers and letters from King Philip and after he had deeply moved the princes of our army through his personal entreaties and extravagant promises, everyone gradually began, as we said, to lean in his favor and toward support of his case. This tendency was encouraged by various factors: first, out of consideration for the influence of King Philip, who was imploring our people so urgently on his behalf; next, because it seemed to them right (if they could effect it) to restore the kingdom's legitimate heir to his throne, from which he had been cruelly deposed; then also because of the youth's entreaties and his promises that, if he were restored, he would be able, both then and afterward, to offer significant assistance to all pilgrims. Moreover, it helped that they knew that this very city was rebellious and offensive to the Holy Roman Church, and they did not think its conquest by our people would displease very much either the supreme pontiff or even God. Also the Venetians, whose fleet they were using, were particularly urging it, partly in hope of the promised money (for which that race is extremely greedy) and partly because their city, supported by a large navy, was, in fact, arrogating to itself sovereign mastery over that entire sea. Through the union of all of these factors and, perhaps, of others, it happened that all unanimously found in favor of the young man and promised him their aid.

Yet there was also, we believe, another far older and more powerful reason than all of these, namely the decision of Divine Goodness which so arranged, through this pattern of events, that this people, proud because of its wealth, should be humbled by their very pride and recalled to the peace and concord of the holy Catholic Church. It certainly seemed proper that this people, which otherwise could not be corrected, should be punished by the death of a few and the loss of those temporal goods with which it had puffed itself up; that a pilgrim people should grow rich on spoils from the rich and the entire land pass into our power; and that the Western Church, illuminated by the inviolable[135] relics of which these people had shown themselves unworthy, should rejoice forever. It is, in any case, significant that the oft-mentioned city, which had always been faithless to pilgrims,[136] following (by God's will) a change of citizenry, will remain faithful and supportive and render us aid in fighting the barbarians and in capturing and holding the Holy Land—an aid that is more significant because of its closer proximity. Anyway, all of these matters would be unsettled had that people been conquered by persons of another faith, heathen or heretic, or (what would have been most disastrous) had it been forced to convert to their error.[137] Therefore, I believe these considerations, surely hidden from us, yet manifest to Him who foresees all, were of utmost importance to God. It was because of them that those monumental and miraculous events of which we shall speak were conducted to their outcome along a fixed but secret path.

There are, indeed, purposes sealed in the divine breast,
Ever constant from eternity in a paternal heart,
Which *Noys* so arranges in calm succession

That nothing transpires, nothing happens here in time,
Which does not receive from that Seal, immediate in all,
A Form and Pattern, subject to a fixed order—
What or where, when or how it is to be forestalled
Or effected; to what end, finally, it is to be directed.
So, in the living, eternal, pure universe of the Divine
Mind, without beginning, without end,
All changes (as I said) happen within a predetermined and
 fixed
Equilibrium, every movement and each sequence
Of changing events, or of time and even days;
By which all phenomena executed in diverse ages
Proceed according to a law, constant but known to absolutely
 no one,
Save One, whose secrets, if one is wise,
One does not desire to investigate, because it is not allowed,
 and the learned
Show it is unholy. Even as light cannot be permeated
By true night, so they cannot lay bare
Secrets of the Celestial Mind, however much they try.

12. Therefore, all things that are created or happen in time proceed along a fixed path and an immutable course in accordance with that so secret and unfathomable Idea within the Divine Mind, which comprehends the Forms of all things[138] and from which neither the number of grains of sand, nor of drops of water in the sea, nor of leaves in the forest can hide. For this reason Greek philosophers generally call the Idea the "archetype," that is, the First Form; John, in his Gospel, calls it "life" when he says: "What was created was life in Him, and life was the light of humanity."[139] For just as those things which a mortal human now conceives, whether they are present or just anticipated for the future, live, after a fashion, in the human's mind, so in fact—indeed, much more so—have all things—those which were later created or, as yet, will be created, right up to the end of time—lived in the Divine Mind even before they came into being. The Greeks call the Divine Mind *Noys*[140]; it is totally alive or, rather, is life itself; it can ignore nothing nor forget anything. Since the conceptual power of the Divine Mind contains the Ideas (that is, Forms) of everything, even the least of things, so much more has it comprehended from all eternity this affair (which we intend to narrate)—so monumental, so novel, so wondrous—just as it would happen.

Therefore, we have to believe that it followed from the uncontrovertible Providence of God that our army, which directly following Zara's capture made haste to head to Alexandria,[141] by a change of plans declared war against this great city. Following[142] a non-stop sea voyage,[143] the army belligerently invaded its territory, set up camp not very far from the city ramparts,[144] and settled down, ready for battle.[145] Alexius, the usurper who sat upon his brother's throne, attacked the camp with a large mass of armed soldiers.[146] Hardly had he tested the military prowess of our people in a brief battle, when he shamefully turned to flight,[147] distrusting his cause and the cowardice of his companions, whom he did not deem sufficiently loyal to himself because of the disgraceful acts he had committed.

What are you doing, you coward, king most undeserving of
    regalia?
What are you doing, you subverter of laws, basest of kings,
Oppressor of rights? Now and in the future
A despised name, a polluted token of a name!
You have the name Alexis, you filthy disease on humanity,
Which in this, our work resounds as "speechless,"[148]
Meaning that no one may rightfully speak
Any longer of you, a deceitful man full of tricks.
Of such a man, so debased, so horrid,
Let no one speak, nor let there be after this any further
    mention
Made of you, who perpetrated such a crime,
Who blinded a brother, who consecrated to yourself a
    brother's *regalia*.

So now, therefore, do you wantonly flee, showing your
backside?
Defeated only by panic resulting from first battle,
In the first battle terrified by scarcely a blow,
You are disgracefully defeated, and you shamelessly flee a
rejected throne,
Which you purchased for yourself at the price of such
loathsome wickedness.[149]

13. Consequently, the citizens of this magnificent city were terrified at the flight of their king, even though most had hardly been partial to him earlier because of the crimes he had perpetrated, and at the same time they were assailed by messengers with repeated promises and entreaties from Alexius the Younger.[150] Also, to their despair, our people were threatening destruction of the city unless they accepted him, the legal heir to the kingdom, as king. So they opened the gates and peacefully admitted him, along with the entire army, within the walls. Furthermore, this youth, bedecked in royal apparel and, as was proper, placed on the royal throne without delay,[151] kindly and freely ordered one-half of the promised money paid out to our leaders, while expressing the hope that he would be paying the remainder in a very short while.[152] Therefore our people tarried in that city for several days[153] and used restraint in availing themselves of the services of both the new king and the citizens, being exceedingly careful not to appear burdensome guests to him. However, because that city, albeit grand and splendid,[154] could not meet the needs of such a large contingent of men and horses, and given that these were two people of such diverse language and customs who did not have much love for one another,[155] they were satisfied, upon leaving the city, to relocate themselves on a wide expanse of flat land.[156] Here they pitched camp and politely awaited fulfillment of the king's pledges.

After they had left the city, a secret citizens' rebellion began to take root against the king; most were grumbling that he showed inordinate affection for people who were pilgrims and strangers to their customs, had already handed over to them, without cause, almost all the wealth of Greece, and proposed to lavish yet as much or perhaps even more on them, although his kingdom was already despoiled.[157] Since virtually everyone deplored this state of affairs, they even dared to censure the king himself openly, telling him publicly not to despoil his kingdom in order to reward foreigners and not to turn the profit of others into their own impoverishment. Rather, he should, along with them, attack and destroy those strangers, as though they were invaders greedy for the possessions of others.[158]

This rebellion of theirs deeply frightened the new king, partly because of the faithlessness of these citizens who had accepted him under compulsion, partly because of the affection he had for our people, and partly because of the oath to discharge payment which he had assumed in good faith. You could see him severely disturbed, as though torn between the wickedness of his people and the love of ours and the favor of King Philip, whom he feared he would severely offend should he cheat or injure our people.[159]

Because he could not easily be goaded into such villainy, Morciflo, whom we mentioned above,[160] through whose advice his father had been blinded and he himself put away in jail, strangled him with his own hands,[161] stating: "It is a lesser evil for this one man to be removed from this life than for the riches of all of Greece to be handed over to baseborn persons because of his stupidity." Once Alexius had been put out of the way, Morciflo crowned himself with the diadem, as though he were a man of royal lineage and even related by blood.[162] Occupying the royal throne with both audacity and insolence, he began to deliberate mercilessly on the affairs of the kingdom and the destruction of our people. We, greatly repelled by the impiety of his deed, are thus compelled to cry out:

Oh, crime! Oh, madness! Oh, fraud! A tyranny to be feared!
Oh, new barbarism, unknown in earlier years!
What race, what land, what age has known the equal of that
Which God and reason have far removed from piety?
What raging beast could be believed to dare such against
other beasts:
To have killed one of its own kind, and without cause?

No brute would do to his own what the Achaean[163] has done,
A man noxious and harmful to innocent kings.
By his cunning,[164] the father was unjustly robbed of his sight
And the son killed, although he was so very close to both.
But he will pay, and soon he will suffer what he has earned by his services.
Savage and cruel, he will experience whatever he himself has done.
Dishonorably driven from royal power, he will forsake ill-gotten gains.
Hated by all, no one will draw close to him in spirit.
An exile, indigent, soon he will flee, blind in each eye.
He will become the laughingstock of our people and his.
Sad and tormented, a criminal to his associates and vile to us,
On this side he will suffer blows, on that side abuse, insults, jeers.
Thus attacked from every side, he will be led to a height;
From here he will be hurled headlong, and will leap through the air.
The birds will feed on his body; and it will pollute the wastelands with its rot,
And he will pay bitter penalties for so great a crime.

14. After the vicious parricide had fallen upon and usurped the kingdom by strangling the young man, he ordained that, for the time being, word of his crime be suppressed and kept secret,[165] lest, immediately making its way into the encampment, it reach the ears of our people before he could try out the master strokes of deceit he had devised. So without delay he sent messengers in the name of Alexius the Younger, summoning the leaders of our army from the camp and into his presence under the pretext that they would receive the promised money and even greater tokens of royal generosity.[166] When this message was communicated to them, they suspected no deceit in it, since they were men of Christian simplicity,[167] and they hastened to enter the city. Naturally, they feared nothing so remote as the new king, whom they themselves had created, being put out of the way in such a short space of time.

There was, however, a certain, especially prudent man there, namely the doge of Venice.[168] He was, to be sure, sightless of eye[169] but most perceptive of mind and compensated for physical blindness with a lively intellect and, best of all, foresight. In the case of matters that were unclear, the others always took every care to seek his advice, and they usually followed his lead in public affairs.[170] Consequently, when the others, as they were accustomed to do, asked how the matter appeared to him, he argued that they should not expose themselves to Greek trickery out of a love of money. He said he feared the very thing which had taken place, namely that the young Alexius either had been killed by his own people or, just like a Greek by nature, had been corrupted by them and was conspiring to destroy our people.

While the leaders discussed this matter at length and the messengers prodded them insistently, word of the murder burst out from the midst of the city[171] and filled the whole army with deep fear. For they saw themselves confined in a hostile land, in the midst of the wickedest race of people, with that man killed whom they had imposed as king on these people by means of force and terror. Had he, at least, lived, he might have been able to curb their folly, give substantial comfort to our people, and send them out of his kingdom safe and well-provisioned for the completion of their pilgrimage journey. Deep down inside they knew they had now been cheated of all these things, to the extent that they could, most certainly, expect nothing but death from the new king and the inhabitants of the city. For what could the pilgrims do, or what hope could they have at such a moment, trapped as they were, with no secure haven in which for even an hour they could catch their breath from enemy attack? Should they declare war on those whom they knew to be their enemies and who previously had been secretly so, thereby inciting them to open attack? Yet the number of Greeks was endless[172] and grew daily through reinforcements.[173] Moreover, they were in their own country, where everything was available to them in great quantity. On the other hand, our people were few,[174] and impoverished, in the midst of enemies from whom they could hope for nothing other than whatever, as the saying goes, they might be able to cut away from them with their swords. It also tremendously disturbed them that they had been cheated of a large part of the promised money, in expectation of which they had prolonged their journey and had spent their pilgrimage travel funds in foreign ventures.

They elected as the best policy in such a situation to conceal their fear (which, surely, they could not possibly be without), to threaten menacingly the besieging enemy and, in revenge for the strangled king whom they had installed, to exact a penalty from the whole city, along with its citizens and that execrable parricide: for the city, destruction; for the Greeks, the sure penalty of death. In acting so offensively against these Greeks, our people incited such terror in them that they scarcely dared venture outside their hiding places.[175] Most of all, however, it was because of our crossbows. Insofar as the Greeks use them less frequently, they deem them more terrifying and dangerous.[176] Meanwhile our people, strengthened in spirit, were prepared for either eventuality: to retreat, if an honorable and practical opportunity presented itself,[177] or to strike at the enemy and court death from and with them, if the Greeks should dare to burst forth from their walls to fight. For no hope could smile upon our people when it came either to gaining victory over such a multitude or storming the city, since it was extremely well fortified and its countless number of defenders was increasing daily. Yet with an eagerness equal to our army's desire to close and die with the enemy, the Greeks avoided pairing victory over our people with their own deaths, for they saw them suffering from deprivation[178] in a hostile land, while they were at home, enjoying every sort of commodity in profusion.

Learn now of novel deeds and wondrous phenomena,
Such as the monuments of ancient days do not record.
Who remembers a multitude, well-supported, shut up behind walls
By a few, unharmed but shamefully hiding?

Here a few brave men oppose a thousand cohorts,
Partners in bloodshed, whom they choose to join in death.
They prefer a natural death and, mixing blood with blood,
    choose
To give their breasts to a victor rather than their backs to fear.
If Greek blood pours out equally with their own,
They deem the deadly square more decorous.
They stand, well united for battle, and threaten a sluggish
    people
With destruction of their walls, since now they are certain of
    death.
They stand with eager countenance and soberly amid
    reverberating clamor,
But with a secret throbbing and pounding of heart.
It becomes the brave and self-possessed to disguise fear,
To feign a happy countenance, to keep the secret.
As often happens, when hope is totally unreasonable
And fate uncertain, joyful prayers come to mind.
Indeed, for those inwardly despairing and prepared for death
Total success became their lot through a change of fate.

15. So our army had taken up a position before the royal city, as was said, but without any hope of taking it by storm, because it overflowed not only with an innumerable mass of citizens but with every sort of commodity, and had been fortified with such care that it could be defended against innumerable enemies by a small body of men. For the city is triangular (so those who have seen it say), extending on any one side a generous mile or more. On that side touching land it is triply enclosed by an enormous rampart and an especially strong wall.[179] It has lofty, strong towers all along its circumference, so close to one another that a seven-year-old boy could toss an apple from one turret to the next.[180] Moreover, one can hardly describe the type of buildings within the body of the city, namely its churches, towers, and the homes of its great people, or believe a description of them, unless he came to learn of them through sharp-eyed faith.[181] On the side on which the

Hellespont, which separates Asia from Europe, washes against the city, it is so narrow in some places that one can see from one continent to the other. Because it is not possible to have a rampart[182] on that side, due to the traffic of an extremely secure and heavily used harbor, there are high walls of astonishing thickness, with towers close together and raised to such a height that anyone would shudder in horror at directing a gaze at their summit.[183]

Yet the great strength and beauty which it now has it did not possess at its first foundation. For once, long ago, it was like any other city and was called by the Greek name *Byzantion*, and for that reason the gold coins that had been customarily minted in that city are called *byzants* by modern people.[184] Only later, because of a certain king's vision, about which we are going to say a few words, was it raised to that splendor and magnificence which it now has. Although this vision appeared[185] to be brief and insignificant, its subsequent effect showed it to have been the omen of a great event. Just as far lesser elements are sometimes represented by a vision of great phenomena (as in Joseph's dream when his father, mother, and eleven brothers were represented by the sun, moon, and eleven stars),[186] so occasionally the great and honored are symbolized by the trivial (as in the vision of Daniel, where we find the most powerful kingdoms symbolized by certain beasts).[187] For this reason they who think there is no basis for distinguishing among the things they imagine while sleeping, but believe all dreams are illusory and contain absolutely no hidden truth, are simply mistaken.

Let no one think that absolutely no truth is to be discerned
In the forms which you, O man, perceive while asleep in
 body.
Truths appear in sleep; we are not led astray by every image
Which we sense while we submit to sleep.
Behold Joseph as proof.[188] His clothing, smeared with blood,
Along with the deceit of fraternal words, invented a death
Under the fangs of a wild beast, but the dreams were true.
I offer as proof him who, because of a seven-fold symbol,

Foresaw a time of bounty and the ruin of famine;
And him,[189] who gave his dreams for interpretation to his servant Daniel,
Who had already professed the God of heaven, whom this insolent man had scorned.
Insofar as he believes them valid signs of his ruin,
He will also be a truthful witness.
Many an image comes to us in the course of the night,
At the time when we take in dreams with full intensity.
Some are fantasies, called in Greek *fantasmata*;
If a dream betokens reality or indisputable events to any extent,
It is usually accorded one of two names: vision or prophetic dream.
I believe the vision that, I have often read, was seen by the king
Was such an image of the city's promised splendor.

16. That vision of which we speak, which served as the occasion for that city's considerable beauty and glory, was a dream of this sort. The story goes as follows: In the wake of that famous donation,[190] by which Constantine, emperor of the Greeks and Romans, his good health restored to him and cured of leprosy by a heavenly miracle, regally honored Christ, the Author of his deliverance, the blessed apostles Peter and Paul, who had been His messengers, Pope Sylvester,[191] who had become His minister, and, in fact, the entire Church of Christ, that same Constantine handed over to blessed Peter the dignity of the royal throne, which he had held in Rome, and traveled to Greece. And he chose, in preference to all other places, to live in that city which was then called *Bisancion*. There one night he lay down on the royal bed, rested, and fell asleep. It seemed to him that he saw a little old woman, quite aged and dead, and the blessed Pope Sylvester (who also appeared to be there in person) said she would be resuscitated by Constantine. When the emperor reawakened her by his prayer, she had been transformed into a very beautiful maiden, who excited a chaste love in his eyes. He adorned her with a royal cape and, when he had placed his diadem on her head, his mother Helena[192] appeared to say to him: "Son, until the end of time you will have this wife, who will remain this beautiful forever." When he had related this vision to many people and one interpreted it this way and another that, the king resolved to fast without break until Christ provided him with an interpretation of his vision through His servant Sylvester. When he had fasted for seven days, the blessed Sylvester appeared to him in a vision on that seventh night and said to him: "That hag whom you saw is this city, which is presently almost dead from neglect and old age. Through you it is to be renovated to such a state of beauty that it will be called queen among all the cities of Greece." The king was not so much terrified as delighted by this vision.

After carpenters and masons had been gathered from the entire region, he ordered the city enlarged, fortified with walls and towers, and adorned with churches and other buildings until, growing into that refined beauty which it now has, it came to resemble, as they say, a copy of Rome. For this reason that city is sometimes called the Second Rome, and the land adjoining it is frequently called today *Romania*. And lest any vestige of its past survive, he suppressed the former name, which could remind people of its youthful abjection, and he ordered it called *Constantinople*, a composite of his name and the Greek *polis*, which is translated as "city."

Therefore, as was said,[193] our people besieged this city from the land side,[194] more out of disgust with their situation, because (for reasons given earlier) they did not dare do anything else, than out of any hope of gaining victory, since it seemed impregnable. However, after they had made little or no progress on this side,[195] they decided, in the face of their considerable danger, to test, on the other side hemmed in by the sea, not so much fortune as the efficacy of divine power, without which, they knew, entrance could in no way be effected. And so, to the enemy's horror, they jumped into their ships, as though in a hostile frenzy, and crossed the sea,[196] which is narrow there. On the shore opposite the city they manfully pitched camp and, in a change of strategy, began to deliberate with greater shrewdness on how to bring this business to term in either death or victory.

But what should they do? What plan or resolute action
Might they find? By what force, hope, even accident might
they succeed?
They are a band small in number, a weak pilgrim army.
The majority are footsoldiers; a cohort unprotected
By breastplates, helmets, shields—useful items for those
Attacking a city, by which to withstand the blows of stones
falling from above
And missiles forcefully hurled by strong arms.
They ward off as many deaths as the missiles they deflect.
Opposite them they discern, on a well-protected shore,
innumerable ships
Filled with courageous soldiers and Greek militia,
Who threaten naval attack.
In the lofty towers and high along the crest of the wall
Citizens stand packed together, prepared in soul and hand
To hurl rocks, pikes, spears, javelins, and arrows
And to destroy the enemy along with their ships.
And in the face of so many mortal dangers,
The pilgrims are not able to hold a stable position, denied a
foothold on land,
And their unsteady vessels roll about in the surging tide.
Neither are they able to set up on firm foundations
Siegeworks or machines to hurl heavy whirlwinds of stones.

17. In addition, the lighter and faster of those innumerable ships would frequently break out to attack our people and test their courage. Meeting them with javelins, arrows, and especially the terror of crossbows, our men easily repelled the Greeks.

Then they sought the advice of the doge of Venice, whom we mentioned a short while ago—a man, to be sure, blind of eye but most perceptive of mind—and they formed a plan to erect on their individual ships additional beams of extraordinary height[197] and strength adjoining both sides of the mast of each vessel. Once they had been securely fixed to the keel, they would link them alternately with the mast and one another into such an enormous network that the wooden towers, so to speak, would, almost like battlements, serve them as a fort. As these beams stood an appreciable distance from one another, they could also fasten on steps, just like those of ladders, so that four or six spirited young men could ascend and descend to watch for hostile ships and assault them from above.[198] When that was done, these towers, or ladders if you prefer, were raised to such a height that at their apex they exceeded every Greek tower and structure.[199] Our men also fortified them, along with all the ships, so artfully on every side that they did not fear missiles, stones, or fire[200]—either regular fire or that which is called Greek fire.[201]

Therefore, after the ships had been reinforced[202] and steered toward the city, it seemed proper for them to test God's favor first in an attack on the harbor and fleet so that, secure on this front, they might attack the men on the wall and in the towers more safely and easily. However, that harbor was enclosed by a certain, very well-protected inlet[203] and by enormous iron chains which, extending from one forward side of the harbor to the other, confined all ships, as it were, in one enclosure.[204] After the chains had been broken with a good deal of effort on the part of our people,[205] the Greeks fled in great panic because of the crossbows, which they could not endure, and abandoned their ships to capture by the victors, who eagerly seized them and turned them to their own use, as very welcome spoils of war.

Next,[206] when the ships outfitted with towers had advanced to the wall, as far as possible,[207] and all of the bravest had climbed the ladders, it was announced through a herald's voice that he who leaped onto the enemy walls first would receive one hundred marks as a reward.[208] You could see everyone ardently strive for a prize reserved solely for one, not so much out of a desire for the promised money as for the honor of God, the gain of their common cause, and to make short work of a task begun. As soon as they occupied the top of the ladders, others followed behind at a quick pace, as if to push them forward into the enemy's midst, and they would hasten to follow them down. Then you could see them rain down onto the enemy below an odious storm of spears, javelins, and arrows from on high; confused and shaken, the Greeks could not retaliate, since they were very tightly packed together. Still, it was the horror and assault of the crossbows that mainly took their breath away, as that race is timid by nature. After one man was seen to take the lead in leaping onto the wall, others very quickly followed him; immediately the faint-hearted and frightened citizens, seeing the enemy now in their midst, scatter all over the wall wherever they can. They jump down in headlong flight, as though by abandoning the walls they might safely take a stand in their city—they who could not be protected by their own defense! Yet nonetheless, our people running along the wall quickly captured their towers.[209]

When they had wrested fifteen or more towers from them, the enemy, as if with a renewed spirit, began to breath a certain boldness again, motivated partly by shame, partly by the danger; encouraging one another, they violently pressed in upon our men with a simultaneous shout and barrage of missiles of every sort.[210] A certain German count,[211] seeing this, ordered that quarter of the city set on fire, so that the Greeks, laboring under a double handicap—battle and fire—might be more easily defeated. This was done and, overcome by this tactic, they were completely routed.[212] Moreover, those of our people who were already sheltered under the walls, after removing every obstruction, either cut down or smashed in the gates that the Greeks had carefully sealed up with a great barricade of wood and stone, and forced the desired entrance for those who were still on board ship.[213]

This happened around Palm Sunday.[214] If we are not mistaken, God so arranged it that the army of Christ would triumphantly break into this faithless city on the very day on which Christ, arriving for the triumph of the Passion, entered the Holy City.[215]

Break in! Now, honored soldier of Christ, Break in!
Break into the city that Christ has given to the conqueror.
Imagine for yourself Christ, seated on a gentle ass,

The King of Peace, radiant in countenance, leading the way.
You fight Christ's battles. You execute Christ's vengeance,
By Christ's judgment. His will precedes your onslaught.
Break in! Rout menaces; crush cowards; press on more bravely;
Shout in thundering voice; brandish iron, but spare the blood.
Instill terror, yet remember they are brothers
Whom you overwhelm, who by their guilt have merited it for sometime.
Christ wished to enrich you with the wrongdoers' spoils,
Lest some other conquering people despoil them.
Behold, homes lie open, filled with enemy riches,
And an ancient hoard will have new masters.
Yet you, meanwhile, curbing heart and hand,
Postpone and disdain the pillage of goods until the right moment!
Throw yourself on the timorous; press firmly upon the conquered;
Do not allow the fatigued to recover and regain strength.
Immediately upon the enemy's expulsion from the entire city,
There will be time for looting; it will be proper to despoil the conquered.

18. Consequently, when the gates opened, those on board the ships rushed in with joyful cries and, for the sake of appearances, threatened a terrified enemy with death by pikes, swords, crossbows, arrows, and every manner of missile. Yet, having absolutely no wish to spill blood, they drove them, like scattering sheep, through all the avenues of the city. The Greeks fled in such numbers that the avenues, although very spacious, were scarcely able to afford sufficient room for flight. In fact, our people threatened them with such terror and violence that the Greeks could neither catch their breath nor glance back. Although our people could have effected a massive carnage such as they never could have hoped for, they actually killed very few.[216] They spontaneously refrained from killing, since they had often been admonished by the clerics living with them—Martin and others—that, insofar as it was possible, they should stay their hands from blood. Even so, almost two thousand citizens fell that day, not, assuredly, at our hands but at the hands of some Franks, Italians,[217] Venetians, Germans, and men of other nationalities, who formerly had lived in that city with them but had been expelled at the time of the siege because they were suspected of treason by the citizens. They had joined our people.[218] Mindful of their injury, they mercilessly inflicted the bitter scourge of revenge on the Greeks. From our ranks, however, absolutely no one is known to have fallen there, with the exception of one extremely noble and famous knight. While he hotly pursued the enemy, this reckless man, along with the horse on which he was mounted, unexpectedly plunged into a pit.[219] In the midst of happy events, the loss brought great grief to every comrade.

After all the enemy were defeated, routed, and quite pitifully driven out of the entire city and the gates also barred, only then were the victors allowed to hurry off for plunder—not before. It had been prohibited almost under threat of death for anyone to presume to think about plunder before total victory. They discovered in abundance, here, there, and everywhere, so great a wealth of gold and silver, so great a magnificence of gems and clothing, so great a profusion of valuable trade goods, so great a bounty of foodstuffs, homes so exceptional and so filled with commodities of every sort, that they were all suddenly transformed from aliens and paupers into very rich citizens.[220]

Meanwhile, the aforementioned fire had devastated almost one-third of the city,[221] since with everyone—citizens as well as pilgrims—occupied with the more pressing danger, there were none who could extinguish the freely spreading flames. Women, children, and superannuated old persons, who were not able to flee, had remained in the city.[222] On meeting any of our people, they would entwine one finger over another to form a cross and quite tearfully chant, "*Aiios phasileos marchio*," which in Latin means "*sanctus rex marchio*."[223] They did so because they thought the marquis,[224] whom the Greeks had known well[225] (and consequently they considered him the greatest of our people), was undoubtedly about to be king of the captured city.[226] God, however, disposed otherwise.

Now it is clear by what has been laid bare that fickle fortune by such sport
Treats human affairs as though they were vile and vain.
Nothing remains or has endured; quickly it is acquired and quickly it passes away—
The vainglory of sufficient earthly prosperity.
Him, whom the wheel of fortune carried to the foyer of heaven,
It hurls back headlong. Sometimes it impoverishes; sometimes it enriches.
Him, who first was poor, it leads aloft from the depths.
Him, stuffed with wealth,[227] it returns to poverty from riches.
Fear does not intimidate it; rather, it always wanders about freely.
Compassion does not soften it; rather, it will give you what it takes from me.
The golden mass of metal that the Gauls[228] now pillage
And the old silver, stained with Trojan blood,
Conquered Troy, glistening with bounteous wealth, once surrendered
To the victorious Argives. Let me not hide the past.
Likewise, the earlier city[229] took new possessions from the old one[230]
And, with a change of name,[231] was given a better fate.
Rich Greece gave her distinguished and wealthy
Citizens, and it offered the lady[232] trophies of ancient rapine
And plunder still gory with Phrygian[233] blood:
The immense ransom which Pergamum[234] had paid;
The utensils of ancient people, gilded and set with gems;
And ancient bars of silver, heavy with weight.
So God, for hidden reasons, I believe,
Enriched Constantinople long ago with multitudinous spoils

So that, as soon as they were secure within the walls,
The happy victors could then bear away all that earlier folk had plundered.
Thus, divine power ordains hidden reasons;
All things that God wills happen, and things foreordained become reality.

19. While the victors were rapidly plundering the conquered[235] city, which they had made their own by right of battle, Abbot Martin began to think also about his own booty and, lest he remain empty-handed while everyone else got rich, he resolved to use his own consecrated hands for pillage. But because he thought it improper to touch secular spoils with those same hands, he began to plan how he might scrape together for himself some portion of those relics of the saints, which he knew to be in great quantity there.

Accordingly, foreseeing something grand,[236] he took along with him one of his two chaplains and headed for a certain church which was greatly venerated because the mother of the extremely famous Emperor Emmanuel[237] had her splendid tomb there.[238] Although this seemed to be significant to the Greeks, our people considered it inconsequential. A large hoard of money from the entire surrounding countryside was stored there and also precious relics, which, in the vain hope of security, the Greeks had brought to the same spot from neighboring churches and monasteries. Before the city was stormed this fact had also been told to our people by those whom the Greeks had expelled. Since many pilgrims were simultaneously breaking into this church and others were greedily occupied with other matters, such as stealing gold, silver, and every sort of precious article, Martin, thinking it improper to commit sacrilege except in a holy cause, sought out a more remote spot, where the very sanctity of the place seemed to promise that it was possible to find there those objects he so greatly desired.

There he found a certain old man, handsome of face and with a long white beard—definitely a priest, but quite different in appearance from our priests,[239] and for this reason the abbot thought

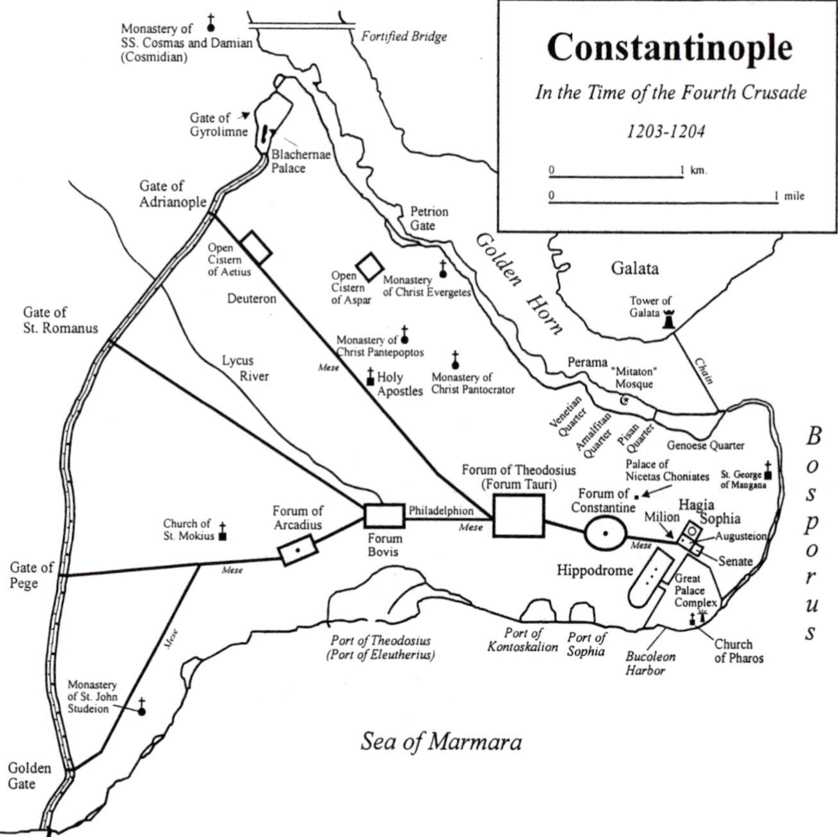

Constantinople
In the Time of the Fourth Crusade
1203-1204
0 1 km.
0 1 mile
Monastery of SS. Cosmas and Damian (Cosmidian)
Fortified Bridge
Gate of Gyrolimne
Blachernae Palace
Gate of Adrianople
Petrion Gate
Golden Horn
Galata
Tower of Galata
Chain
Open Cistern of Aetius
Open Cistern of Aspar
Monastery of Christ Evergetes
Deuteron
Gate of St. Romanus
Monastery of Christ Pantepoptos
Lycus River
Mese
Holy Apostles
Monastery of Christ Pantocrator
Perama
"Mitaton" Mosque
Venetian Quarter
Amalfitan Quarter
Pisan Quarter
Genoese Quarter
Bosporus
Palace of Nicetas Choniates
St. George of Mangana
Forum of Theodosius (Forum Tauri)
Forum of Constantine
Hagia Sophia
Milion
Augusteion
Senate
Church of St. Mokius
Forum of Arcadius
Philadelphion
Forum Bovis
Hippodrome
Great Palace Complex
Gate of Pege
Port of Theodosius (Port of Eleutherius)
Port of Kontoskalion
Port of Sophia
Bucoleon Harbor
Church of Pharos
Monastery of St. John Studeion
Sea of Marmara
Golden Gate

him a layman. With an inward calmness yet in a truly terrifying voice, Martin thundered violently: "Come, faithless old man, show me the more powerful of the relics you guard. Otherwise, understand that you will be punished immediately with death." The old man was truly terrified by the shouting rather than by the words, inasmuch as he heard the former but could not understand the latter. Knowing that Martin could not communicate in the Greek tongue, the old man began to speak in the Roman language,[240] which he had learned to an extent, in order to appease the man with flattery and mollify his anger (which really did not exist). In reply, the abbot was barely able to force out a few words of the same language, in order to communicate to the old man what he demanded of him. Then, examining Martin's face and dress and thinking it more tolerable that a man of religion violate[241] the holy relics in awe and reverence, rather than that worldly men should pollute them, possibly, with bloodstained hands, the old man opened for Martin an iron chest and showed him the desired treasure, which Abbot Martin judged pleasing and more desirable to him than all the riches of Greece. On seeing it, the abbot hurriedly and greedily thrust in both hands, and, as he was girded for action, both he and the chaplain filled the folds of their habits with sacred sacrilege. He wisely concealed those relics which seemed to him the most powerful and left at once. What those relics are which the holy robber appropriated for himself, and how worthy they are of veneration, is set forth more appropriately at the end of this little work.[242]

Therefore, as he was hurrying back toward the ships, so overstuffed, so to speak, those who had come to know and love him saw him from the ships, even as they were hurrying toward the pillage. They light-heartedly asked whether he had looted anything or with what articles he was so loaded down. He, as always was the case, said with smiling countenance and merry words: "We have done well." To which they replied: "Thanks be to God." Quickly passing by, and enduring with annoyance every reason for delay, he returned to the ship. There he stored those prayed-for spoils of his personal military exploit in his sleeping quarter, which he kept neat and clean, until that wild commotion in the city should subside.

He remained there for three days of deeply devout homage; no one was aware of this act of his, save one of his two chaplains and that old man who had handed over these holy objects to him and who, perceiving Martin to be a kindly and generous person, now clung to him in a quite friendly manner. Meanwhile through his efforts, the old Greek priest also arranged quite decent and suitable lodgings for Martin, as befit his profession, in the vicinity of a certain church within that same city.[243]

Consequently, after the aforementioned uproar had subsided, the abbot, accompanied by the chaplain whom we mentioned, sought out the quarters prepared for him, taking his secret along with him. There he lingered the entire summer, unceasingly cherishing those holy relics. To be sure, they were venerated in secret,[244] but with great love, and by his respectful devotion he made up for what was lacking externally.

In addition, he remained in that locality more willingly since he had learned that the peace treaty, which the pagans had violated,[245] was renewed,[246] but owing to the significant turn of new events,[247] navigation through that sea was less than safe. He was also held back by the love of his associates; at the same time, he awaited the structuring of the city and kingdom that was due, so that he might give a true picture of these matters to those who had sent him.

And so, as we have said, that royal city—the most renowned of all Greek cities—was captured and despoiled within a very brief space of time and occupied by its conquerors. Let others view this achievement from whatever perspective they might judge it. I confess that among everything recorded by historians or even by poets, I have read of nothing like it or of anything so splendid. I also do not believe that without the indisputable miracle of divine favor this exceedingly well-fortified city, to which all of Greece was subject, could have been surrendered into the hands of a few, so suddenly, so openly,[248] and so easily. Moreover, I see that here in a single instant, so to speak, a few brave men are found[249] to have done as much as the poets of old falsely claim that numberless thousands of men effected in ten years at Troy.

Let poetic deception cease to plague the unsophisticated!
Let it cease and let the lies of ancient poets stop.[250]
Maro[251] does not deceive the Romans, or Homer the
Greeks;
Each is sufficiently skilled in blending truth with poetry.
We sing a simple truth, and in an honest account
We present what has happened in our day.
If not as elegantly, certainly we write more truthfully
Than they, and we do not adorn triflings with rouge.
And yet we reveal, in an indisputably true narrative,
Events greater than those which such great poets have
invented.
Who or what, I pray, can be compared to our triumphs?
The son of Atreus?[252] Thousands of Greeks? Troy?
He had ships numbering almost twelve hundred,[253]
And yet he barely overthrew Troy in the tenth year;
We, with a few ships on which high towers had been raised,
Took a heavily populated city on the first assault—
A city to which the continent of Asia,
This, our homeland Europe, and Africa have known few equals.
A shameful woman[254] was the cause of its[255] wars
And a sense of conscience ours—to punish a regicide.
Through Sinon's[256] deceit, a horse duped that walled city,
back then;
Just now, our youths took these walls by storm, through their
gallantry.
The Trojans cut down many Greeks in the ten-year war;
From our ranks only one fell, engulfed in a pit.
And the sea swallowed up most of the Greeks on the return
voyage,
While our people happily rule in the conquered city.
Therefore, let the ancient fable of the Trojan War cease;
Let new deeds of splendid triumph be recounted.

20. Once the city was captured and pillaged and its buildings distributed among its new citizens,[257] they began to discuss the issue of establishing a king, so that they would not remain without a prince—like Acephali.[258] However, there were two highly renowned and distinguished men in our army: Boniface, marquis of Montferrat, and Count Baldwin of Flanders.[259] The situation seemed to demand that one or the other should be elected king,[260] and the entire army was loud in its concurrence. Since each enjoyed the support and approval of many persons, and since one could not easily be preferred over the other (because both men were deemed quite worthy), it occurred to everyone to transfer the burden and power of election to twelve men who were highly regarded by everyone for integrity and considered to have good judgment.[261] After a good deal of deliberation,[262] they named the count of Flanders.[263] He was seated on the royal throne and a diadem was placed on his head.[264]

Moreover, the provinces of this same kingdom were divided into three parts: one should belong exclusively to the king's demesne; another the Venetians took possession of; the third was given to the marquis, namely Thessalonica and its farthest frontiers.[265] When the marquis also proposed to take our Martin along with him and make him a bishop,[266] as was most assuredly disclosed to us, Martin declined with thanks. Mindful of his vows, he preferred to return to his brothers, should God permit it, as a humble person without rank.[267] Finally the lesser properties, such as castles, villages, towns, and other such things, were distributed to those persons considered especially deserving in this regard.[268] In addition, urban and rural laws, rights, and other institutions regarded from ancient times as commendable were allowed to remain as they had been formerly. Those, however, perceived as unacceptable were either corrected for the better or totally changed.[269]

While these things were being done in the city, that pestilential Morciflo, perpetrator of a very vicious crime and emperor for a very brief time,[270] aware of his misdeeds and consequently fearful of punishment, had fled the city before its conquest.[271] Not knowing where to turn or in what person or place to put his hope, he went to the elder Alexius.[272] In the division of the kingdom, our princes had granted Alexius possession of a certain small portion of land because, even though a nefarious person, he was still of royal blood.[273] When he saw the accursed man coming to him, even though he himself was not much different, Alexius was barely prevented by his people from inflicting on him the ultimate punishment of death. He ordered him blinded and expelled him, remembering him as the author of a good deal of destructive mischief: He had induced Alexius to blind his own brother, incarcerate his nephew, and steal the kingdom from both; finally, to add to his crime, he had strangled this same nephew with his own hands. So Morciflo was dishonorably expelled. He who formerly had been blind mentally was now also deprived[274] of his corporeal vision.[275] Poor, wretched, and hated by all, as long as he was a vagabond in that region he led a miserable life. When our people heard this, they dispatched men to capture him for their inspection.[276]

When this was accomplished,[277] all of our people, as well as the Greeks who had been left behind in the city, began to taunt the wretch with insults, abuse, and invectives, crying out as one that he was a parricide, a subverter of the fatherland, and worthy of punishment. Although everyone agreed on his sentence of death, there was still a good deal of disagreement among them concerning the manner of execution. Some held the opinion he should be strangled with a rope, just as he had slain his lord. According to others he should be: thrown alive into a fire; tied to a rock and drowned in the sea; buried in the earth; flayed of his skin, thereby exposing all of his viscera; completely dismembered; or, if it were possible, some other, more horrible punishment should be devised by someone for the accursed man.[278] What do you imagine was the wretch's emotion when he heard them discussing his death in such detail (unless the pain of lost sight mitigated the terror of approaching death)?

At last the princes decided, in consideration of the fact that, even though he was a nefarious man, he was still of high[279] blood, he would be led to the top of the highest pyramid and hurled headlong, tied to a long beam. The reason for this was that he who had fallen with such a sudden plummet from the lofty office of kingship, notwithstanding plunging from a summit, would experience a death that would be, while admittedly very pitiful, nevertheless, not entirely disgraceful. When this sentence was carried out, his whole body was smashed, and he breathed out his unhappy soul in pain and misery.

Now come on, blind man, fly. You do not deserve a single execution,
But also by cross, rope, and millstone. Now come on, blind man, fly.
You deserve to die by fire, fuel for sizzling flame.
By the indisputable law of the court, you deserve to die by fire.
And you deserve to be broken on the wheel or to have your skin stripped
From your whole body, and you deserve the wheel
(Or torn limb from limb by beasts). Would that you were either cast into the sea
Or sawn into pieces (or torn limb from limb by beasts).
You deserve to die and to see, in shame and misery,
Your limbs hacked off. You deserve to die.
Savage! Dregs of humanity! Your heart is pitiless and beastly
While you kill your lord. Savage! Dregs of humanity!
Both you and all your kind I detest and loathe;
You and all your kind deserve to be planted in a grave.
I call you a blasphemer,[280] faithless butcher of kings;
Despiser of laws, I call you a blasphemer.
Justly you fall suddenly, since deceitfully you rush for the heights,
And in imitation of your fall,[281] justly you fall suddenly.
Faithless, gruesome bandit, worthily will you spend eternity
In the stinking, black Abyss, faithless, gruesome bandit.

21. Something noteworthy can be said about the pyramid from which that man was hurled and which many call a column.[282] Constructed of gigantic stones solidly joined together with iron interlacing, it rises from a very thick base, gradually tapering to a point at an immense height.[283] They recall that some hermit once had a hiding place on its summit.[284] Having rejected a terrestrial home for himself and by no means having reached a heavenly one, he constructed a hermitage for himself midway, as it were, between the two in the midst of a heavily populated city. Also, so they say, various representations of events since antiquity were sculpted on it, which are said to depict in sundry scenes the prophecies of a Sibyl, largely concerning their kingdom. Among these were scenes of ships, with ladders of a sort projecting from them, on which armed men were climbing. They seemed to be storming and capturing a city which was also sculpted there.[285] Until that time the Greeks had disregarded the sculpture, thinking that nothing was less possible than that such a thing could ever befall a city such as their own. However, when they saw the ladders erected on our ships, they finally then pondered this sculpture and began to fear more seriously what they had held in contempt for so long. As a consequence, some people smashed these images with stones and iron hammers and largely deformed them, believing that in this way they could turn an unfavorable omen back on us.[286] Anyway, this was an absolutely vain hope, and the foreordained[287] outcome of events demonstrated that the aforementioned sculpture had been a token of truth.

While all these events were transpiring and a good part of the interim time was slipping away, Martin concluded that our army, occupied with enormous tasks relating to the affairs of the kingdom, would not be able to complete for quite a long time the pilgrimage journey it had begun, and that, because of this, the primary business of the Cross was being obstructed by a variety of unforeseen events. As a result, he directed all the powers of his mind to the purpose of returning to his brothers, so that he might again submit himself to the claustral discipline which, in this great uproar of events, he had not been able to observe as well as he wished.[288] Although he could have taken an easy short cut by sailing straight to Venice from his present location, he preferred to return first (along with the things God had given him) to those who had sent him. In this way he might faithfully report to them about the state of that kingdom[289] and of all that he had personally heard and seen. Only then, after taking leave of everyone, might he happily begin his return journey from the Holy Land, which he had reached as he had vowed to.

Reader, reflect on this man, steadfast and resolute in all things.
A man who weighs everything by his own standards of measurement.
Behold, he spurns the ready advantages of a short trip—
Not before he has discharged the duties entrusted to him.
He chooses to set sail on a return voyage and to revisit his colleagues,
Insofar as he wishes always to keep true faith.
He does not fear to face again the toils of the sea—
Toils which a soul totally sure of itself bears well.
He fears only that by some accident he might lose
The sacred gifts which God, Himself, bestowed.
And yet, in the face of holy fear, hope is not small.
In no way could the gifts be snatched from him.
If God should wish the gifts taken away, I ask, for what purpose?
Why would He first make the gift? What is the reason?
With so many strong men about, why would He give sacred tokens of victory
To an unwarlike man, if they are to be immediately snatched away?
Good hope and a certain faith greatly strengthen his will,
And he believes that little vessel safe by reason of its cargo.
Who would imagine or fear that one could lose
To watery disasters a ship so laden with sacred goods?

22. Martin, consequently, boarded ship around the Nativity of Blessed Mary,[290] almost unwilling yet willing, composed yet timid, he was not without fear and a good deal of apprehension. On the first day of October he landed at Acre,[291] where he was happily received by his associates, especially the Germans, who were particularly fond of him. He faithfully[292] reported in detail the kingdom's situation[293] and everything he had observed in person or had heard from unimpeachable sources.

Yet he wished to reveal his secret to no one, except for a certain very forthright and honorable man named Werner,[294] who was German by birth (indeed, a native of Alsace), of noble blood and, above all, noted for manly excellence. He had acquired such a great reputation in that land that the policies of the king[295] himself rested in large part on him. He had always been close to our abbot, who had come to know and love him back home and who, embracing him here with even greater affection, honored him above almost all others. When the abbot showed him those gifts of God which he had borne with him, Werner immediately trembled, seized with a joyous fear, and began to marvel exceedingly at the favor which God had bestowed on His servant. Yet when he heard the abbot's proposal concerning his return voyage, he resolutely tried to dissuade him, saying: "It is not very likely that such articles, as precious as they are, could arrive in the land of Germany unplundered, given the numerous dangers of land and sea, given the numerous pirates and highwaymen, given the numerous calamities which so frequently occur." As a result, he advised him to honor the Holy Land with these articles in piety and humility; furthermore, he suggested that Martin stay there with them and not be reluctant to accept from the king and the other princes either a bishopric or whatever other ecclesiastical offices he might desire. Should Martin wish to lead a more secluded life and one more congruent with the monastic profession, Werner would also arrange that to the abbot's liking with the king, with whom he was especially close. For there is in those parts a region which, both in modern usage and in the old records, is called Mount Carmel—a place abundantly rich in every sort of bounty, fertile in the fruits of the earth, well covered with vineyards, gracefully planted with olive and other species of trees, abounding in large areas of pasture land. There are three monastic communities on that mountain, each separate from one another and each having extensive holdings. Martin could preside as abbot and lord over these monasteries, either individually, as they were, or combined into one. Should he prefer to preside over brethren of his own Order rather than over others, these cenobites could be transported quite conveniently to other locations. As a matter of fact, once the abbot had received men from his Order—whomever he might wish and however many he might desire—the abbot and his successors would hold the entire area of the aforementioned mountain forever in free tenure.[296] Finally, should he accept none of this, he could receive from the king and princes wealth in gold and silver in a quantity that he could never imagine requesting or desiring, and he could transport it more safely and conceal it more unobtrusively, thereby enriching his own church through this simple expedient.

When the abbot declined all of this, saying he wished only to deliver faithfully to his monastery those sacred articles that God had given him,[297] Werner, being a trustworthy man, kept the secret. Consequently, both Werner and a considerable number of others escorted Martin with due honor to the ship which lay ready in the harbor.[298] After Martin had boarded, farewells were exchanged with reciprocal affection. On the third day before Palm Sunday[299] these people returned home. Martin, with sails unfurled, embarked on the sea voyage he had desired.

I should like to interject certain things at this point in our narrative. Even if everything else were false, they would adequately prove that the things effected through Abbot Martin—both those deeds which we have already narrated and those which still remain to be told—received direction from the font of Divine Providence. Specifically, on the third night before Martin began his return voyage,[300] a certain cleric with whom he was quite friendly, Aegidius by name, a native of Bohemia,[301] whose words the abbot was unable to understand except when Latin was spoken, and who intended to return in the same ship with the abbot—indeed not while sleeping but while wide-awake—saw very clearly (as he vehemently asserted) two angels at the very spot where the sacred relics were stored. This was also the place where he and the abbot had sleeping quarters—the abbot, of course, in order to guard the sacred articles closely. Aegidius, however, was totally ignorant of what was stored there. These angels[302] were seen in the vicinity of the chest in which God's holy gifts were hidden, engaged in a service of wondrous devotion, praising with every reverence God, who had bestowed these articles on His servant. Moreover, when that service of divine veneration ended, with one encouraging the other, they determinedly called upon God to place under His protection that very man to whom He had given such goods, along with all who were attached to him.

Anyway, when morning came and Aegidius related this indisputable vision to the abbot, suddenly in the midst of his words he burst into tears from the great stirring within his heart, and he said: "I do not know who you might be, where you have come from, or what you are guarding in that chest of yours. What I do know for certain, however, is that the hand of God is with you. For this reason I ought not leave the company of Your Holiness during this voyage, since I believe most certainly that I could not possibly be in any jeopardy while aboard the ship on which you are traveling." The abbot was struck by the miracle of this man's holy vision, especially considering the faith of the man, whom he had come to perceive as devout and truthful, and Martin himself told of another vision, one which had come to him in his sleep that very same night. It seemed to him as though from that place where he then was, namely Acre, all the way to the village neighboring his monastery, Sigolsheim[303] by name, there was nothing other than sea. However, it was so tranquil and trifling that not even a skiff, no matter how small, could fear shipwreck on it. Moreover, there seemed to be constructed overhead, in a straight line from Acre to the aforementioned village, canopied roofs of some sort, so that neither the wind, the rains, nor any other adverse circumstance of sea or ship had the power to harm the abbot in any way while under sail.

We can interpret this vision of the abbot in the following manner. Although surrounded by many dangers on land and sea from this point all the way to his monastery, he would still enjoy safe passage on his homeward journey by reason of divine protection, and the populace of the aforementioned village, both men and women, would be the first among all to visit the sacred relics at the cloister of Pairis, just as the plain truth of the situation afterwards demonstrated.

Now work is prayer; now use all your powers.
Now beseech, now pray; now, Martin, toil with true devotion
To have merited it from the Lord in heaven;
Pray that it please Him to complete your joys with the
celestial gift
Of a good end and that He take care to bring you back safe.
Over so many seas, over so many lands you wander for love of
Him.
So many adversities (there are so many), each in turn
Troubling this journey; so many dangers remain
On the seas and on land. Who can relate them all?
There are, indeed, winds, exceedingly stormy and violent.
There are mighty ocean waves and the distant rage of the sea,
While the wind arouses a hostile tide.
There are visible reefs, and there are hidden ones,
And straight ahead Ceraunian shores[304] for incautious sailors
to dread.
Pirates, a race filled with impiety, harass the seas,
Bandits and other highwaymen the land.
You do what you do willingly. You embrace the sacred
plunder,
As if it provided certain guarantees of your security.
With it leading you, you will be safe, you will fulfill your vow,
And you will render thanks to the Lord. So I, the soothsayer,
pledge.

23. It is not easy to recount all the mischances and dangers before which the abbot and those sailing with him in the same vessel repeatedly shrank. But his fear was greater than theirs, insofar as his love for the things he feared losing was deeper. Yet in the face of such fear and danger, the Lord rendered him the grace of His protection to a degree almost greater than he could hope for. Pirate vessels, which even after plundering some ships desired to plunder still others, frequently crossed his path.[305] Once his ship was sighted, they turned tame and gentle, hailing it with every peaceful salute. It was not so much that they allowed it to pass by unharmed, as they were compelled to give it leave. For such was God's power, which could restrain pirates and guide Martin's ship to port on a safe course.

So, after a good deal of effort and not a few dangers, Martin's ship (or, rather, the ship of God and His sacred relics) was piloted into the port of Venice on the vigil of Pentecost.[306] Once the abbot had disembarked there and inquired quite discreetly about the state of affairs on land, he discovered that no less danger and fear abounded on land than had been the case earlier at sea. In fact, they claimed that all of Italy, through which his route lay, was beset by the heat and uproar of warfare.[307] However, he knew that since the same God rules on land and sea, He who had protected him on the sea would also protect him on land. Purchasing horses to transport himself and his baggage, he began the journey toward the Alps certainly with confidence, but not without fear and anxiety.

Yet even though bands of armed men, on the march for nothing less than plunder and rapine, frequently confronted him, they were struck by sudden terror. They timidly shrank away from the priceless booty that offered itself, as though they were unworthy of it. Moving out of the way, they gave safe passage through their midst to the pack animal carrying the chest with the sacred relics.[308] So our Martin, traveling across all of Italy and after that the rugged Alps and, beyond them, many other dangerous, thief-filled spots, joyously entered the city of Basel, from which he had begun his pilgrimage.

First of all he sought out the church of the Blessed Virgin,[309] to whom he had devoutly commended himself upon setting out for foreign lands, and repaid her with as many acts of gratitude as he could, because she had honored him before her beloved Son with relics of that Son and had brought him back happy and whole, delivered from so many extreme dangers. For these reasons he adorned the highly venerated altar which she has in that church with a magnificent altarcloth. He also liberally distributed personal offerings to the city's bishop, Lord Luthold,[310] and to certain other persons and churches of this same locality.

He remained there but a few days before his brethren, who had now learned of his return, came to meet him respectfully, as was his due. With these and numerous other persons from the city, who attended him with great pleasure, this man betook himself to the monastery of Pairis, to be sure in grand style but with the great humility of piety. Here, as the entire convent of brothers humbly rushed out to the gate to meet him and the sacred relics that he was bearing, he carried those triumphal spoils of holy plunder into the church on the birthday of St. John the Baptist[311] before terce.[312] While everyone rejoiced and praised God aloud and in their hearts, he placed them with all possible respect on the high altar.

Now come on,[313] Martin. You see you have now reached, at last,
The final end and the goal of your great labor.
Now, in safety, you can, with carefree heart,
Be free from fear and breathe quietly.
Now, indeed, at last, the remarkable—in fact—magnificent feat
Which God Himself effected through you is patently proved.
Oh, constrained in so many situations, for so many days,
Your uneasy mind occupied itself with oppressive cares.
Now you fear seas, now winds, now conflicts, and now
Cruel pirates everywhere, always ready
For crime, cohorts of homicide and despoliation!
Behold, with the extraordinary devotion of a spotless heart,
You have found an abode for the holy rewards of a happy robbery.

Behold, the cohort[314] of brothers, Christ's special audience!
You hear them raising canticles of divine praise.
Behold, you truly see those whom you once thought
You would never be able to see, when you despaired of return;
And they see you, whom they heard had been seized
By the darkness of death,[315] no more to enjoy the returning light,
Now safe, everything fulfilled as prayed for.
Good man, worthy of being entreated, return to your accustomed peace.
Be a tutor to the brethren, as a model of goodness, as the tinder
Of fraternal peace, as the light and beam of a lamp.
Pour out supplications, pray, joyfully honor your gifts
And the Cross of Christ, through whose guidance, assuredly, you have returned
Healthy—a beloved Deliverer and a useful Guest.

24. Blessed be God! He alone effects wondrous miracles. In His unspeakable power and mercy, He looked upon and glorified the church at Pairis through certain gifts of His grace, which He deigned to transmit to us through the venerable man, the already frequently mentioned Abbot Martin. The church of Pairis now exults in their presence, and any soul faithful to God is assisted by and profits from their protection.[316] In order to encourage a firmer belief in them in our readers, we have decided to list some by name.

The first, truly unique and by all means most worthy of every veneration, is a trace of the Blood of our Lord Jesus Christ, which was shed for the redemption of the entire human race.

The second is wood from our Lord's Cross, on which the Son of the Father was sacrificed for us, the New Adam who paid the debt of the old Adam.

The third is a not inconsiderable piece of St. John,[317] forerunner of the Lord.

Fourth, the arm of St. James the Apostle, whose memory is held in veneration by the entire Church.

There are also relics of other saints, whose names follow:

Christopher, martyr
George, martyr
Theodore, martyr
Item: the foot of St. Cosmas, martyr
Item: a relic from the head of Cyprian, martyr
Item: a relic of Pantaleon, martyr
Item: a tooth of St. Lawrence
Item: a relic of Demetrius, martyr
Item: a relic of Stephan, protomartyr
Item: relics of Vincentius, Adjustus, and of Mauritius, and his companions
Item: relics of Crisantius and Darius, martyrs
Item: relics of Gervasius and Protasius, martyrs
Item: a relic of Primus, martyr
Item: relics of Sergius and Bacchus, martyrs
Item: a relic of Protus, martyr
Item: relics of John and Paul, martyrs
Item: a relic from the place of the Lord's Nativity[318]
Item: a relic from the area of Calvary
Item: a relic from the Lord's Sepulcher
Item: a relic from the stone rolled away[319]
Item: a relic from the spot of the Lord's Ascension
Item: a relic from the stone where John stood when he baptized the Lord
Item: a relic from the spot where Christ raised Lazarus
Item: a relic from the stone on which Christ was presented in the temple
Item: a relic from the stone on which Jacob slept
Item: a relic from the stone where Christ fasted
Item: a relic from the stone where Christ prayed[320]

Item: a relic from the table on which Christ ate the Supper
Item: a relic from the place where He was taken captive
Item: a relic from the spot where the Lord's mother departed from her sepulcher[321]
Item: a relic from the sepulcher of the apostle Saint Peter
Item: relics of the holy apostles Andrew and Philip
Item: a relic from the place where the Lord gave Moses the law
Item: relics of the holy patriarchs Abraham, Isaac, and Jacob
Item: a relic of St. Nicholas, bishop
Item: a relic of Adelasius, bishop
Item: a relic of Agricius, bishop
Item: a relic of John Chrysostom
Item: a relic of John the Almsgiver
Item: a relic of the milk of the Lord's mother
Item: a relic of Margaret, virgin
Item: a relic of Perpetua, virgin
Item: a relic of Agatha, virgin
Item: a relic of Agnes, virgin
Item: a relic of Lucy, virgin
Item: a relic of Cecilia, virgin
Item: a relic of Adelgunde, virgin
Item: a relic of Euphemia, virgin

This was written and executed in the year of the Lord's Incarnation, 1205, in the reign of Philip, king the Romans,[322] when Innocent presided as supreme pontiff over the Holy Roman Church, in the time of Luthold, bishop of Basel, and Henry, bishop of Strassburg.[323]

None of the faithful ought, therefore, to believe or even imagine anything other than that this was done under the shelter of divine grace,[324] in order that so many important, deeply venerated relics would arrive at our church by the agency of a man who retained his great modesty in the face of numerous obstacles. With their arrival, all of Germany, we believe, began to be adjudged happier in its own eyes, more famous before humanity, and more blessed before God. No one ought, therefore, to imagine that this, like many other phenomena, happened by chance. That would be nothing more than falsely denying God's great deeds their deserved honor. For if we carefully consider the utterly unbelievable and sudden capture of this very great city, from which all of these relics were translated, and the pattern of events as they happened, and Abbot Martin's journey on land and sea—filled with peril and yet, through God's protection, undisturbed at every point—it will appear clearer than day that all of these were surely not matters of chance, but divine gifts. For this reason, all who either witnessed these events or heard of them should in every way venerate the work of God, by whose authorship these things were done, and believe, and look forward to a reward from Him for their faith and devotion.

These matters of which I have written—which we have come to know for ourselves,
And have accepted as certain and absolutely indubitable—
It is not as though they were brought about by chance, in the usual manner,
Like pointless things which time turns vain.
Neither is it accidental that I note the truth of things done
By order of the Highest Father, the Author of the events.
For who is so filled with envy in his heart, who is so devoid of reason,
To be able to say that this could have been effected by chance?
Should one believe it accidental, should one change the proper words for the events,
Attributing to earthly destiny what is clearly celestial?
Whoever you are who deviates toward this opinion, you are not perceiving things correctly,
And I do not agree with you. What earthly law or order
Can bring it about that such events happen, that such significant things take place?

In every which way the mind of the writer is amazed at such
things:
An undermanned and ill-informed army, far from its native
soil,
Besieged, within their own walls, hostile squadrons
And thousands of armed soldiers. Who would believe such
things?
And yet it conquered the great number (one may speak only
the truth)
Of the citizen mob that it penned up in the sheltered city
(Which, doubtless, could have been fully one hundred times
its size),
And it cast out the conquered. It made the walls its own.
And, delighting in enemy spoils and treasure stores
That God Himself bestowed, the conqueror now resides in
the city.
In this conquest, not sluggishly or without trouble,
The man of religion was enriched with an opulent treasure,
Not in coin or gold but sacred wares, and Martin
Merited the honor of being remembered for his zealous
character.[325]
He brought us divine goods, the rich plunder of piety,
Safe[326] in the service[327] of the Divine Will through so many
evils,
Inasmuch as God guided him well.
Indeed, he has suffered much, yet although exhausted in
body,
He is alive, with a spirit ever quick, hearty, and keen.[328]
Well did he complete the task. This decent man would not rest
Until he had borne the sacred goods to that abode of Christ.

25. From those gifts of celestial grace, moreover, that the Lord had conferred on His now often-mentioned servant, Abbot Martin, and through him on the church of Pairis, that same church gave quite a valuable share to Lord Philip, the most serene emperor,[329] for the honor of God and of the whole Roman empire, specifically: a certain tablet of nearly incalculable value, sumptuously decorated with gold and precious stones and containing numerous sorts of holy relics (by far more precious than the gold or gems) which had been artfully hidden within it. On solemn feast days the emperor of the Greeks[330] used to wear this tablet on a golden chain hanging from his neck, as a sort of indisputable token of his imperial power. In addition to the gold and the many other gems, a single jasper of amazing size is set into this tablet. On it is carved the Lord's Passion, and standing on either side are representations of the Blessed Virgin and John the Evangelist. There is also a sapphire there of amazing weight on which the majesty of God is engraved.[331] (Certainly this cannot be adequately represented by any image. Yet it was done as skillfully as possible.)

In any case, the unconquered King Philip, young in age, to be sure, but mature in his fear of God and in the nobility of his total character,[332] accepted this gift in such a spirit of good will and with such a show of gratitude that he placed the church of Pairis, along with all of its holdings, under his protection. In addition, he authorized, by imperial privilege,[333] its perpetual possession of all the other relics which Martin had brought back.

A certain Master Gunther wrote this history. Then[334] a monk, but previously a master of studies, he was quite widely educated. Heartily applauding the matters about which he wrote, he desired and believed that even he, the narrator of divine actions, would receive life eternal from Him who had deigned to perform them through His faithful servants.

So the victor, a man worthy of love for all his virtues,
Brought us these sacred trophies from the Argive people.
Truly, a good part of the joyous palm—
A prize certainly joyous and bountiful, which, with much praise,
Enriched the crown of the kingdom—the man (with no slow heart)
Gave to you, Philip, king of the Romans!

An ornament of Greek kings and a decorous burden,
No necklace like it to be found in the world.
An exceptional gift, in which is set a single stone
Of ultimate price and workmanship (which one could scarcely buy
With countless wares or any amount of coin),
It is the dearer for its beauty and rarity.
This was done almost as soon as his vessel touched port.
Martin, by just judgment, has merited the esteem of laity and clergy,
Of kings and of all the brethren joined to him within the Order,
Or, rather, be they near or far,
Of everyone of German stock.
May the court over which Christ presides judge this man righteous and beloved.
Let him who has read this say: Amen.

Nor may Gunther, the trustworthy author of this story,
Be any less absolved by Christ of every sin.
May he gain Life. Say, Reader, say: Let it be so!

Notes

Introduction

1. Wilhelm Wattenbach, ed., "Le *Solymarius* de Günther de Pairis," *Archives de l'Orient Latin* 1 (1881): 551–561. A reprint of the *Solimarius* also accompanies Erwin Assmann's edition of the *Ligurinus*: 501–512 (note 2).

2. Gunther der Dichter, *Ligurinus*, ed. Erwin Assmann, MGH, Script. rer. Germ. 63 (Hanover: Hahn, 1987), 151–495.

3. Gunther von Pairis, *Hystoria Constantinopolitana: Untersuchung und kritische Ausgabe*, ed. Peter Orth (Hildesheim and Zurich: Weidmann, 1994). An earlier, less satisfactory edition can be found in Paul Riant, ed., *Exuviae sacrae Constantinopolitanae*, 2 vols. (Geneva: I. G. Fick, 1877–1878), 1: 57–126. This latter edition is a reprint of *Guntheri Alemanni, scholastici, monarchi et prioris Parisiensis, De expugnatione urbis Constantinopolitane, unde, inter alias reliquias, magna pars sancte crucis in Alemanniam est allata; seu, Historia Constantinopolitana*, ed. Paul Riant (Geneva: I. G. Fick, 1875).

4. PL 212: 101–222.

5. See the epilogue in chapter 25.

6. Assmann, *Ligurinus*, 17.

7. *Ligurinus*, 1: 14, 729; 10: 648 (pp. 151, 193, 494).

8. PL 212: 101–102.

9. See Peter Orth's introduction to his recent edition of the *HC* for a good overview of the history of scholarly debate on this issue and the reasons why one must conclude that Gunther of Pairis composed all four works: "Die Verfasserfrage," *Hystoria Constantinopolitana*, 1–42.

10. For quite different biographies of Gunther, see Erwin Assmann, *Ligurinus*, 58–102, and Hans Bayer, "Gunther von Pairis und Gottfried von Strassburg," *Mittellateinisches Jahrbuch* 13 (1978): 140–183. Assmann argues that there were three Gunthers: the Gunther of the *Solimarius* and the *Ligurinus*; a Gunther of the *HC*; and a Gunther of the *De oratione*. Bayer believes that Gunther and Gottfried von Strassburg, the author of *Tristan*, were the same person. Gunther/Gottfried, a Cathar heretic, took refuge in Pairis in 1211/1212 and composed the *HC* in 1218/1219 as an occult anti-crusade parody.

11. *Ligurinus*, 1: 82–88; 10: 648–649 (pp. 157, 494).

12. Jean-Marie Jenn, "L'Abbaye cistercienne de Pairis en Alsace des origines à 1452" (diss., École des Chartes, 1968), 104–123.

13. Jenn, ibid., 322, following the lead of Albert Pannenborg, "Magister Guntherus und seine Schriften," *Forschungen zur deutschen Geschichte* 13 (1873): 331, contends that Pairis enjoyed a reputation for scholarship and general cultural activities at this time, and he concludes that this was a prime reason for Gunther's attraction to the abbey. Jenn's sole piece of evidence is a single, somewhat disconnected sentence in the anonymous *De rebus Alsaticis ineuntis saeculi XIII*, MGH, SS, 17: 236, no. 10, which states that Pairis (or Paris; the Latin is *Parisius*) was noted for the studies that flourished there. It is far from certain that this statement, which follows a short paragraph dealing with the state of Alsatian monasticism in the mid- and late thirteenth century, even refers to Pairis. The editor, Philippe Jaffe, assumed the reference was to the university of Paris, which had been dealt with at great length in an earlier, not especially relevant section of this Dominican document. Even if we assume that the abbey of Pairis is referred to here, the assertion proves virtually nothing, as far as the monastery's intellectual life in the age of Martin and Gunther is concerned. The context of the entire *De rebus* makes obvious that the author is describing Alsace after the coming of the Dominican friars—that is, after the probable death date of Gunther.

My own survey of all known manuscripts from Pairis, which today reside in the municipal library of Colmar, leads to the conclusion that thirteenth-century Pairis was conventionally Cistercian and not a center of learning. Although a fair number of standard Cistercian liturgical texts and a Bible survive, there is only one work which might in any way be termed a piece of secular learning—an incomplete treatise on meteorology dating from either the thirteenth or fourteenth century. Significantly, this text, which is more practical than academic, is bound with a commentary on the Song of Songs and other devotional materials: *Catalogue général des manuscripts des bibliothèques publiques de France*: 56, Colmar (Paris: Bibliothèque Nationale, 1969), no. 10. See also, nos. 3, 222, 227, 228, 235, 237–240, 270, 285, 286, 357, 360, and 361.

14. *Ligurinus*, 10: 576–577 (p. 491); *De oratione*, 13: 3 (col. 220).

15. *De oratione*, 12: 1 (col. 207).

16. Philippe André Grandidier, *Histoire de l'église et des évêques-princes de Strasbourg*, Oeuvres historiques inédites, 3 vols. (Colmar: Georg, 1865), 3: 12.

17. A survey of Grandidier's notes, which were posthumously published as *Alsatia sacra ou statistique ecclésiastique et religieuse de l'Alsace avant la Révolution avec des notes inédites de Schoepflin*, Nouvelles oeuvres

inédites de Grandidier, 3, 4, ed. Augustin M. P. Ingold (Colmar: Huffel, 1899), reveals no other Gunther functioning as a canon in Alsace during the late twelfth or early thirteenth century.

18. There is some uncertainty over the dates of their respective tenures. In *Alsatia sacra*, 1: 48 (vol. 3 of Nouvelles oeuvres) the single date of 1171 appears next to Henry's name, while Morand's dates are given as 1181–1203. In *Histoire de l'église . . . de Strasbourg*, 50, n. 5, Grandidier notes that Morand was *scholasticus* from 1185 to 1203. On p. 12, n. 6, he cites a charter of 1157 witnessed by *Henricus Magister scolarum* and a donation of 1162 witnessed by Henry de Hasenburch, "*scholasticus* and later also bishop." Henry was elected bishop of Strassburg late in 1180 and assumed his duties in 1181. In the catalogue of canons of 1181 he is still listed as master of studies: ibid, 9. If Morand became *scholasticus* only in 1185 and not in 1181, one or more of three things could have happened. Bishop Henry might have continued to teach. Possibly he retained the title of *scholasticus* for several years after his election, in order to collect the income from the benefice, while paying a vicar (Morand?) to do the actual teaching. Possibly some unknown person held this position from 1181 to 1185, but an unlikely possibility at best. Whatever the case, it is hardly imaginable that Gunther served as either Bishop Henry's vicar or Strassburg's master of studies during that four year period, since he had to have been tutoring Conrad at that time.

19. *Ligurinus*, 1: 735–736 (p. 194).

20. Assmann, *Ligurinus*, 126, n. 511, disagrees. He argues that *Ligurinus* means *The Book on Liguria*; by extension, *Solimarius* would mean *The Book on Jerusalem*.

21. *Ligurinus*, 1: 73–74 (p. 156), 10: 644–650 (p. 494).

22. Ibid., 10: 650 (p. 494).

23. In the *Ligurinus* Gunther now mentions the wedding that had taken place, "in our time": ibid., 5: 419 (p. 319). This certainly seems to suggest that Gunther completed and dedicated the *Solimarius* sometime in 1186 or early 1187 and finished work on the *Ligurinus* in either 1186 or 1187.

24. Henry, Frederick, Otto, Conrad, and Philip: *Ligurinus*, 1: 56–101 (pp. 155–158).

25. Ibid., 10: 652 (p. 494).

26. The thirteenth-century rhetorician Eberhard the German listed the *Solimarius* among a select group of literary works representative of the highest standards of rhetorical excellence: Evrardus Alemannus, *Laborintus*, lines 647–48, in *Les Arts poétiques du XIIe et du XIIIe siècle*, Bibliothéque de l'École des Hautes Études 238, ed. Edmond Faral (1924; Paris: Champion, 1958), 360.

27. *Ligurinus*, 1: 34–37 (p. 153); 3: 219–224 (pp. 242–243).

28. Ibid., 10: 586–590 (p.491).

29. Ibid., 1: 33 (p. 153), where he compares Frederick to Charles the Great.

30. See especially ibid., 3: 369–580 (pp. 251–261), where Gunther paraphrases Barbarossa's speech to the citizens of Rome, as reported by Otto of Freising. Karl Langosch, *Politische Dichtung um Friedrich Barbarossa* (Berlin: Schneider, 1943), 76, states that Gunther's work is more German in outlook than its model, the *Gesta* of Otto of Freising and Rahewin. That is, the *Ligurinus*'s concept of empire is consonant with Carolingian and Ottonian traditions.

31. While he branded Arnold of Brescia a heretic and "false doctor," Gunther agreed that Arnold had been correct in calling for a moral reformation of the clergy: *Ligurinus*, 3: 263–348 (pp. 246–250).

32. Otto of Freising and Rahewin, *The Deeds of Frederick Barbarossa*, trans. Charles C. Mierow, Records of Civilization, Sources and Studies 49 (New York: Columbia University Press, 1953), 294–297 and 308–330.

33. *Ligurinus*, 10: 117–126 (pp. 470–471).

34. Ibid., 10: 576–585 (p. 491).

35. Walter Stach, "Politische Dichtung im Zeitalter Friedrichs I. Der *Ligurinus* im Widerstreit mit Otto und Rahewin," *Neue Jahrbücher fur deutsche Wissenschaft* 13 (1937): 385–410, disagrees. He argues that the differences between the *Ligurinus* and the *Gesta* of Otto of Freising and Rahewin must be understood in the light of the critical political situation of late 1186 and early 1187. A Milanese, Urban III (1185–1187), was on the papal throne, and his violently anti-Hohenstaufen prejudices were precipitating the last of Frederick I's conflicts with the papacy. It was in this context that Gunther composed the *Ligurinus*, a tale of earlier imperial victories in the face of the hostility of Pope Hadrian IV. To the contrary, if Gunther was revising Otto of Freising and Rahewin to fit the circumstances of a new papal-imperial crisis, he was proving to be singularly inept in his execution of the project, since his treatment of the papal schism could only embarrass the emperor.

36. Langosch, *Politische*, passim; William C. McDonald, *German Medieval Literary Patronage from Charlemagne to Maximilian I*, Amsterdamer Publikationen zur Sprache und Literatur 10 (Amsterdam: Rodopi, 1973), 66–75.

37. Frederic J. E. Raby, *A History of Secular Latin Poetry in the Middle Ages*, 2nd ed., 2 vols. (1957; rpt. Oxford: Clarendon, 1967), 1: 186–187.

38. Raby, *Secular*, 2: 159–160; Robert Holtzmann, "Das *Carmen de Federico I imperatore* aus Bergamo und die Anfänge einer staufischen Hofhistoriographie," *Neues Archiv der Gesellschaft für ältere deutsche Geschichtskunde* 44 (1922): 252–313.

39. McDonald, *Patronage*, 73–75.

40. Peter Munz, *Frederick Barbarossa: A Study in Medieval Politics* (Ithaca, N. Y.: Cornell University Press, 1969), 369, n. 1, has come to the opposite conclusion. He argues that during the 1180s Frederick was at the height of his success, and we must view the *Ligurinus* in the light of these triumphs.

41. *Ligurinus*, 1: 56–68 (pp. 155–156).

42. Francis R. Swietek, "Gunther of Pairis and the *Historia Constantinopolitana*," *Speculum* 53 (1978): 58; Riant, *Exuviae*, 1: lxxvi–lxxvii.

43. *De oratione*, 3: 5 (col. 128).

44. Ibid., 13: 3 (cols. 220–221).

45. Ibid., 12: 1 (col. 207).

46. For example, 1: 3; 5: 1; 8: 1; 9: 6 (cols. 108, 141, 163, 175).

47. Respectively 1: 1; 8: 3 (cols. 105, 165); 1: 2 (col. 106); 1: 3 (col. 108); 1: 3 (col. 113); 4: 1 (col. 133).

48. Ibid., 13: 3 (cols. 220–221).

49. Ibid., 12: 1 (col. 207).

50. Ibid.

51. *De oratione*, Prooemium (cols. 99–100); 13: 3 (col. 220).

52. Patrick J. Geary, *Furta Sacra: Thefts of Relics in the Central Middle Ages, 800–1100* (Princeton, N. J.: Princeton University Press, 1978).

53. Otto of St. Blasien, *Ad librum VII chronici Ottonis Frisingensis Episcopi continuatae historiae appendix* in MGH, SS, 21: 331–332.

54. For a contrary interpretation, see Swietek, "Gunther," 70–71, who writes: "Martin's removal of the Constantinopolitan relics to Pairis, for example, had been attacked with some vigor by the chronicler Burchard of Ursperg: 'whether these relics were stolen, or whether the lord pope can really justify such thievery in the Christian community, the reader may decide.'"

55. Burchard of Ursberg, *Chronicon*, MGH, SS, 23:369.

56. Reg. VII 154 of November 13, 1204 to the clergy with the army at Constantinople: PL 215: 456.

57. Reg. IX 139 of August 5, 1206 to Doge Peter Ziani: PL, 215: 957–958.

58. Robert de Clari, *La Conquête de Constantinople*, ed. Philippe Lauer (Paris: Champion, 1924), 69, sec. LXVIII.

59. Ibid., 68–69; Geoffrey de Villehardouin, *La Conquête de Constantinople*, ed. Edmond Faral, 2. vols., 2nd rev. ed. (Paris: Société d'Édition Les Belles Lettres, 1961), 2: 56, sec. 252.

60. Villehardouin, *Conquête*, 2: 56–58, secs. 252–253.

61. Geary, *Furta*, 138.

62. Poem 17, lines 11–12.

63. Ibid., lines 9–10.

64. Chap. 8.
65. Poem 10.
66. Chap. 1, verse lines 3–5, and passim.
67. Chap. 19.
68. Geary, *Furta*, 139–140.
69. Chaps. 5 and 19.
70. Geary, *Furta*, 139.
71. Chaps. 1 and 24.
72. *Statuta Capitulorum Generalium Ordinis Cisterciensis ab anno 1116 ad annum 1786*, ed. Joseph Canivez (Louvain: Bureaux de la Revue, 1933), 1: 333.
73. Ibid.
74. Ibid., 1: 205.
75. Chaps. 1, 2, 5, and 20, and poem 5.
76. Chaps. 5, 9, 19, and 22.
77. Chaps. 2, 4, 5, 20, 21, and 22.
78. Chapter 5 and its verse specifically link the two Martins. Sherry L. Reames, "Saint Martin of Tours in the 'Legenda Aurea' and Before," *Viator* 12 (1981): 143–146, provides an analysis of Bernard's vision of the saintly qualities of St. Martin, especially as seen in Bernard's sermon "In festivitate sancti Martini episcopi." Here Reames expands upon the insights of Jean Leclercq, "S. Martin dans l'hagiographie monastique du moyen age," *Saint Martin et son temps: Memorial du XVIe centenaire des debuts du monachisme en Gaule, 361–1961*, Studia Anselmiana 46 (1961): 175–187.
79. Erwin Assmann, trans., *Die Geschichte der Eroberung von Konstantinopel* (Cologne: Böhlau, 1956), 43, n. 37; Swietek, "Gunther," 74–76.
80. Chap. 19.
81. Chap. 23.
82. Peter Orth, *Hystoria*, 7, n. 8, deals with some of the conflicting, unsatisfactory evidence regarding Martin's death date.
83. Riant, *Exuviae*, l: lxxix.
84. Alfred J. Andrea, "Conrad of Krosigk, Bishop of Halberstadt, Crusader, and Monk of Sittichenbach: His Ecclesiastical Career, 1184–1225," *Analecta Cisterciensia* 43 (1987): 20–25.
85. Chaps. 8, 11, and 13.
86. Alfred J. Andrea, "The *Historia Constantinopolitana*: An Early Thirteenth-Century Cistercian Looks at Byzantium," *Analecta Cisterciensia* 36 (1980): 298–301.
87. Orth, *Hystoria*, 8, has missed my argument regarding this title in "*Historia*," 277, n. 34, and, therefore, misunderstands my argument for dating chapter 25 to the period August 1207–June 21, 1208.

88. Canivez, *Statuta*, 1: 270.

89. *HC*, chapter 2.

90. Ralph of Coggeshall, *Chronicon Anglicanum*, ed. Joseph Stevenson (London, 1875), 133.

91. Ibid., 130, n.1. In addition to the evidence of Statute 37, there is also the geographic factor to consider. La Columba was located in northern Italy, Cercanceaux in France. It is not likely that a north Italian monk would have been assigned to Fulk's retinue.

92. Ibid., 129–130. Italics added.

93. Elizabeth A. R. Brown, "The Cistercians in the Latin Empire of Constantinople and Greece, 1204–1276." *Traditio* 14 (1958): 68.

94. Leopold Janauschek, *Originum Cisterciensium* (1877; rpt. Ridgewood, N. J.: Gregg, 1964), 11.

95. Ibid.

96. Ibid., 23.

97. Angel Manrique, *Cistercienses seu verius ecclesiastici annales a condito Cistercio*, 4 vols. (Lyons: Anisson, 1649), 3: 386.

98. Brown, "Cistercians," 67, n. 17; Swietek, "Gunther," 75.

99. Brown, "Cistercians," 67, n. 15.

100. Alfred J. Andrea, "Walter, Archdeacon of London, and the *Historia Occidentalis* of Jacques de Vitry," *Church History* 50 (1981): 141–151.

101. Andrea, "Conrad," 60–63; see also 85–87 for a treatment of Conrad's crusade preaching.

102. *HC*, chapter 2.

103. PL 216: 822–823.

104. The work is edited in Riant, *Exuviae*, 1: 10–21, and MGH, SS, 23: 117–121, where it is an integral part of the *Gesta episcoporum Halberstadensium* (hereafter, *GeH*). It is translated and analyzed in A. J. Andrea, "The Anonymous Chronicler of Halberstadt's Account of the Fourth Crusade: Popular Religiosity in the Early Thirteenth Century," *Historical Reflections/Réflexions Historiques* 22 (1996): 447–477.

105. Andrea, "Conrad," 63–69.

106. *Exuviae*, 1: 12; *GeH*, MGH, SS, 23: 117.

107. Abbot Peter of Locedio was with Boniface de Montferrat, who was in Rome at the time: *Gesta Innocentii III*, PL 214: cxxxix. Abbot Adam of Perseigne never went to Venice: Alfred J. Andrea, "Adam of Perseigne and the Fourth Crusade," *Cîteaux* 36 (1985): 21–37.

108. Villehardouin, *Conquête*, 2: 22–24, secs. 224–225.

109. Ralph of Coggeshall, *Chronicon*, 82–83.

110. Note 88 above.

111. Canivez, *Statuta*, 1: 294.

112. Chap. 7.

113. Chap. 9.

114. Ibid.

115. Chap. 10.

116. Alfred J. Andrea and Ilona Motsiff, "Pope Innocent III and the Diversion of the Fourth Crusade Army to Zara," *Byzantinoslavica* 33 (1972): 19, n. 66.

117. Canivez, *Statuta*, 1: 106.

118. Ibid., 1:65.

119. Ibid., 1:263–264.

120. Ibid., 284.

121. Swietek, "Gunther," 78–79.

122. Thomas F. Madden, "Outside and Inside the Fourth Crusade," *International History Review* 17 (1995): 726–743, provides a good overview of recent historiography.

123. *HC*, chapters 6 and 11, mentions Venetian commercial-imperial designs. See Innocent III's letter of ca. September 1205 to Boniface de Montferrat in which the pope questions the crusaders' motives: Reg. VIII 133: PL 215: 710–714. Donald E. Queller and Irene B. Katele, "Attitudes towards the Venetians in the Fourth Crusade: The Western Sources," *International History Review* 4 (1982): 1–36, maintain that an inability to appreciate mercantile values led most thirteenth-century clerical writers on the Fourth Crusade to treat the Venetians unsympathetically: 21–23, 26–28, 30–34. Alfred J. Andrea, "Cistercian Accounts of the Fourth Crusade: Were They Anti-Venetian?" *Analecta Cisterciensia* 41 (1985): 3–41, questions this conclusion.

124. For example, Andrea, "Anonymous," passim.

125. *GeH*, MGH, SS, 23: 118.

126. Andrea and Motsiff, "Zara," 18–19.

127. Clari, *Conquête*, 72, sec. LXXIII.

128. Andrea and Motsiff, "Zara," 18.

129. Innocent was deliberately ambiguous on this point, probably because he wished to keep his options open in order to gain some semblance of control over a very fluid, potentially promising, yet still dangerous situation: Reg. VI 230–232 of late February 1204: PL 215: 260–263.

130. Clari, *Conquête*, 40, sec. XXXIX; 71–72, sec. LXXIII; Villehardouin, *Conquête*, 1: 97–98, sec. 97; 2: 22–24. secs. 224–225.

131. Villehardouin, *Conquête*, 1:92, sec. 93; 1: 190, sec. 188; 2: 24, sec. 224. Clari, *Conquête*, 71, sec. LXXII. Clari actually states that the clergy had assured the army that it was licit to punish the Greeks because of their disobedience to Rome.

132. Donald E. Queller and Susan J. Stratton, "A Century of Controversy on the Fourth Crusade." *Studies in Medieval and Renaissance History* 6 (1969): 236 and passim.

133. One of the subthemes that runs through his account is the conviction that: "If God had not loved this army, it could never have been able to keep together when so many people wished it evil.": *Conquête*, 1: 104, sec. 104. See also 1: 64, sec. 61; 1: 78, sec. 77; 1: 86, sec. 86; 1: 184–186, secs. 182–183; 1: 196–198, sec. 194; 1: 202, sec. 199; 2: 54, sec. 251. Secs. 61, 77, and 86 allude to God's role in their taking of Zara; the others relate to the crusaders' successes at Constantinople.

134. Clari, *Conquête*, 32–39, secs. XXXIII–XXXIX.

135. Villehardouin, *Conquête*, 1: 62–64, secs. 60–61; 1: 84, secs. 83–84; 1: 94–98, secs. 95–98. See ibid,, 2: 8–14, secs. 208–215, which contrasts the crusaders, who honor their sworn word and play by all the rules of proper feudal behavior, with the treacherous Greeks.

136. Villehardouin, *Conquête*, 1: 92, sec. 92; 1: 144–148, secs. 144–146. Clari, *Conquête*, 40, sec. XXXIX; 40–41, sec. XLI; 61–62, sec. LXII; 71–72, sec. LXXIII.

137. Villehardouin, *Conquête*, 1: 96, sec. 96; Clari, *Conquête*, 32, sec. XXXIII.

138. Villehardouin, *Conquête*, 1: 92, sec. 93; 1: 90, sec. 188; 1: 198–202, secs. 195–198. Clari, *Conquête*, 15–16, secs. XVI and XVII; 32, sec. XXXIII.

139. Villehardouin, *Conquête*, 1: 92–94, sec. 93; 1: 190, sec. 188.

140. Ibid., 1: 106, sec. 106; 1: 118, sec. 115.

141. Chap. 9.

142. Chap. 6.

143. Chap. 8.

144. Chap. 6.

145. Chaps. 6 and 11. See Andrea, "Cistercian Accounts," 17–31.

146. Chap. 8.

147. Chap. 14.

148. Chaps. 14 and 16, and poem 16.

149. Raymond H. Schmandt, "The Fourth Crusade and the Just War Theory," *Catholic Historical Review* 61 (1975): 216–217.

150. Chaps. 8 and 11.

151. Chap. 11 and poem 19. See also chapter 8 and poem 12, which detail the crimes of Alexius III and Morciflo against Isaac and Alexius.

152. Chap. 14.

153. Poem 10; chap. 13 and verse; chap. 14; chap. 20 and verse.

154. Chaps. 7 and 18 and poem 17.

155. Chap. 1.

156. Various copies of the letter exist, addressed to different recipients. Here we quote from the copy addressed to Innocent III in PL 215: 447. See the copy addressed to the Abbot of Cîteaux and all the abbots of his order in *De Oorkonden der graven van Vlaaanderen (1191–aanvang 1206)*, ed. W. Prevenier, 3 vols. (Brussels: Palais der Academien, 1964, 1971), 2:

583–591, no. 273, which contains the same sentiment. Peter Orth, *Hystoria*, 85–86, argues that certain parallels between the *HC* and Baldwin's letter to the West suggest that Gunther used the Cistercian copy of the letter as one of his sources. That is possible, but the parallels Orth cites to buttress his point fail to convince.

157. Note 56 above.

158. Arnold of Lübeck, *Chronica Slavorum*, ed. J.M. Lappenberg, MGH, Script. rer. Germ. 14 (Hanover: Hahn, 1868), VI, 19, p. 240.

159. Giles Constable, "The Second Crusade as Seen by Contemporaries," *Traditio* 9 (1953): 269–270; Jean Leclercq, "Saint Bernard's Attitude Toward War," *Studies in Medieval Cistercian History*, Vol. 2, ed. John R. Sommerfeldt, Cistercian Studies 24 (Kalamazoo, Michigan: Cistercian Publications, 1976), 12; B. Flood, "St. Bernard's View of the Crusade," *Australasian Catholic Record* 47 (1970): 135–137; Thomas M. Prymak, "The Role of the Cistercian Order in the Third Crusade" (MA thesis, University of Manitoba, 1972), 21–22.

160. James A. Brundage, "A Transformed Angel (*X*.3.31,18): The Problem of the Crusading Monk," *Studies in Medieval Cistercian History Presented to Jeremiah F. O'Sullivan*, ed. M. Basil Pennington, Cistercian Studies 13 (Spencer, Mass.: Cistercian Publications, 1971), 55–62.

161. Bruno Scott James, trans., *The Letters of St. Bernard of Clairvaux* (Chicago: Regnery, 1953), letters 4–6, pp. 19–25.

162. Janauschek, *Originum*, 139.

163. William M. Daly, "Christian Fraternity, the Crusaders, and the Security of Constantinople: 1097–1204: The Precarious Survival of an Ideal," *Mediaeval Studies* 22 (1960): 66–69.

164. C. C. Mierow, trans., "Introduction," *The Two Cities* (1928; rpt. New York: Octagon, 1966), 16.

165. Prymak, "Third Crusade," 45–46.

166. Ibid., 52–83.

167. Ibid., 82–96.

168. Ibid., 102–103.

169. Ibid., 115–120.

170. Ibid., 110–111. Mgr. Vautrey, *Histoire des Évêques de Bâle* (Einsiedeln: Benziger, 1884–1886), 1: 178–184, deals with the pontificate of Bishop Henry. Raised to the see in 1180, he proved a generous patron to Pairis. See Jenn, *Pairis*, 95, 101, 166, for Bishop Henry's dealings with Pairis.

171. Prymak, "Third Crusade," 108–110.

172. J. C. Didier, "Garnier de Rochefort, sa vie et son oeuvre," *Collectanea Ordinis Cisterciensium Reformatorum* 17 (1955): 145–158.

173. Prymak, "Third Crusade," 111–112.

174. Abbot Robert of Ford, who died while on crusade, was penanced

in absentia in 1190 for being absent from the Chapter General without proper authority: Canivez, *Statuta*, 1: 126. At the same meeting the abbots of Morimond and La Creste were given three days each of bread and water for having sent lay brothers "to Jerusalem" without sufficient cause, and the abbot of Tully, who had dared do the same, despite the contrary advice of the abbot of Morimond, was sentenced to an exile of forty days from his cell and given six days penance with one of bread and water: ibid., 128–129. In 1192 the abbot of Savigny was sentenced to three days light penance for having received back a monk who had sailed overseas, and the monk was permanently assigned to another house: ibid., 152.

175. Otto of Freising and Rahewin, *Deeds*, in Mierow, 79.

176. *Historia peregrinorum, expeditio asiatica Friderici I*, ed. Anton Croust in *Quellen zur Geschichte des Kreuzzuges Kaiser Friedricks I*, MGH, SS, N.S., 5, pt. 2 (Berlin: Weidmann, 1928), 116–172.

177. Albert Pannenborg, *Der Verfasser des Ligurinus, Studien zu den Schriften des Magister Gunther* (Göttimgen: Peppmuller, 1883), 8, n. 3.

178. Despite certain striking parallels, Peter Orth, *Hystoria*, 19, n. 2, 54, n. 8, and 56, concludes that internal evidence suggests that Gunther was not the author of the *HP*.

179. See Chroust's Introduction to the *HP*: lxxxi–xcv, especially lxxxii–lxxxviii.

180. Peter Orth, *Hystoria*, 56, n. 19, notes that this theory is far from proven.

181. *Ligurinus*, 10: 576–577 (p. 491).

182. *HI*, RHC. H. Occ. 3: 717–882.

183. Guibert was the author of the *Gesta Dei per Francos*. See *Historia quae dicitur Gesta Dei per Francos edita a venerabili domno Guiberto, abbati monasterii Sanctae Mariae Novigenti*, RHC. H. Occ. 4: 113–263.

184. Radulfus Cadomensis, *Gesta Tancredi in expeditione Hierosolymitana*, RHC. H. Occ. 3: 587–716.

185. Nancy F. Partner, *Serious Entertainments: The Writing of History in Twelfth-Century England* (Chicago: University of Chicago Press, 1977), 194–211.

186. Ibid., 221. See 212–230, "The Question of Christian History."

187. Robert of Reims, *HI*, 723.

188. Bernard Silvestris, *Cosmographia*, trans. Winthrop Wetherbee, (New York: Columbia University Press, 1973). See Winthrop Wetherbee, *Platonism and Poetry in the Twelfth Century: The Literary Influence of the School of Chartres* (Princeton, N. J.: Princeton University Press, 1972), 158–186, and Brian Stock, *Myth and Science in the Twelfth Century: A Study of Bernard Silvester* (Princeton, N. J.: Princeton University Press, 1972), 63–226.

189. Alan of Lille, *De planctu naturae*, ed. Thomas Wright in *Anglo-*

Latin Satirical Poets of the Twelfth Century Rolls Series 59, 2 vols. (London: Longman and Trübner, 1872), 2: 429–522. It has been rendered into English as *The Complaint of Nature*, trans. Douglas M. Moffat, Yale Studies in English 36 (Hamden, Conn.: Archon, 1972) and, with fuller commentary, as *The Plaint of Nature*, trans. and ed. James J. Sheridan (Toronto: Pontifical Institute of Mediaeval Studies, 1980). See Wetherbee, *Platonism*, 188–211; and Richard H. Green, "Alan of Lille's *De planctu naturae*," *Speculum* 31 (1956): 649–674.

190. Macrobius, *Commentary on the Dream of Scipio*, trans. William Harris Stahl (New York: Columbia University Press, 1952).

191. Bernard Silvestris, *Cosmographia*, 69.

192. For treatment of the twelfth-century marriage between literature and Neo-Platonism, see Wetherbee, *Platonism*, 66–73; and Richard McKeon, "Poetry and Philosophy in the Twelfth Century: The Renaissance of Rhetoric," *Modern Philology* 43 (1946): 217–234.

193. Swietek, "Gunther," 59–62, provides a survey of the origins and uses of prosimetry. On pages 66–71 he discusses the Neo-Platonic philosophy of history that runs throughout the *HC* and Gunther's debt to Bernard Silvestris.

194. Edmund Reiss, *Boethius* (Boston: Twayne, 1982) provides a good introduction to the author and his masterwork. The argument that follows is a synopsis of Alfred J. Andrea, "Boethian Influence on Gunther of Pairis's *Historia Constantinopolitana*," *Carmina Philosophiae* 1 (1992): 19–33.

195. Howard R. Patch, *The Tradition of Boethius: A Study of His Importance in Medieval Culture* (New York: Oxford University Press, 1935).

196. Boethius, *The Consolation of Philosophy*, trans. Richard Green (Indianapolis: Bobbs-Merrill, 1962), 89, 93.

197. Ibid., 24.

198. Poem 18. See also poem 14 where Gunther discourses on fate.

199. Boethius, *Consolation*, 91.

200. Frederick P. Pickering, *Augustinus oder Boethius? Geschichtsschreibung und epische Dichtung im Mittelalter-und in der Neuzeit*, 2 vols. (Berlin: E. Schmidt, 1967, 1976).

201. Orth, *Hystoria*, 165.

202. Andrea, "*Historia*," 282–283, analyzes in detail Gunther's treatment of Morciflo.

203. Actually this phrase appears in only one of the three extant MSS. See chapter 19, n. 242.

204. Additional parallels can be found in Andrea, "*Historia*," 278–298; idem, "Accounts," 21–35; idem, "Boethian," 26–30.

205. Poem 18.

206. Peter Burke, *The Renaissance Sense of the Past* (New York: St. Martin's, 1969), 1–6.

207. Manrique, *Cistercienses*, 3: 386–387.

208. Anna Maria Nada Patrone, *La quarta crociata e l'impero latino di Romania (1198–1261)* (Turin: Giappichelli, 1972), 27–28.

209. Swietek, "Gunther," 79. See also 56.

210. Donald E. Queller, *The Fourth Crusade. The Conquest of Constantinople, 1201–1204* (Philadelphia: University of Pennsylvania Press, 1977), 179, n. 69; 220.

211. Chap. 6. Swietek, "Gunther," 51, has pointed this out. The best studies of the Venetian role in the diversions of the crusade to Zara and Constantinople are Donald E. Queller and Gerald W. Day, "Some Arguments in Defense of the Venetians on the Fourth Crusade," *American Historical Review* 81 (1976): 717–737, and Donald E. Queller and Thomas F. Madden, "Some Further Arguments in Defense of the Venetians on the Fourth Crusade," *Byzantion* 62 (1992): 1–36.

212. Chap. 7.

213. Chaps. 8 and 11.

214. Chap. 12.

215. Ibid.

216. Chap. 8.

217. Chap. 13. Actually, although his murder might not be directly attributable to his putative pro-crusader sympathies, Alexius IV's deposition probably was due to the likely correct perception that he was seeking Latin aid against his domestic enemies during the confused days of late January 1204: Thomas F. Madden, "Vows and Contracts in the Fourth Crusade: The Treaty of Zara and the Attack on Constantinople in 1204," *International History Review* 15 (1993): 454.

218. Poem 16; Chap. 7.

219. Chaps. 14 and 17.

220. Chap. 18.

221. See Swietek's catalogues: "Gunther," 51–56, 71–78.

222. Ibid., 56.

223. Reg. VI 102 in PL 215: 109–110. See Andrea and Motsiff, "Zara," 22, n. 72.

224. See A. J. Andrea's study, "Pope Innocent III and the Diversion of the Fourth Crusade to Constantinople," which is tentatively scheduled to be published in *Venice: Society and Crusade: Studies in Honor of Donald E. Queller*, ed. Thomas F. Madden and Ellen E. Kittel (Urbana, Ill.: University of Illinois Press, 1997).

225. Ernoul et Bernard le Trésorier, *Chronique*, ed. Louis de Mas Latrie (Paris, Renouard: 1871), 340–341, mentions the treaty. Roger de Hove-

den, *Chronica*, ed. William Stubbs (London: Longman, 1868–1871), 4: 186, quotes a letter of 1201 from the Master of the Hospital at Jerusalem to the prior of the Order in England in which he mentions the Nile's failure to flood and the resultant famine in Egypt.

226. See pp. 24–25 above.

227. See the last line of poem 2.

228. Penny J. Cole, *The Preaching of Crusades to the Holy Land, 1095–1270* (Cambridge, Mass.: Medieval Academy of America, 1991), 92–97, has provided the most complete analysis of the sermon. Assuming that Gunther has faithfully recorded the abbot's words, Cole characterizes the sermon as unique and possessing "a peculiar forcefulness, coherence, and balanced viewpoint which have been missing in many previous sermons" (p. 93).

229. Chap. 19.

230. Andrea, "Adam," 25–33.

231. Andrea, "Historia," 269–302, passim.

232. Queller and Katele, "Attitudes," 30–31, 35–36, characterize the *HC* as anti-Venetian, because Gunther, as was true of most clerical commentators on the Fourth Crusade, did not understand or appreciate mercantile values. Andrea, "Cistercian Accounts," 17–31, argues for a modification of these conclusions.

233. Chaps. 15, 16, 21, 22, and poem 15. See also chapters 4 and 19 and poem 2 (possibly also poem 21), where Martin has presentiments of success. Abbot Martin's crusade sermon in chapter 3 is also prophetic.

234. Steven F. Kruger, *Dreaming in the Middle Ages* (Cambridge: Cambridge University Press, 1992), 57–82.

235. See Orth, *Hystoria*, 95–99, for a discussion of the three MSS.

236. Riant, *Guntheri*.

237. Riant, *Exuviae*, 1: 57–126.

238. Theodor Vulpinus (pseud.), trans., "Günthers von Pairis *Historia Constantinopolitana* oder *Die Eroberung Constantinopels 1205 von wo, unter anderen Reliquien, ein grosses Stück des heiligen Kreuzes nach Deutschland gebracht worden ist*," *Jahrbuch für Geschichte, Sprache und Litteratur Elsass-Lothringens* 5 (1889): 1–56.

239. Dana C. Munro, ed., and trans., "The Fourth Crusade," *Translations and Reprints from the Original Sources of European History*, Published for the Department of History of the University of Pennsylvania, vol. 3 (Philadelphia: University of Pennsylvania Press, 1901), No. 1: 16–19. Edward Peters, ed., *Christian Society and the Crusades, 198–1229* (Philadelphia: University of Pennsylvania Press, 1971), 18–21, has reprinted Munro's translation.

240. Charles Homer Haskins, *The Renaissance of the Twelfth Century* (1927; Cleveland: World, 1957), 234.

241. Louise and Jonathan Riley-Smith, eds. and trans., *The Crusades: Idea and Reality, 1095–1274*, Documents of Medieval History 4 (London: Edward Arnold, 1981), 70–71, 172–173.

242. Assmann, *Geschichte*.

243. Minor corrections to Riant's edition were suggested by Gaston Paris in his review of the 1875 edition in *Revue Critique d'Histoire et de Littérature* 9, 2nd semestre (1875): 85–88; Albert Pannenborg, "Die Verse in der *Historia Constantinopolitana* und der Dichter des *Ligurinus*," *Forschungen zur Deutschen Geschichte* 19 (1879): 611–624, and *Verfasser*, 29; and Assmann, *Eroberung*, passim. Riant provided his own emendations in *Exuviae*, 2: 303.

Translation

1. The title *Hystoria Constantinopolitana* appears only in I; M has only this second title; C has no title.

2. Literally, *a private and humble man*. See chapter 20, where the same term is used to describe Abbot Martin.

3. Compare with the prologue to Sulpicius Severus's *Life of St. Martin*.

4. Compare Robert of Reims, *HI*, prologue.

5. Compare Robert of Reims, *HI*, introduction.

6. This phrase might seem to imply that Martin is dead, but the poem makes it clear that the abbot was still alive while Gunther was composing the *HC*.

7. Compare Robert of Reims, *HI*, prologue.

8. Compare Sulpicius Severus, *Life of St. Martin*, chap. 25.

9. Abbot Martin.

10. Compare Boethius, *Consolation of Philosophy*, 4: prose 5.

11. Compare Robert of Reims, *HI*, prologue.

12. Compare *HP*, prologue.

13. Fulk of Neuilly, the primary preacher of the Fourth Crusade: Milton R. Gutsch, "A Twelfth-Century Preacher—Fulk of Neuilly, " *Crusades and Other Historical Essays Presented to Dana C. Munro by His Former Students*, ed. Louis J. Paetow (New York: Crofts, 1928), 183–206; John M. O'Brien, "Fulk of Neuilly," *Proceedings of the Leeds Philosophical and Literary Society* 13 (1969): 109–148. Gunther is the only medieval or modern author to refer to him as Fulk of Paris. His reason is obvious.

14. The Île de France, which was centered on Paris.

15. Jerusalem capitulated to Saladin on October 2, 1187.

16. *Oberdeutschland*, or southern Germany.

17. *Parisius*. By modern convention, we spell the name of the abbey Pairis, to differentiate it from Paris, France.

18. Martin can hardly be termed Fulk's equal when it came to preaching the Fourth Crusade. Scores of contemporary chroniclers, including the Cistercians Alberic of Trois Fontaines and Ralph of Coggeshall, recognized Fulk as the single most important preacher of the crusade. Ralph went so far as to credit the French priest with personally investing two hundred thousand people with the Cross. Abbot Martin's preaching efforts were overlooked by these same fellow Cistercians.

19. Fulk's birthplace is unknown.

20. Paris derives its name from the Parisii, a Celtic tribe that inhabited a fortified site on the present Île de la Cité.

21. Lucelle, known in modern German as Lützel, was founded on March 25, 1124 as a daughter abbey of Bellevaux and a granddaughter of Morimond. Between 1130 and 1139 Lucelle established six daughter houses of its own. Either the fifth or sixth of these was Pairis. Here Tegenhard, first superior of the new cloister, and eleven brothers settled in late 1138 or early 1139 on land donated by Ulrich, count of Egisheim: Jenn, "Pairis," 52–86.

22. The Latin is *puram glaciem* (pure ice), which would mean little to any reader unaware of the German pun here. In Middle High German *puram glaciem* could be translated as *Bar Îs*. As noted in the introduction, this would be pronounced "par is" in the dialect of Alsace. Gunther, probably expecting his reader to chuckle at this joke, suggests that the original twelve founders of the cloister named their monastery for the most striking feature of its natural environment, the cold desolation of the Vosges Mountains. Modern scholars have proposed more sober etymological explanations. Wulf Müller, *Die Siedlungs- und Flurnamen von Urbeis (Orbey) im Oberelsass* (Bern: Lang, 1973), 152–159, argues the name derives from *Paradies* (paradise), which was transformed into Paris or Parys, as we see in a number of Middle High German plant names, such as *parysappfel* (apple of paradise, or pomegranate) and *pariskörner* (paradise grains, or cardamoms).

23. *Prediis*. A pun, inasmuch as Martin enriched the abbey with spoils (*preda*).

24. Innocent III (r. 1198–1216).

25. Basel founded in A.D. 44 and originally named *Robur* (Latin: *roburetum: oak grove*), was renamed *Basilia* (Greek: *basileus: emperor*) in 374 in honor of Valentinian I (r. 364–375), who used it as a frontier encampment.

26. Clergy and laity.

27. The cathedral, known to the residents of Basel as the Münster. An

earlier Romanesque structure had burned down on October 25, 1185, so the church was probably still being rebuilt when Martin preached his sermon: Wilhelm Streuber, *Die Stadt Basel, historish- topagraphisch Beschrieben* (Basel, 1854), 43.

28. The *Annals* of the Alsatian monastery of Marbach indicates otherwise. According to this source, Basel's bishop, Luthold I von Rötelen (1190–1213), publicly supported the cause of the Holy Land as early as 1200 and in May of that year took the Cross himself, along with a large number of abbots and religious: *Annales Marbacenses*, ed. Roger Wilmans, MGH SS, 17:170.

St. Bernard of Clairvaux had brought word of the Second Crusade to the people of Basel when he preached the Cross in the city on December 6, 1146: Vautrey, *Évêques de Bâle*, 1: 160. It seems clear that Gunther attempts to underscore the parallels between Martin and St. Bernard by making it appear that the abbot of Pairis was the first person to preach the Fourth Crusade in that city. See also chapter 3, note 32.

29. Martin probably delivered his sermon between late spring and mid-summer of 1201. It had to have been given well before Martin's appearance at the Chapter General which convened at Cîteaux on September 14. Chapter 4 indicates that a fair amount of time lapsed between Martin's sermon at Basel and his journey to Cîteaux.

30. Orth, *Hystoria*, 111, prints *munere*, following M 117v and C 34v, col. 1. The word makes no sense here, and Riant's correction of *munera* is preferable: *Exuviae*, 1: 62.

31. Apparently Gunther was not in the audience.

32. *Verbum mihi ad vos*. With these opening words Gunther brings to mind St. Bernard of Clairvaux's famous encyclical in support of the Second Crusade, which begins *Sermo mihi ad vos* (Heed my sermon to you). Bernard's letter, numbered 363, is edited in Jean Leclercq, "L'Encyclique de Saint Bernard en faveur de la croisade," *Revue Bénédictine* 81 (1971) 295–300. James, *Letters of St. Bernard*, 460–463, translates the copy addressed to the people of England.

Gunther intends his reader to see parallels between St. Bernard and Abbot Martin and to draw the obvious conclusions. Whereas Bernard in his letter refers to himself as a person of little account, Martin calls himself a fragile instrument. With the same exclamation of sorrow (*Proh dolor!*), both men recount in detail how Christ had blessed, through his actions, lands that the impious were now defiling and polluting. Both speak of Jerusalem as the city made sacred by Christ's blood. Whereas Bernard called his audience men of valor (*viri fortes*), Martin calls them true warriors (*validi bellatores*) and renowned warriors (*incliti bellatores*). Gunther also borrows for Martin St. Bernard's promise of payment. Compare the following passage from St Bernard's letter with the last two paragraphs of Martin's sermon:

> If you are a prudent merchant, if you seek the things of this world, I will tell you of some great bargains. See that they not escape you. Take up the sign of the Cross and you will equally obtain indulgence for all of the sins you confess with a contrite heart. Such goods are purchased for a cheap price. When the Cross is devoutly taken onto one's shoulders, no doubt the kingdom of God is merited. Consequently they have done well who have taken up this heavenly sign. Others will do well and will not be foolish should they hurry to seize what will be for them a sign of salvation.

33. The church of the Holy Sepulcher.

34. Saladin captured a major portion of what was believed to be the True Cross at Hattin in 1187. The Christians never recovered it.

35. Crusader forces recaptured the port city of Acre in 1191, and it currently served as the royal capital of the Latin kingdom of Jerusalem in exile.

36. Note the ironic parallel between the crusaders' ultimate goal—to restore Christ to his patrimony—and the proximate cause that will lead the crusaders to Constantinople—the restoration of Alexius the Younger to his patrimony: chapters 8 and 11.

37. The First Crusade, 1096–1099.

38. Compare Robert of Reims, *HI*, 1:1.

39. Orth, *Hystoria*, 114, accepts the reading of all three MSS and prints *atterritis*. I have adopted Assmann's suggestion, *Geschichte*, 39, n. 29, that the word should be *attritis*.

40. *Tollere signa*. Here Gunther indulges in wordplay. Normally this is an idiomatic expression that is best translated "to break camp." In this particular case its primary meaning has to be "to assume tokens [of the Cross]," but undoubtedly Gunther also wished to convey the notion of their preparing to depart from Basel.

41. In this ambiguous passage Gunther tries to explain the origin and original meaning of the practice of wearing the crusader's cross on both breast and back. His source is Robert of Rheims's recreation of Urban II's speech at Clermont. There, according to Robert, the pope instructed his audience:

> Whoever, therefore, sets his mind on this holy pilgrimage and would, thereby, make a commitment to God and would offer himself to Him as a living sacrifice, holy and pleasing, let him display the sign of

> the Lord's Cross on his forehead or on his breast. Then, indeed, let him, who has fulfilled his vow and who wishes to return home, place [it] on his back, between his shoulders. (RHC. H. Occ. 3: 729–730)

As we can see by comparing Gunther's explanation with his source, he has distorted the meaning of the passage. Gunther appears to be saying that originally one elected to wear the cross on either the front or the back, from the moment one took the vow. He who wore the cross on his chest showed he intended to stay in *Outremer*; he who displayed it on his back signified a desire to return home to Europe once the pilgrimage was completed.

42. This has to be read in the light of the opening sentence of chapter 4. The papal order Gunther refers to is the commission to preach the crusade.

43. This might be another example of Gunther's exaggeration of Martin's role in the crusade, but it is possible the crusaders from Basel did ask the abbot to be their leader. Both popular sentiment and canon law did not totally preclude a cleric's leading troops to the Holy Land. Basel also had a tradition of active clerical leadership in the crusades. Bishop Ortlieb led a contingent from Basel under his banner on the Second Crusade: Vautrey, *Évêques de Bâle*, 1: 162. We have also seen where one of his successors, Henry of Horburg, a member of the Cistercian Order, died on the Third Crusade. It is possible that Abbot Martin took the place of Bishop Luthold, who might not have been able to fulfill his crusade vow (Chapter 2, n. 28; Chapter 23, n. 310).

44. In chapter 19 Abbot Martin returns to his ship loaded down with relics and, "with smiling countenance and merry words [states], 'We have done well.'"

45. Swietek, "Gunther," 62, n. 105, points out that line 13 of poem 19 describes the Greeks at Troy as having had almost twelve hundred ships. He concludes: "The coincidence of the same numerical phrase in exactly the same metrical position in two hexameters raises the suspicion that it may simply be a conveniently scanned formula without evidential value in either case."

46. Gunther might mean that other southwest German crusaders opted for an alternate route to Venice.

47. The Brenner Pass, which normally opens in May, which means the contingent left Basel no earlier than April 1202.

48. As recently as 1196, the Chapter General had prohibited the Cistercians of Germany and Hungary from leading armed retainers: Canivez, *Statuta*, 203. Apparently Gunther and Martin believed this crusade command did not fall under that prohibition.

49. Sulpicius Severus, *Life of St. Martin*, chap. 2.

50. Abbot Martin.

51. Cistercian monks who became prelates were still expected to observe all regular fasts, recite the Cistercian canonical hours, wear the Order's habit, and generally comport themselves as Cistercians: Canivez, *Statuta*, 27. Nothing less could be expected of an abbot traveling on a pilgrimage.

52. Sulpicius Severus, *Life of St. Martin*, chap. 3.

53. Chap. 9.

54. Sulpicius Severus, *Life of St. Martin*, chap. 10.

55. Chap. 20.

56. Chap. 22.

57. *Plenus*. Compare this to chapter 19 where Martin is "overstuffed" (*suffarcinatus*) with relics.

58. St. Martin of Tours.

59. November 11.

60. Martin of Pairis.

61. Cf. Mt. 19:29.

62. Alexius the Younger was in Verona during the summer of 1202, where he met a fair number of pilgrims there on their way to join the army: Villehardouin, *Conquête*, 1: 70–72, sec. 70. Possibly Abbot Martin met Alexius at this time, which could explain some of Gunther's knowledge of Byzantine court intrigue and his obvious sympathy for the young Greek.

63. Cardinal Adelardo Cataneo, bishop of Verona from 1188 to 1211 or 1212. Adelardo had served as a papal cardinal-legate on the Third Crusade.

64. Probably from late May to late July: *FC*[1], 44; *FC*[2], 50.

65. Ernoul-Bernard, *Chronique*, 353; Roger de Hoveden, *Chronica*, 4: 68. A five and a half year truce (Hoveden says six years) was entered into on June 21, 1198, but it would be broken in November of 1203 (see chapter 10). The treaty was quite important to the Latins in Syria, because it provided them a measure of security, and, for this reason, King Amalric II took special pains to honor it: *L'Estoire de Eracles Empereur et la conqueste de la terre d'Outremer*, RHC. H. Occ., 2: 247. Gunther surely reflects here the thinking of the besieged Latins in the Holy Land, attitudes that Martin learned during his two visits to Acre (chapters 9, 10, and 22), and not necessarily the reasoning behind the strategic decision of the crusade leaders to attack Egypt. The only reason Villehardouin offers for the decision is that: "from Babylon [Egypt] they could better destroy the Turks than from any other land": *Conquête*, 1: 30, sec, 30.

66. Baldwin IX, count of Flanders and Hainaut, swore the Cross on Ash Wednesday, February 23, 1200 in Bruges. He would subsequently be crowned Latin emperor of Constantinople on May 16, 1204: chapter 20.

67. During the summer of 1201 the crusade barons offered the position of crusade leadership to Boniface, prince of the north Italian marquisate of Montferrat: Villehardouin, *Conquête*, 1: 40–42, secs. 40–42.

68. Roger de Hoveden, *Chronica*, 4: 186, quotes a letter from Jerusalem describing the famine. In 1201–1202 a plague followed the famine, wiping out a large percentage of Egypt's population. See also Queller and Madden, "Further Arguments," 436–444.

69. It was not that simple. See Queller and Day, "Some Arguments," 724–728; Queller and Madden, "Further Arguments," 444–450.

70. This is confirmed by other sources: *Historia ducum Veneticorum, Supplementum*, ed. H. Simonsfeld, MGH, SS, 14: 90; Thomas of Spalato, *Historia Spalatina*, ed. L. de Heinemann, MGH, SS, 29: 576; and Alberic of Trois-Fontaines, *Chronica*, ed. P. Scheffer-Boichorst, MGH, SS, 23: 880.

71. Villehardouin, *Conquête*, 1: 66, sec. 63, notes that some barons, "who wished the army disbanded," raised objections to this proposal when it was presented in Venice. In fact, a number of leading knights defected from the army, rather than sail to Zara.

72. King Imre (Emeric) I (r. 1196–1204): James Ross Sweeney, "Hungary in the Crusades, 1169–1218," *International History Review* 3 (1981): 475–476. For the Venetian answer to this charge, see Queller and Madden, "Further Arguments," 449–450.

73. Villehardouin, *Conquête*, 1: 80, sec. 79. The marshal of Champagne interpreted their actions differently. To him they were deserters who acted badly and were justly blamed for their actions.

74. Werner Maleczek, *Petrus Capuanus: Kardinal, Legat am vierten Kreuzzug, Theologe (+1214)* (Vienna: Verlag der österreichischen Akademie der Wissenschaften, 1988), pp. 117–157.

75. Schmandt, "Just War," 204–208, deals with the moral issues surrounding the affair at Zara. The *GeH* tells how Cardinal Peter helped Bishop Conrad of Halberstadt to resolve this quandary: MGH, SS, 23: 117.

76. There is no evidence in any other source that Cardinal Peter gave Abbot Martin or any other cleric military command over any crusaders.

77. The *GeH* notes that Cardinal Peter commissioned Bishop Conrad of Halberstadt and four Cistercian abbots to stay with the army, instructing it by example and sermon: MGH, SS, 23: 117.

78. A city of northeastern Italy.

79. Ariadne, daughter of Minos of Crete. Gunther has managed to mutilate her name and, thereby, associate it with the Adriatic Sea.

80. The fleet took roughly forty days to cover the fairly short distance to Zara, because of a number of stops along the way: *FC*[1], 61–62; *FC*[2], 68–72.

81. According to Villehardouin, *Conquête*, 1: 78–86, secs. 78–85, the

siege began on November 11. On November 13 the army commenced firing on the walls, and this lasted for a period of about five days. After clearing the walls of opposing fire, the crusaders began to undermine one of the towers. Upon seeing this, the citizens of Zara surrendered. The *GeH* (MGH, SS, 23:117) and Thomas of Spalato, *Historia*, 576, both tell us that the city capitulated on the feast day of St. Chrysogonus, November 24. An anonymous eyewitness source known as the *Devastatio Constantinopolitana* (hereafter *DC*) notes that the city surrendered on the fifteenth day of operations, or November 25: Alfred J. Andrea, "The *Devastatio Constantinopolitana*, A Special Perspective on the Fourth Crusade: An Analysis, New Edition, and Translation," *Historical Reflections/Réflexions Historiques* 19 (1993): 132.

82. Compare Sulpicius Severus, *Life of St. Martin*, chap. 4. Innocent III charged otherwise. In early 1203 he accusingly wrote to the crusaders: "You surrounded the city and undermined its walls, not without shedding a good deal of blood.": Reg. V 160 (161 in PL 214) in Othmar Hageneder et al., *Die Register Innocenz' III.* (Vienna: Verlag der Österreichischen Akademie der Wissenschaften, 1993), 5: 316.

83. This makes no sense, since the army and fleet wintered over in Zara. Upon their capture of the city, the two major groups of crusaders, the Venetians and the non-Venetians, divided the city between themselves: Villehardouin, *Conquête*, 1: 86–88, secs. 86–87; *DC* in Andrea, 132–133; Clari, *Conquête*, 15, sec. XIV; *GeH* in MGH, SS, 23: 117. They seem, however, to have pulled down at least portions of the walls and destroyed some buildings upon their capture of the city. In early 1203 Innocent III accused the crusaders of having idly stood by while the Venetians toppled walls, despoiled churches, and destroyed buildings: Reg. V 160 (161) in Hageneder, *Register*, 5: 316. This corresponds to evidence supplied by Andrea Dandolo, *Chronica*, ed. E. Pastorello, RIS[2], 2nd ed., Vol. 12, 1: 277, which suggests that the walls were destroyed before winter. Yet Villehardouin, *Conquête*, 1: 110, sec. 108, notes that the walls were toppled as the Venetians prepared to evacuate the city in early April 1203. Certainly, the Venetians only leveled the entire city as they prepared to leave in the spring of 1203: Villehardouin, ibid; *GeH* in MGH, SS, 23:118; *DC* in Andrea, 133; Thomas of Spalato, *Historia*, 576.

84. Abbot Martin clearly was not an elected member of this delegation. Villehardouin, *Conquête*, 1: 106, sec. 105, tells us the legation consisted of four persons: two clerics, Bishop Nevelon of Soissons and John de Noyon, and two knights, John de Friaize and Robert de Boves. Absolutely no source, other than the *HC*, mentions Abbot Martin's presence in the legation. He appears to have been a self-appointed representative of the German contingent, who tagged along in the hope of gaining a papal dispensation from his vow.

85. Nevelon de Chérisy (r. 1176–1207). See Alfred J. Andrea and Paul I. Rachlin, "Holy War, Holy Relics, Holy Theft: The Anonymous of Soissons's *De terra Iherosolimitana*: An Analysis, Edition, and Translation," *Historical Reflections/Réflexions Historiques* 18 (1992): 147–175, for Bishop Nevelon's own relic translation history of the Fourth Crusade.

86. John Faicete of Noyon, future chancellor of the Latin empire of Constantinople and bishop-elect of Acre. Gunther is the only source to call him John of Paris.

87. Reg. V 161 (162) in Hageneder, *Register*, 5: 318–320.

88. Innocent was forty-two in early 1203.

89. Compare poem 12, lines 4–6.

90. Isaac II Angelus (r. 1185–1195; 1203–1204).

91. Philip of Hohenstaufen's claim to the crown was contested by Otto of Brunswick.

92. Alexius did not reach Zara until April 25, 1203, where he was greeted by Montferrat, Dandolo, and a small retinue. The bulk of the army had already set sail on April 20: *DC* in Andrea, 133. Accompanied by the doge and marquis, the Greek prince joined the main elements of the army and fleet at Corfu in mid to late May. Bishop Nevelon and his colleagues had left Rome well before Alexius's arrival at Zara and arrived back in time to set sail with the main army. Reg. VI 99, dated April of 1203, from the crusade leaders to the pope, is an obvious reply to instructions the pope had sent back to the army with its returning legates.

Although Alexius had not yet visited the army, he had quite a bit of contact with it and its leaders. Alexius had been at Verona, where he met many crusaders (chapter 6, n. 62). From Verona he also sent messengers to Montferrat and the other crusader leaders in Venice, and they responded by sending envoys to him, to accompany him back to the court of his brother-in-law, Philip of Swabia: Villehardouin, *Conquête*, 1: 70–74, secs. 70–72. Earlier Alexius had met Boniface de Montferrat at that same court during the Christmas holidays of 1201: *FC*[1], 30, 172–173, n. 70; *FC*[2], 33–37. While the army was encamped at Zara, King Philip answered the barons' apparent request for further guarantees and information by sending his own envoys back in the company of the crusader legates who had traveled to Germany with Alexius: Villehardouin, *Conquête*, 1: 90–94, secs. 91–94; *DC* in Andrea, 133; *GeH* in MGH, SS, 23: 118. Villehardouin dates the arrival of this embassy toward the very end of December of 1202 (four weeks after November 28); the *DC* dates it as January 1, 1203. It was this legation, bargaining in the name of Alexius, that occasioned the rumor to which the pope responded.

93. Alexius III Angelus (r. 1195–1203).

94. The future Alexius IV (r. 1203–1204).

95. Alexius "Mourtzouphlos" Ducas, the future Alexius V (r. 1204).

Alexius Ducas was not related by blood to the imperial family but was the lover of Alexius III's daughter Eudokia: Nicetas Choniates, *Historia*, ed. Aloysius van Dieten (Berlin: de Gruyter, 1975), 571. Nicetas, a contemporary of Alexius Ducas, informs us that Ducas's nickname was due to the fact that his dark, bushy eyebrows almost covered his eyes. In a piece of undated correspondence, Professor Renée Kahane of the University of Illinois at Urbana-Champagne pointed out that Μούτζουφλος is a variant of *Μουτζότυφλος*, or "blackened and blind." One of Byzantium's major punishments was to blind and blacken the face of a felon and to lead him through the streets. Francis Swietek kindly forwarded to me a copy of Professor Kahane's letter.

Gunther's translation of this nickname as *flos cordis* (blossom of the heart) seems to be a pun on the phrase *motus flos* (blossom of passion) since *cor* and *motus* are metaphorically synonymous. *Motus*'s primary meaning is "movement" and, therefore, it can also mean "revolution" or "sedition." To Gunther's mind, this would be a fitting name for such a traitor.

96. The only other source that implicates Alexius Ducas in the palace coup of 1195 is the Cistercian Alberic of Trois-Fontaines, *Chronica*, 870, who lists "Morcuflus" as one of the eight principal conspirators who encouraged Alexius Angelus to depose his brother. Although Alberic is late (d. 1251) and a Westerner, Charles M. Brand, *Byzantium Confronts the West, 1180–1204* (Cambridge, Mass.: Harvard University Press, 1968), 111, characterizes his history as "frequently well-informed on Byzantine affairs." Alberic's treatment of the Fourth Crusade clearly shows that he did not use the *HC* as one of his sources: Andrea, "Cistercian Accounts," 9–10. There is also no reason to believe he and Gunther utilized a common, now lost source. Even though these two independent Cistercian histories were far removed in space and time from the events of 1195, they should not be dismissed lightly. Undoubtedly each author had opportunities to learn of events in the East.

97. Alexius arrived in Germany around October of 1201.

98. Irene.

99. Boniface de Montferrat traced his matrilineal line back to his great-grandfather, Emperor Henry IV, by way of Henry's daughter Agnes. King Philip, on his father's side, claimed Henry IV as a great-great-grandfather through the same Agnes. Boniface was also one of the great lords of the empire and exceedingly loyal to the Hohenstaufen cause.

100. Villehardouin, *Conquête*, 1: 92, sec. 93, Clari, *Conquête*, 31, sec. XXXII, and the *GeH* in MGH, SS, 23: 118, all say two hundred thousand marks. Hugh, count of St.-Pol, in a letter to Henry, duke of Louvain, states that Alexius promised equal payments of one hundred thousand

marks of silver each to the doge of Venice and the army: RHGH, 18: 517.

101. Satan.

102. See Wilhelm De Vries, "Innocenz III. (1198–1216) und der christliche Osten," *Archivum Historiae Pontificae* 3 (1965): 87–126; Gerd Hagedorn, "Papst Innocenz III. und Byzanz am Vorabend des Vierten Kreuzzugs (1198–1203)," *Ostkirchliche Studien* 23 (1974): 3–20, 105–136; Joseph Gill, *Byzantium and the Roman Papacy* (New Brunswick, N. J.: Rutgers University Press, 1979), 1–23.

103. Leading studies in English on the schism between the churches of Rome and Constantinople include: Yves Congar, *After Nine Hundred Years* (New York: Fordham University Press, 1959); Francis Dvornik, *Byzantium and the Roman Primacy* (New York: Fordham University Press, 1966) and "Constantinople and Rome," *The Cambridge Medieval History* 4, 1 (1966) 431–472; George Every, *The Byzantine Patriarchate*, 2nd ed. rev. (London: Society for Promoting Christian Knowledge, 1962) and *Misunderstandings between East and West*, Ecumenical Studies in History Series 4 (Richmond, Va.: Knox, 1966).

104. This is known as the *filioque* controversy, due to the Western Church's addition to the Creed of the Latin phrase *filioque* ("and from the Son") in the passage concerning the procession of the Holy Spirit. See Gill, "Greeks, Latins, and the *Filioque*" in *Byzantium*, 142–160.

105. Latin Christians had used unfermented bread (*azyme*) since at least the eleventh century. In his treatise *De sacro altaris mysterio* (*On the Sacred Mystery of the Altar*), which Innocent began while a cardinal but completed during his papacy, the pope twice addressed the question of the Greek use of fermented bread for the sacrament of the Holy Eucharist. In the first passage, written probably during the period of his cardinalate, he stated that the Greeks were stubbornly in error on this point: PL 217: 855. The second passage, which dates no earlier than 1208, declares that, although Christ used *azyme* when he instituted the sacrament, nevertheless many true Catholics, in communion with the Roman Church, today sacrificed with fermented bread: ibid., 878. The reason for the change in attitude is clear. Innocent was forced to compromise with the Greeks of the captive church of the Latin empire of Constantinople.

106. According to tradition, St. Peter was crucified upside down.

107. This probably refers to Cardinal John whom Pope Alexander III had sent to Constantinople to negotiate with Emperor Manuel. He was killed during the Latin Massacre of 1182, and his severed head was dragged through the streets, tied to a dog's tail: Brand, *Byzantium*, 41, 223.

108. This was the *hyperperon* (pl. *hyperpera*), Constantinople's standard gold coin since 1092.

109. Gunther was correct. Four hyperpera equaled one mark, or a half pound, of silver.

110. According to Nicetas, *Historia*, 540–541, when Alexius III heard rumors of the crusaders' sailing to Constantinople, he feverishly began to repair his war fleet, which at that time numbered barely twenty, largely unseaworthy vessels. Time, however, ran out. Even if Nicetas is guilty of some exaggeration, it is clear that the Byzantine fleet was no match for the Venetians, and at no time in the period 1203–1204 was it able to offer any effective resistance.

111. The Latin term for the Byzantine empire.

112. Reg. VI 102 in PL 215: 109, provides this license.

113. Both C 38r, col. 2, and M 126r clearly have *exequenda*. Orth, *Hystoria*, 130 and Assmann, *Geschichte*, 56, n. 92, believe the word should be *exequanda*, which would result in: *So that victory can hardly be justified by fearful losses and a double catastrophe*.

114. Reg. V 161 (162) and VI 102. There is no way that Abbot Martin could ever have been entrusted with bearing these letters to the army. He was not even an official member of the legation, and Bishop Nevelon was the mission's ranking ecclesiastic, as Innocent's letter V 161 (162) makes clear. Here the pope refers to the embassy as "our venerable brother, the bishop of Soissons, and others who came with him," and a bit farther on the pope informs the army that he has given the bishop oral instructions for the army: Hageneder, *Register*, 5: 318–320. See also the *Gesta Innocentii III*. in PL 214: cxxxix.

115. Benevento, a port in southeast Italy, is not on the route to Zara, which makes it appear highly unlikely that Bishop Nevelon, John of Noyon, or John de Friaize accompanied Martin as he traveled southward from Rome. It is more likely that Martin and Robert de Boves, who also left the embassy in order to make his separate way to Syria (Villehardouin, *Conquête*, 1:106, sec. 106), bade farewell to the legates at Rome and set out together to find passage to the Holy Land. If Martin sent any message back to the Germans at Zara, he had to have done so at Rome.

116. On April 21, 1203 Innocent dispatched letter VI 48 to Cardinal Peter, in which the pope instructed him on how he was to deal with the Venetian refusal to seek absolution for the transgression at Zara: Othmar Hageneder et al., *Die Register Innocenz' III*. (Vienna: Verlag der Österreichischen Akademie der Wissenschaften, 1995), 6: 71–72. Although it is possible that Peter left for Syria before receiving this papal reply to his now-lost request for papal guidance, which he had sent off in late winter/early spring, it does not seem likely. Certainly the author of Innocent's *Gesta* seems to imply that Cardinal Peter left for the province of Jerusalem only after receiving Innocent's letter of instruction: PL 214: cxl. Conse-

quently, it seems likely that Capuano and Martin departed no earlier than very late April or early May of 1203. As note 118 suggests, April 25 is a likely date for Martin and Peter's embarkation.

117. Manfredonia.

118. In a comparative analysis of the relative speeds of several long sea voyages in the eastern Mediterranean in the period of the Fourth Crusade, Erwin Assmann, *Geschichte*, 95, n. 202, concludes that Capuano's vessel could be reasonably expected to have averaged 1.7 kmph for the roughly 2,000 kilometer trip from Italy to Syria-Palestine by way of Cyprus. To have made the voyage in only twenty-two days would have necessitated the incredible speed of almost 4 kmph. Doubting this reported speed, he suggests that the *HC* erroneously reads *septimo kal. maii* (the seventh day before the kalends, or first, of May—April 25) instead of the correct *septimo kal. Junii* (May 26), because Gunther, being more at home with the ecclesiastical calendar, made an understandable mistake when using the old Roman system of dating: ibid., 57, n. 97. Assmann assumes that the reported date of departure, April 4, is essentially correct, which seems unlikely. As note 116 argues, Martin probably set sail from Italy no earlier than around April 25. It seems likely, therefore, that Gunther confused Abbot Martin's embarkation date with the date of his arrival.

119. Ernoul-Bernard, *Chronique*, 359, mentions this epidemic and notes it severely depleted the Latin ranks. The disease's speedy course and high mortality rate suggest cholera.

120. A mark was a weight of silver, or money of account, and not a coin. The mark of Cologne, the most widely accepted monetary standard in medieval Germany, weighed a bit over 3,600 grains and had considerable purchasing power. The Crusader-Venetian Treaty of 1201 stipulated payment of two marks of Cologne for each man and four for each horse in return for transportation from Venice to the crusade's final destination and provisions for an entire year.

121. According to Ernoul-Bernard, *Chronique*, 354–355, an Egyptian emir from Sidon sent armed galleys into the seas around Cyprus, where they captured two Christian vessels. After fruitless appeals to the sultan, King Amalric II countered with a raid that netted two hundred or more Saracen captives, twenty ships, and 60,000 gold coins.

122. Only C 38v, col. 2, has "our"; it is missing in the other two MSS and in Orth, *Hystoria*, 134, and Riant, *Exuviae*, 1: 82.

123. Riant, *Exuviae*, l: lxxxiii, n. 2, points out that the *HC* is the sole source to mention this supposed legation and concludes that it is possibly another example of Abbot Martin's masquerading an independent action as an official duty. According to Riant, had Amalric II wished to send a legation to the crusaders, it is likely he would have preferred to send Re-

naud of Montmirail, who had been dispatched to Syria by the army on Palm Sunday (March 30) 1203: *DC* in Andrea, 133; Villehardouin, *Conquête*, 1: 102, sec. 102.

124. Secular patron and defender. A hereditary feudal office.

125. See Orth, *Hystoria*, 9, for a sketch of Conrad.

126. November 8, 1203.

127. January 1, 1204.

128. Gunther wants us to believe that Alexius IV has already been deposed and murdered. However, if Martin actually arrived on January 1, he came to the crusader camp before Alexius IV's deposition. What is more, the *DC* (Andrea, 135) states that on January 1, during the first period of sleep, the Greeks attacked the Venetian fleet by setting loose fifteen burning vessels. The anonymous eyewitness who recorded his memories of these events in the *Chronicle of Novgorod* tells us that ten fire ships were sent against the Latin fleet at midnight on St Vasilij's day (January 1): Jared Gordon, trans., "The Novgorod Account of the Fourth Crusade," *Byzantion* 43 (1973): 309. Villehardouin, *Conquête*, 2: 16, sec. 217, numbers the fire ships at seventeen and simply notes that this event took place "one night at midnight." It is curious that Gunther does not mention this attack.

129. Gunther consistently uses the word *virtus* (excellence; moral perfection; strength) for both God's (chapter 1) and the crusaders' power and *potentia* (worldly dominion; political or ruling power) for Greek might. The message clearly is that these crusaders are serving unconsciously as divine agents, whereas the Greeks only enjoy worldly strength: Andrea, "*Historia*," 301.

130. This word is missing in all three MSS, but the sense of the sentence demands we supply it.

131. Chap. 8.

132. *De re devota*. *Devota* is an ambiguous word and was chosen for the irony contained in that ambiguity. Normally Christian authors used it in the sense of *faithful* and *pious*. However, clearly the reference here is to Morciflo's murder of Alexius IV, so Gunther intends the word to be understood in the classical, poetic sense of "accursed" or "bewitched."

133. Gunther failed to mention in chapter 8 that Alexius III had blinded Isaac II after deposing him. See chapter 13 and its accompanying poem, line 9, which both mention the blinding of Isaac.

134. Chap. 8.

135. *Sacrosanctis*. Compare chapter 19.

136. Crusaders. Greek treachery toward the crusaders was a major complaint among the Latins since the First Crusade: B. Ebels-Hoving, *Byzantium in Westerse Ogen, 1096–1204* (Assen, Netherlands: Van Gorcum,

1971), passim; Martin G. Arbagi, "Byzantium in Latin Eyes: 800–1204" (PhD diss., Rutgers University, 1970), passim.

137. Compare Otto of St. Blasien, quoted in the introduction, p. 15.

138. *Omnia formaliter comprehendit*. Gunther expounds on this below when he states that the conceptual power of the Divine Mind contains, from all eternity, the Forms, or Ideas, of all reality, and those Forms have life by reason of their being known by the Divine Mind.

139. The Gospel of John, 1: 3–4.

140. *Noyn*. The accusative form of the Greek noun *Noys* (*Nous*) is demanded here, and Gunther provides it, indicating at least a minimal knowledge of Greek grammar, but see note 148 below.

141. Once Zara was taken, there was no haste to push on to Alexandria. Because of winter sailing conditions, the army stayed at Zara until the early spring of 1203, occupying the city until April 7 but not setting sail until the twentieth. During the winter bivouac the army's leaders decided to detour to Constantinople: *DC* in Andrea, 133; Clari, *Conquête*, 16, sec. XVII; 40, secs. XXXIX–XL.

142. *Ex*, which appears in all three MSS, is preferable to the *et* in Orth, *Hystoria*, 140, and Riant, *Exuviae*, 1: 87.

143. It was not non-stop, as many other sources, such as Villehardouin, the *DC*, and the *GeH*, bear witness.

144. On June 23, 1203 the crusaders sighted Constantinople, and for the next two days they anchored at Chalcedon, across the Bosporus from Constantinople. From June 26 through July 4 they were encamped a few miles to the north at Scutari. On July 5 they invaded the north shore of the Golden Horn and quickly captured most of this wealthy suburb. The following day they secured their beachhead by storming and taking the tower of Galata (note 146 below). They now were safely on Constantinople's European shore and, by virtue of having taken the tower and broken the great chain across the harbor entrance, were able to sail their vessels against Constantinople's weakest walls, those facing its protected harbor.

145. Queller and Madden, *FC*², 110–114, argue convincingly that the crusaders sailed to Constantinople ingenuously believing that its citizens would welcome the young Alexius, once they saw him, and would throw out his evil uncle. Expecting to be received as friends and liberators, it came as a shock to them to learn that they would have to fight to gain the city for the prince.

146. The first skirmish was on July 1 when a Latin scouting party attacked and routed a larger Greek force encamped near Scutari. On the following day, Alexius III tried unsuccessfully to buy the crusaders off by offering them supplies, if they would leave peacefully. After the cru-

saders discovered that Alexius III would not abdicate nor would the people of Constantinople depose him, they decided to capture the north shore of the Golden Horn. On the morning of July 6 the Greeks made their first offensive gesture when a combined force of soldiers from the besieged tower of Galata and troops who had sailed across the harbor from Constantinople attacked the crusader camp. After intense fighting the Greeks were repulsed with heavy losses and the tower was taken.

147. The Greek reverses of July 5 and 6 did not precipitate the emperor's flight. On July 11 (or possibly July 12; Villehardouin, *Conquête*, 1: 162–164, sec. 163, is ambiguous), the crusaders crossed the harbor by bridge and set up a siege of the northern corner of the city. Once the Latins were encamped underneath the city's walls, the Greeks began sending out numerous sallies. Nicetas Choniates, *Historia*, 544, claims the Greeks fought well in these engagements. Finally, on July 16 the crusaders decided to assault the city, their present position being untenable. The following day they attacked by both land and water. The soldiers attacking the land walls suffered numerous casualties and were repulsed. The Venetian sailors were more successful and captured a number of harbor wall towers. As they moved off of the towers, the Venetians suffered a Greek counterattack. In order to blunt the attack, the Venetians set fire to nearby buildings. Soon, this small tactical action metamorphosed into an uncontrollable inferno that destroyed about 125 acres of city property: Thomas F. Madden, "The Fires of the Fourth Crusade in Constantinople. 1203–1204: A Damage Assessment," *Byzantinische Zeitscrift* 84/85, Heft 1 (1991/1992): 73–74. Notwithstanding the fire's destruction, the Greek counterattack succeeded in forcing the Venetians to quit the city and the towers they held on the harbor wall. Despite the day's success, Emperor Alexius III secretly fled Constantinople that evening. Had Alexius shown more spirit, he conceivably could have destroyed the crusader army, which was in a sorry state following its setback on the seventeenth.

148. Gunther provides a fanciful Greek etymology for the name Alexis/Alexius. He puns that it is derived from a combination of *a privativum*, the prefix that negates the word to which it is joined (as in "amoral"), and *λέξις* (speech or speaking)—hence, *sine sermone*, or "speechless." The name actually derives from *'αλέξω* (to defend). Had Gunther known this, he would have surely highlighted its irony in this poem. We can only conclude that his ignorance of the true root of Alexius's name betrays the shallowness of his knowledge of Greek.

149. *Tam fasti sceleris* is in both M 130v and C 40r, col. 1, but Orth, *Hystoria*, 141, and Riant, *Exuviae*, 1: 88, favor *tam vasti sceleris* (so vast a crime). *Fasti* makes sense here, but only if we understand it to be either a

poetic neologism, in which Gunther has shortened the rare Late Latin *fastidibilis* (loathsome), or as part of the oxymoron "so legal a crime," since *fasti* normally means "legal" or "lawful." The former possibility seems preferable.

150. No other source mentions Alexius initiating such negotiations. To the contrary, Clari, *Conquête*, 52, sec. LII, reports that following Alexius III's flight the citizenry of the city informed the Latins of the new state of affairs and invited Prince Alexius into the city. Villehardouin, *Conquête*, 1: 184, sec. 182, and Nicetas, *Historia*, 550, add that it was the restored Emperor Isaac II who sent the message to his son.

151. Actually, young Alexius's father, Isaac II, was restored to his throne either during the night of July 17 or in the predawn of the next morning, almost as soon as Greek officials learned of Alexius III's flight. Our unimpeachable sources on this point are Villehardouin, *Conquête*, 1: 184, sec. 182, and 1: 186–188, sec. 184, who negotiated with Emperor Isaac before the Latins allowed his son to enter the city, and Nicetas Choniates, *Historia*, 550, a high-born Greek statesman and eyewitness to the events. Prince Alexius was not crowned co-emperor until August 1, the feast of St. Peter.

152. Before the crusaders even allowed Prince Alexius to enter the city they demanded and received Emperor Isaac's ratification of the terms of payment promised by his son: Villehardouin, *Conquête*, 1: 186–192, secs. 184–189. Shortly thereafter Isaac and Alexius began paying the debt.

153. How long we do not know. Villehardouin, *Conquête*, 1: 194, sec. 191, states that on July 19 Isaac and Alexius begged the crusaders to encamp on the far side of the harbor, and he implies they did so shortly thereafter and before Alexius's coronation on August 1. Clari, *Conquête*, 55–56, sec. LV, asserts that the crusaders did not begin to make arrangements to take up residence in Pera until after the coronation.

154. Orth, *Hystoria*, 142, prefers the reading *spaciosa* (spacious) of C 40r, col. 2, rather than *speciosa*, which appears in the other two MSS.

155. This is quite an understatement. Mid-August of 1203 saw two major clashes between Greeks and Latins. A brawl on August 19 ended with certain crusaders and a number of Italian residents of Constantinople setting a series of fires that soon became an inferno. The fire was spent only after destroying some of the city's most opulent areas, and its embers were still smoldering at least a week later. Villehardouin, *Conquête*, 1: 210, sec. 205, estimates that some fifteen thousand Latin inhabitants of Constantinople felt it wise to leave the city for the security of the crusader encampment. Madden, "Fires," 74–89, concludes that this, the second and greatest of three fires set in Constantinople by the crusaders, destroyed about 450 acres, or about thirteen percent of the city's total

walled-in area. Shortly before this disaster, the city had exploded in a frenzy of anti-Western hostility, resulting in another of what were becoming Constantinople's periodic anti-Latin riots. Later, in early December 1203 there was, apparently, another riot, in which the Latin quarters were again attacked, buildings destroyed, and persons butchered with no regard to age or sex. By early winter mutual hatred was at a fever pitch, with Latins equally attacking Greeks. Yet, despite all of this misunderstanding and conflict, which grew sharper as the months wore on, both the *DC* (Andrea, 134) and Villehardouin, *Conquête*, 1: 194, sec. 192, indicate that in July 1203 there had been, at least on the surface, a short interlude of concord between the Byzantines and the crusaders.

156. Across the harbor, in the neighborhood of Estanor and the tower of Galata.

157. Byzantine sources agree that Isaac II and Alexius IV were forced to plunder churches, monasteries, and private estates in order to try to meet the Latins' demands: e.g. Nicetas Choniates, *Historia*, 551–552: 555–556; 559–560.

158. Charles M. Brand has translated and analyzed a speech prepared by Nicephorus Chyrsoberges for presentation to Alexius IV: "A Byzantine Plan for the Fourth Crusade," *Speculum* 43 (1968): 462–475. Brand believes that the speech was never delivered, because by the date of its intended delivery, January 6, 1204, the emperor was already at war with the Latins. The value of this rhetorical piece, which is heavy with military images, is that it shows Chyrsoberges, although then a moderate who believed some sort of ecclesiastical accommodation with the West was necessary, was ready to advise the emperor to deal with the immediate problem of the crusaders through military action, if necessary.

159. Alexius IV was at first quite friendly with his crusader patrons and went so far as to convince the Latins to stay in Constantinople until March of 1204 in order to help him secure his throne. During the high summer and early fall of 1203 he appears to have seriously attempted to keep all his promises to the crusaders, but soon he discovered that his promises and the Latin demands were equally unrealistic, and he suspended payments. Events came to a head, perhaps as early as mid-November 1203, when six Latin envoys, including Villehardouin, formally defied the young emperor and his father at the Blachernae palace. According to the rules of feudal protocol, Alexius IV was now an enemy, and the conflict between crusaders and Greeks began anew, as a fierce anti-Latin faction led by Alexius Ducas Mourtzouphlos gained control of the city. However, Nicetas Choniates, *Historia*, 560–561, maintains that even then the young emperor refused to take part in assaults against his Latin friends.

160. Chap. 8.

161. Around the turn of the year Isaac II faded into the background, suffering apparently from impaired mental faculties, and Alexius had to bear alone the anger of the people of Constantinople who blamed him for the fire of August 19 and the despoliation of the monasteries. In the last days of January, 1204 a large crowd gathered in *Hagia Sophia* where it proclaimed an anti-emperor, Nicholas Canabus. Alexius panicked and called upon the Latins in an effort to shore up his hold on the crown. When this was discovered by the Greeks he was even more deeply discredited, despite his attempts to save the situation by insulting Boniface de Montferrat when the marquis arrived at the palace. An anonymous source close to Bishop Nevelon of Soissons tells us that Alexius IV was killed because the Greeks learned that he wanted to reestablish his dependence on the Latins: Andrea and Rachlin, "Holy War," 160. It might not have been that simple, but the young emperor's desperate situation gave Mourtzouphlos the opening he needed to seize power from both the Angeli and the mob at *Hagia Sophia*. On the night of January 28 he staged his palace coup and threw young Alexius into jail. On or around February 5 Mourtzouphlos was acclaimed emperor as Alexius V Ducas, and on February 8 he personally strangled Alexius IV. Alexius V also disposed of his rival, Nicholas Canabus, by having him decapitated. Isaac II died around this same time, under unknown circumstances.

162. Alexius Ducas was descended through the female line from the imperial dynasty of the Comneni. Gunther describes Morciflo as a "certain relative" of Alexius III in chapter 8.

163. A Homeric term for "Greek" and a reference here to Morciflo.

164. MR 131v and C 40v, col. 1, both have *doce per hunc*, which makes no sense. Orth, *Hystoria*, 143, corrects *doce* to *dote*, which results in the ironic "by his 'gift.'" A preferable correction is *docte per hunc* (skillfully through him; by his cunning).

165. Villehardouin, *Conquête*, 2: 22, secs. 223–224, tells us that Alexius V attempted unsuccessfully to disguise the murder as death due to natural causes. His public display of mourning, however, did not deceive the Greeks.

166. No other source mentions this stratagem. The story seems to be another product of either Gunther's artistic imagination or of his incomplete and flawed knowledge of the course of events at Constantinople.

167. The crusaders were not as ingenuous as Gunther would have us believe. Clari, *Conquête*, 55–56, sec. LV, notes that following the coronation of Alexius IV, the army took the precaution of stationing a small garrison in the imperial palace and of tearing down about one hundred meters of the city wall before it evacuated the city—out of fear that the city might someday become hostile. Subsequently, however, the Greeks

repaired the wall (ibid., 57, sec. LVII), and at some unknown point the palace contingent was withdrawn.

168. Enrico Dandolo (r. 1193–1205).

169. Thomas F. Madden, "Venice and Constantinople in 1171 and 1172: Enrico Dandolo's Attitudes towards Byzantium," *Mediterranean Historical Review* 8 (1993): 179–184, discusses the doge's blindness.

170. Villehardouin and Clari praise Dandolo unequivocally and often for his wise leadership. Their silence, on what would have been a sterling example of the doge's wisdom, suggests that we should reject Gunther's story.

171. Villehardouin, *Conquête*, 2: 22, sec. 224, states simply that eventually the Greeks and the French became aware of the murder. Clari, *Conquête*, 62, sec. LXII, claims that a letter was shot into the crusader encampment, informing the Latins of the deed.

172. On one occasion Villehardouin estimated that the city had two hundred people for every crusader: *Conquête*, 1: 164, sec. 163. In another section of his story he stated that the city held four hundred thousand male citizens or more: ibid., 2: 54, sec. 251. Modern estimates of the city's total population in 1203/1204 range from a low of two hundred thousand to a high of one million: Madden, "Fires," 85–86.

173. This is doubtful. No other source mentions reinforcements.

174. Villehardouin, *Conquête*, 2: 54, sec. 251, reports that the combined Latin forces numbered no more than twenty thousand. This figure seems about right. Surprisingly for a medieval historian, Villehardouin's numbers are usually on target.

175. Actually, the Greeks did make some forays. The one that most impressed the crusaders was Alexius V's disastrous attempt to ambush a forage party led by Henry, brother of Baldwin of Flanders.

176. Clari, *Conquête*, 50, sec. XLVIII, notes that in the battle before the landwalls, with the army of Alexius III, the crusaders and Greeks exchanged crossbow fire. He also reports that prior to the July assault on the harbor walls, the Venetians covered their flying bridges with hides to protect their marines and sailors from crossbow bolts (*arbalestes*): ibid., 44, sec. XLIV. So, by the early thirteenth century the Greeks employed, probably in the hands of foreign mercenaries, some of those devilish weapons that had so horrified Anna Comnena during the First Crusade and which, perhaps as late as 1148, she stated were unknown to the Greeks: *Alexiad*, trans. E. R. A. Sewter (Harmondsworth: Penguin, 1969), 316–317, n. 36.

177. Mourtzouphlos offered the army an opportunity to retire from Constantinople, but under conditions that its leaders considered dishonorable and impractical. They were not about to leave without receiving full payment for their services.

178. Clari, *Conquête*, 60, sec. LX, tells us that wine, meat, and eggs were scarce, but there was sufficient bread in camp. Alberic of Trois-Fontaines, *Chronica*, 883, claims the crusaders were reduced to eating their horses.

179. The city is roughly triangular in shape, with only its western perimeter bordered by land. Gunther accurately describes its triple system of land defenses, which consisted of a wide moat surmounted by a low breastwork, a moderately sized outer wall, and a massive inner wall.

180. It would have to be an athletically precocious seven-year-old. The towers of the third, or great, wall on the land side stood approximately fifty-five meters apart.

181. It is tempting to conclude that Gunther is playfully comparing this triangular, triple-encircled city to the mystery of the Trinity. This might be true in part, but we should also understand this as an oblique self-compliment. When commenting on his art in the *Ligurinus*, 4: 609–611 (p. 296), Gunther claims that *oculata fides* (sharp-eyed faith) enables him to narrate these great deeds. In other words, he is an inspired author.

182. An outerwork, such as the moat and breastwork that were on the land side, which would inhibit an enemy from bringing siege machines up to the main wall.

183. This is a great exaggeration. The harbor wall was relatively low, about ten meters in height, and was the weakest part of Constantinople's defenses.

184. The *byzant* was actually the contemporary *hyperperon* (chapter 8, n. 108) not some pre-Constantinian coin.

185. Orth, *Hystoria*, 148, prefers the present tense *appareat* of C 41v, col. 1 and I 14r. M 133v's perfect tense *apparuerit* seems the better reading.

186. Genesis 37: 9–11.

187. The Book of Daniel, chapter 7.

188. See chapters 37–45 of the Book of Genesis for the story of Joseph.

189. King Nebuchadnezzar of Babylon. The story is in The Book of Daniel, chapters 2–4.

190. The forged Donation of Constantine ascribed to Constantine I (r. 306–337) but composed in the eighth or ninth century.

191. Sylvester I (r. 314–335).

192. St. Helena (d. c. 330).

193. Gunther nods here; chapters 14 and 15 do not explicitly place the army at the landwalls.

194. This is untrue. The crusader camp was located across the harbor of the Golden Horn, although sometime after Alexius V's coup, possibly in January of 1204, the army did, for a short while, establish a forward base in front of one of the land wall gates near the Blachernae Palace. Following

a minor skirmish, in which they cut down a solitary Greek noble who was foolish enough to charge their position, they retired.

195. In 1204 the crusaders left the heavily defended land walls alone. Because of the failure of the army to carry the land walls in the battle of July 17, 1203 and the Venetians' relative success in their simultaneous assault on the harbor wall, the crusade leaders decided to concentrate all their forces in an amphibious attack on the harbor wall. They do not appear to have even seriously probed the land defenses, except for the skirmish noted above.

196. Wrong again. The army and fleet had been encamped across the harbor since leaving Constantinople.

197. Hugh of St.-Pol, *Letter*, 518, estimated that the flying bridges constructed for the assault of July of 1203 were one hundred feet high. Clari, *Conquête*, 44, sec. XLIV, states that they were fully thirty *toises* high or more, a medieval *toise* being roughly two meters. On several occasions, Clari overestimated heights and distances by a factor of two. If we halve his estimate in this case, it is close to St.-Pol's figure.

198. The Venetians employed such flying bridges in their assault of July 17, 1203 and reconstructed them for the April attacks. The best description of them is provided by Clari, *Conquête*, 44, sec. XLIV, who tells us that the bridges were wide enough to allow three fully armed soldiers to attack abreast of one another. The *Chronicle of Novgorad*, 309, states that the battle of April 12 saw forty such outfitted ships, lashed together in pairs, lead the assault.

199. The evidence is contradictory on this point. The Greeks, having learned a lesson from the Venetian attack of July 17, 1203, had raised the height of their harbor wall and its towers by building wooden structures upon them. Clari, *Conquête*, 69, sec. LXIX, with his usual exaggeration, states that these wooden additions added five to seven stories to the already high towers; Villehardouin, *Conquête*, 2: 32–34, sec. 233, claims a more believable two or three stories. This added height, at least momentarily, helped shift the tactical advantage to the Greek defenders, if we believe Clari: 70, 73, secs. LXXI, LXXIV. According to this participant, when the Latins attacked on April 9, no Venetian ship could reach the top of the wall or towers, and when the Latins successfully reassaulted the city on the twelfth the bridges of no more than four or five ships could reach the tops of the towers. One might assume that during the two day interlude the crusaders had raised the height of some of their bridges to compensate for the added height of the wall and towers. Clari, *Conquête*, 72, sec. LXXIV, tells us that during this weekend the Latins refitted their flying bridges. Possibly, he refers to their doing more than simply repairing battle damage, but this seems unlikely because adding to the height of the

bridges would have made the ships unstable. The wall, even with its additions, could not have been much higher than eighteen or twenty meters, and the reinforced towers were probably only about twenty-five to thirty meters high. So roughly thirty meter high flying bridges were high enough, if the ships could get close enough to the walls to reduce the bridges' angle of approach to a minimum. On April 9 a strong contrary wind drove the ships away from the walls. Even so, during that battle the Latins were able to engage some Greek defenders in close combat from the flying bridges. Apparently, however, the Latins could not, because of the wind, bring sufficient force to bear on any one point, nor could they reach the tops of any of the towers. On the twelfth, when the fleet had a favorable wind, a few of its flying bridges did prove high enough to allow its men to cross over and capture several towers.

200. Clari, *Conquête*, 44, sec. XLIV, states that the flying bridges of July were covered with various types of sail cloth. Prior to the April assault they covered their ships with timbers and grapevines, which effectively protected them from enemy artillery on the twelfth but had been less effective on the ninth: ibid., 69, 70, 72–73, secs. LXIX, LXXI, LXXIV.

201. H. R. Ellis, "The Secret Weapon of Byzantium," *Byzantinische Zeitschrift* 66 (1973): 61–74. By 1204 Greek fire was no longer exclusively a Greek weapon. Clari, *Conquête*, 72, 75, secs. LXXIV, LXXV, mentions its use by both sides.

202. *Exstructis . . . navibus*. This can also mean: *once the fleet had been formed*.

203. The Golden Horn.

204. A single chain, which Ernoul-Bernard, *Chronique*, 362, claims was longer by far than three bow shots and as thick as a man's arm, was stretched, by means of wooden crossbeams, across the entrance to the Golden Horn from a tower slightly west of Saray (Saraglio) Point on the Byzantine Peninsula to the tower of Galata in Pera.

205. Gunther's account is misleading. The crusader ship *Aquila* (*Eagle*) had broken the harbor chain on July 6, 1203, as the Latins were in the process of capturing the tower of Galata and securing a beachhead on Pera. The crusader fleet had been anchored within the harbor of the Golden Horn since that operation and by April 1204 had swept the harbor of all hostile Greek ships.

206. What follows is Gunther's oversimplified account of the successful attack of April 12/13. He totally ignores the costly setback of April 9, in which the crusaders suffered significant casualties. In the face of this setback, the crusaders had to abandon much of their equipment on the narrow strand of land that ran underneath the harbor wall. In private conversation, Francis Swietek has argued that Gunther had to have known of

the setback of April 9 but left it out of his story to heighten the contrast between the capture of Constantinople and that of Troy. See poem 19.

207. Most of the harbor wall was separated from the water by a narrow strand of beach. It was sufficiently narrow, however, to permit the Latins on their flying bridges to come into contact with the defenders. In the course of the attack of April 12 the fleet benefited from a sudden, strong north wind, which tended to drive the ships onto the strand and closer to the wall.

208. *L'Estoire de Eracles* in RHC. H. Occ., 2: 273, notes that the first man to gain access to a tower won a hundred marks of silver; the man who followed him won fifty.

209. Villehardouin, *Conquête*, 2: 44–46, sec. 243, and Clari, *Conquête*, 73–75, secs. LXXIV–LXXV, give the impression that whatever towers were captured were taken by direct attack from the flying bridges. Upon taking these towers, the Latins found themselves hemmed in by a large force of Greeks on the wall and did not dare step outside of their captured fortifications until relieved by comrades who had broken into the city through several (Villehardouin says about three) gates.

210. Clari, *Conquête*, 74–75, sec. LXXV, tells us the crusaders were initially unwilling to leave the safety of the *two* towers they had captured, due to the large number of enemy on the walls. Peter of Amiens and his men saved the day by breaking into the city through a small gate on the narrow strand of beach that ran under the city's harbor walls. Villehardouin, *Conquête*, 2: 44, sec. 243, states that after the Latins had taken about *five* towers, other crusaders broke down about three of the city's gates and poured into Constantinople.

211. Paul Riant, *Exuviae*, I: xxxiv, asserts this was Count Berthold of Katzenellenbogen, who played an important role in the crusade and the affairs of the subsequent Latin empire of Constantinople. Berthold was the only German count with the army, but there is no compelling evidence to link his name with the fire. Villehardouin, who knew and mentioned Count Berthold in his history, tells us that the identity of the arsonists was not known: *Conquête*, 2: 48, sec. 247.

212. This was the third fire that Constantinople suffered at the hands of the crusaders: Madden, "Fires," 84–85.

213. The forcing of the gates was the turning point in the battle, and Peter of Amiens and his small band of followers, who included Robert of Clari, played a decisive role in this action. Led by Robert's clerical brother Aleaumes of Clari, these crusaders broke into the city through a walled up postern gate and, after routing Alexius V and his body guard, demolished a gate that had been barred with iron. This allowed the army outside to pour into the city and, importantly, to bring horses in from the transports.

214. Palm Sunday fell on April 18; the assault began on Monday, April 12, and the city was secured on Tuesday morning.

215. Jerusalem.

216. Other sources disagree. Nicetas, *Historia*, 570, charged that the Latins spared neither age nor sex. Nicholas Mesarites, another Greek eyewitness, claimed in his highly emotional and equally rhetorical account that the Latins were barbaric to the point that they butchered new born infants and beheaded many other hapless Greeks before the very sacred altars of the city: translated in Brand, *Byzantium*, 269. Even most Latin sources admit that quite a few Greeks were killed. The *DC* (Andrea, 137) speaks of "a tremendous slaughter of Greeks"; Villehardouin, who was not given to exaggerating numbers, claimed that so many Greeks were cut down no one could count them: *Conquête*, 2: 46, sec. 244.

217. Genoese, Pisans, Amalfitans Anconitans et al.

218. Chap. 13.

219. No other source mentions this knight. See line 24 of poem 19 where Gunther again states that this unfortunate man was the sole fatality suffered by the crusaders in the entire battle. This is patently absurd.

220. The pillage lasted three days, from April 13 through April 15. All the sources agree that the amount of booty taken at Constantinople was incredible. Villehardouin, *Conquête*, 2: 58–60, secs. 254–255, almost always sober and careful in his computations, estimates that after paying off its debt to the Venetians, the army's share of the collected booty equaled four hundred thousand marks and ten thousand horses. Of this, one hundred thousand was distributed among the ranks according to the ratio 4:2:1 for knights, mounted sergeants, and footsoldiers respectively. This division, which meant that each footsoldier received only five marks, left at least some of the rank and file dissatisfied and feeling cheated by their leaders: Andrea, "*Devastatio Constantinopolitana*," 128–129. The sums officially handed out, however, were only a small percentage of the wealth taken. Villehardouin, *Conquête*, 2: 60, sec. 255, and Clari, *Conquête*, 81, sec. LXXXI, agree that there was a high degree of pilferage and private hoarding, despite the fact that it was a capital offense.

221. This is an exaggeration. Madden, "Fires," 85 and 89, estimates this third fire devastated an area of about twenty-five acres, or about .007 percent of the city's total space. He calculates that so little was destroyed because sections of the city devastated by the two earlier fires acted as firebreaks. He further concludes that not more than one-sixth of the entire city was consumed in the fires of 1203/1204.

222. Clari, *Conquête*, 79, sec. LXXX, tells us that on the morning of April 13 the crusaders were informed by the imperial Varangian guard that all the Greeks had fled the city, save for the poor. Villehardouin, *Conquête*,

2: 46, 48, secs. 244, 246, states that already by the afternoon of April 12 most of the Greeks who could had fled. Nicetas, *Historia*, 587–593, gives a vivid picture of his own family's harrowing flight from the city on April 17.

223. Blessed king, the marquis. Actually, the correct translation from the Greek is "Blessed emperor, the marquis."

224. Boniface de Montferrat. See chapter 6, n. 67.

225. The House of Montferrat already had a long history of active involvement in eastern affairs. Queller and Madden, *FC*², 25–30, provides a good survey. Clari, *Conquête*, 32–34, sec. XXXIII, gives a somewhat fanciful account of the adventures of Conrad of Montferrat (Boniface's elder brother) at the Byzantine imperial court.

226. The *DC* (Andrea, 137) states: "On the following day [April 13], all the Greeks fell at the feet of the marquis and surrendered themselves and all their possessions into his hands."

227. Compare Gunther's description of Abbot Martin in the next chapter as "overstuffed" with relics.

228. The French crusaders. Compare Clari, *Conquête*, 102, sec. CVI, who reports that Peter of Bracheux defended the crusaders' capture of Constantinople by claiming the Franks were descended from Trojans who had wrongly been driven out of that land by the Greeks. Ebels-Hoving, *Westerse Ogen*, 282, concludes that from ca. 1160 onward Westerners occasionally used the popular stories of Troy and its descendants in the West as support for claims on Byzantine territory.

229. Byzantium.

230. Troy.

231. To Constantinople. See chapter 16.

232. Constantinople. See the dream of Constantine in chapter 16.

233. A gold-smithing people of ancient Asia Minor; here a synonym for Trojan.

234. Troy.

235. C 43r, col. 2 has *invictam* (unconquered). One wonders if Gunther actually wrote *invictam* in order to heighten the chapter's irony.

236. Compare chapter 4.

237. Manuel I (r. 1143–1180).

238. The church of the monastery of Christ Pantokrator (Lord of the World). Clari, *Conquête*, 90, sec., XCII, briefly describes the abbey church.

239. By custom and canon law, Latin priests did not wear beards. Within the Order of Cîteaux beards were worn by lay brothers, which distinguished them from choir monks.

240. Riant, *Guntheri*, 85, and Assmann, *Geschichte*, 85, n. 172, assume

this *romana lingua* was French. It was more likely a north Italian patois used for commercial purposes in the Mediterranean.

241. *Contrectaret* (touch illicitly; purloin; have sexual intercourse with; dishonor; handle). Gunther has chosen a verb with a number of odious overtones, rather than the neutral *caperet* (seize; possess), in order to heighten the passage's ironic humor. Earlier, in chapter 11, Gunther assured his readers that these are "inviolable relics."

242. Orth, *Hystoria*, 160, prefers the *postea* (later on) of C 43v, col. 1, and I 17v; only M 138v reads: *in fines huius opusculi* (at the end of this little work). M seems to be, over all, the best of the three MSS, and its reading is preferable here.

243. Brand, *Byzantium*, 265, incorrectly states that Martin eventually found the old priest a position in a suitable church.

244. Secrecy was needed because Martin had broken the rules established by the lay and ecclesiastical leaders of the army. All members of the army had been forced to swear solemnly that they would not break into any churches or monasteries, and they had also been ordered to place all spoils into a common hoard (introduction, 16). Moreover, Cardinal Peter Capuano, hearing that many persons had stolen relics, expressly commanded, under threat of excommunication, that all relics be handed over to Bishop Garnier of Troyes: Anonymous Canon of Langres, in Riant *Exuviae*, 1: 28. This latter ruling was intended to prevent desecration of and venal commerce in relics: Rostang of Cluny, *Narratio exceptionis apud Cluniacum capitis beati Clementis*, ibid., 134. In Martin's defense, Gunther points out that this man used the relics properly. He venerated them deeply and refused to part with them for any amount of earthly wealth.

245. Chap. 10.

246. It was renewed in September 1204 for five years. Word of its renewal could not have reached Martin until he returned to Acre sometime in the autumn of 1204: chapter 22.

247. The capture of Constantinople and destruction of the Greek fleet.

248. I.e., without a stratagem; see poem 19, lines 21–22.

249. *Inveniantur*. Pannenborg, *Verfasser*, 29, argued that this word, which follows *mentiantur* (falsely claim) is an erroneous transcriptional redundancy and should be rejected. Orth, *Hystoria*, 161, agrees. Inasmuch as the word makes sense and appears in all three MSS, we should accept it.

250. Compare Boethius, *Consolation of Philosophy*, bk. 1, prose 1.

251. Publius Vergilius Maro, or Virgil.

252. Agamemnon, leader of the Greeks at Troy.

253. Compare poem 4.

254. Helen.

255. Troy.

256. The Greek "traitor" who convinced the Trojans to take the horse into their city.

257. Clari, *Conquête*, 79–80, sec. LXXX, complains that the high and rich seized all the best houses for themselves, leaving the commoners to find accommodations as best they could. Even so, he notes, there were more than enough buildings to house everyone. Villehardouin, *Conquête*, 2: 54, sec. 251, agrees that everyone was housed, inasmuch as there was no lack of fine dwellings in the city.

258. A group of ardent Egyptian Monophysites, largely monks, who withdrew their allegiance from the more moderate Monophysite Patriarch of Alexandria in 482, thereby becoming headless (*acephali*).

259. Chap. 6.

260. Villehardouin, *Conquête*, 2: 62, sec. 256, concurs. Robert of Clari, *Conquête*, 91, sec. XCIII, whose account of the election is confused (he states there were twenty electors), strongly implies that Louis of Blois, Hugh of St. Pol, and Enrico Dandolo were also serious candidates.

261. Six Venetians and six from the army: Villehardouin, *Conquête*, 2: 64, sec. 258. The March Pact of 1204 between the Venetians and the baronial leaders provided specifically for such an election process: *Pacta inter Henricum Dandulum et crucesignatos inita*, PL 215: 518. After a good deal of wrangling, the barons named the army's six highest ranking ecclesiastics as their allotted electors: Clari, *Conquête*, 91–92, sec. XCIV. Significantly, Martin was not one of the six: Baldwin of Flanders, "Letter to Pope Innocent," PL 215: 451.

262. According to the *DC* in Andrea, 137, they convened during the octave of Easter (April 25–May 2). Baldwin of Flanders, PL 215: 451, informed the pope that he was elected on Sunday, May 9, 1204. This means their deliberations lasted a minimum of one and a maximum of two weeks.

263. Baldwin I (r. 1204–1205 or 1206).

264. On *Iubilate* Sunday (May 16): Baldwin of Flanders, PL 215: 451; *DC* in Andrea, 137; and Clari, *Conquête*, 93–95, secs. XCVI–XCVII, provide descriptions of the ceremony.

265. The division arrangements were more complex than this. For detailed analyses, see Robert Lee Wolff, "The Latin Empire of Constantinople, 1204–1261," in Kenneth Setton et al., *A History of the Crusades*, 2nd. ed., 6 vols. (Madison: University of Wisconsin Press, 1969–1989), 2: 187–199, and Antonio Carile, "Partitio Terrarum Imperii Romanie," *Studi Veneziani* 7 (1965): 125–305.

266. Boniface might have made some vague promise to Abbot Martin, but it is not likely that there was a bishopric immediately awaiting the abbot in Thessalonica. The marquis rewarded his close friend, loyal supporter, and spiritual adviser, Peter of Locedio, with the monastery of

Chortaiton, not with an episcopal see. It was not until 1208 that Peter, already bishop of Ivrea in Italy, was nominated for the archbishopric of Thessalonica: PL 215: 1425.

267. *Privatus et humilis*. Compare Moses in chapter 1.

268. Clari, *Conquête*, 102–103, sec. CVII, describes the division of the empire into fiefs.

269. Robert Lee Wolff, "Greeks and Latins before and after 1204," *Ricerche di Storia Religiosa, Studi in Onore di Giorgio La Piana*, 1 (1957): 320–334.

270. Note Gunther's ability to turn a pleasing phrase: *gravissimi sceleris perpetrator et brevissimi temporis imperator*.

271. Mourtzouphlos fled the city during the night of 12/13 April.

272. Alexius III.

273. This is nonsense. Alexius III was also a fugitive and spent the rest of his days harried by his Latin and Greek enemies.

274. *Privatus*. Compare Martin above.

275. Compare Dandolo, chapters 14 and 17.

276. The fugitive Mourtzouphlos sought out Alexius III at Mosynopolis in Thrace. After Alexius III had lulled Mourtzouphlos into a sense of security, he had him seized and blinded. With this new setback, Mourtzouphlos now found himself deserted by all but a handful of his supporters. Around November 1204 he was captured by Dietrich von Loos in Asia Minor and sent to Constantinople.

277. Gunther's description of what follows cannot be based upon Martin's personal observations. According to Gunther's account, the abbot left Constantinople around September 8, and he possibly left as early as August 15 (chapter 22, n. 291). Mourtzouphlos would not be captured until sometime around the Feast of All Saints, which falls on November 1.

278. Clari, *Conquête*, 103–104, sec. CIX, also describes, but in less gory detail, the debate over the mode of Mourtzouphlos's execution.

279. According to Clari, ibid., the doge also indulged in similar gallows humor. Stating that Mourtzouphlos was too "high" a man to be hanged, Dandolo claimed that for him only "high justice" (technically the right to impose capital punishment) would suffice. Villehardouin also employed this pun on high justice to describe the execution: *Conquête*, 2: 116, sec. 307.

280. *Sacrilegium*. This and the following line show Morciflo to be an anti-Martin. Note how Gunther juxtaposes Morciflo's sacrilege with Abbot Martin's "sacred sacrilege" of the previous chapter. Note also how Abbot Martin in chapter 20 refuses a bishopric because he is "mindful of his vows."

281. From power.

282. Gunther is the only historian to refer to it as a pyramid, and he is wrong. It was the column of Theodosius the Great, which stood in the Forum of Theodosius (the Tauros). Clari, *Conquête*, 89, 104, secs. XCII, CIX, describes it and its twin, the column of Arcadius in the Forum of Xerolophos.

283. About fifty meters. Clari, *Conquête*, 89, sec. XCII, exaggerates when he estimates that each column stood at least one hundred meters (fifty *toises*) high. Both columns contained interior staircases for access to their summits.

284. Clari, ibid., also notes that hermits had formerly inhabited little shelters on the summits of this column and its twin.

285. Clari, ibid., also reports that the twin columns were covered with sculpted prophetic scenes, some of which related to Constantinople's being captured by shipborne invaders from the West. Villehardouin, *Conquête*, 2: 116, sec. 308, tells us that the column from which Alexius V was cast had incised on it a scene of an emperor falling headlong, and that very column had long ago been the subject of the prophecy that some emperor would be thrown off of it. The columns of Theodosius and Arcadius were actually triumphal memorials. Theodosius's column pictured in bas-relief his victories over the Scythians and other foes. The column of Arcadius celebrated similar successes. Neither column exists today.

286. Nicetas, *Historia*, 558–559, relates a strikingly similar incident. Around the time of the deposition of Alexius IV, a drunken mob, in a frenzy of anti-Latin sentiment, destroyed a statue of Athena, which stood on a column in the forum of Constantine. This sculpture, which some scholars have identified as the work of Phidias, was attacked because it seemed to be beckoning, with its extended right hand, the crusaders who had sailed up from the south.

287. *Certus*.

288. Compare Chapter 5.

289. The Latin empire of Constantinople.

290. September 8, 1204.

291. Once again Gunther's estimate of a sea voyage's length seems wide of the mark (see chapter 7, n. 80, and chapter 9, n. 118). According to Gunther, Martin's trip from Acre to Constantinople had taken about fifty-five days (chapter 10). Now he would have us believe that the return voyage took less than half that time, around twenty-four days. Riant, *Guntheri*, 87, was correct when he saw that this incredible speed was beyond belief. When Conrad of Halberstadt made a similar voyage from Constantinople to Tyre, he left on August 17 and arrived on October 7: Andrea, "Conrad," 47. Assuming that their respective ships followed roughly the same course, we should expect their voyages to be of approximate equal duration. Riant, ibid., offered the theory that we should read

the feast of Mary's Assumption (August 15) in place of the feast of her nativity and October 21 instead of October 1. Assmann, *Geschichte*, 95, n. 202, believes that this would make the trip too long. He suggests adopting the dates August 15 to October 1. This theory gives Martin's ship a believable 1.3 kmph speed, which compares favorably with the speed of similar voyages. It is somewhat faster than Conrad of Halberstadt's trip, but not unduly so. Assmann further points out that we need not take Gunther literally, therefore, when he states in chapter 19 that Martin stayed in Constantinople the entire summer. His arguments seem eminently reasonable.

292. Compare poem 21, line 6.

293. The citizens of Acre had already heard about the events at Constantinople. Baldwin of Flanders's wife, Marie, had sailed from Marseilles to Acre. Here she died suddenly on August 9, 1204, but not before receiving word that she was Constantinople's new empress: Villehardouin, *Conquête*, 2: 124–126, secs. 317–318.

294. Werner of Egisheim. Egisheim (today Eguisheim) is only a few miles from Pairis, and the abbey had a chapel there as early as 1145. Count Ulrich von Egisheim had been Pairis's original lay patron (chapter 2, n. 21), and Werner was in all likelihood a member of his family, possibly a great-grandson.

295. Amalric II (r. 1197–1205).

296. Elias Friedman, *The Latin Hermits of Mount Carmel* (Rome: Teresianum, 1979), 126–128, dismisses this story as "far from . . . sober." Although he doubts the tale's veracity, Friedman points out that one can reasonably suppose the mountain was home to three Greek monasteries around the time of the Fourth Crusade: the convents of St. Margaret, Elijah, and St. John of Tyre. Andrew Jotischky, *The Perfection of Solitude: Hermits and Monks in the Crusader States* (University Park: Pennsylvania State University Press, 1995), 130–134, seems to accept Gunther's story at face value.

297. Gunther has already established the fact that Werner is wise, manly and, in every sense, a true Christian knight. Now by juxtaposing this knight's apparently sound advice with Abbot Martin's resolute determination to push on with his relics, despite the hazards awaiting him, Gunther has highlighted the superior courage of Martin—a courage born of his faith in God's protection.

298. Conrad of Halberstadt was embarking for the West at this same time (note 299). His anonymous chronicler tells us that the German bishop was given a rousing, yet bittersweet send off by the king, members of the two major military orders, and large numbers of clergy and laity: *GeH* in MGH, SS, 23: 119.

299. March 31, 1205. The *GeH* informs us that Conrad of Krosigk sailed

from Acre on March 30, 1205 and arrived in Venice on the Vigil of Pentecost (May 28), the same day that Gunther claimed Martin sailed into this very harbor (chapter 23): MGH, SS, 23: 119. Bishop Conrad and Abbot Martin probably sailed in the same convoy.

300. March 28, 1205.

301. Nothing else is known about this man.

302. On the angelic visions of St. Martin, see Sulpicius Severus, *Dialogues*, 1: 25; 2: 5, 12, 13; 3: 1, 13; and *Life of St. Martin*, chap. 14.

303. In the canton of Kaysersberg, the arrondissement of Colmar. This village was listed among Pairis's possessions as early as October 22, 1179: Jenn, *Pairis*, 89–90.

304. Both M and C clearly read *certamina*, but the word does not easily fit the sense of the sentence, and it ruins the meter of the line. Orth, *Hystoria*, 172, suggests substituting *Ceraunia*, a chain of coastal mountains along the eastern Adriatic.

305. The Levantine waters were filled with pirates. The *GeH* notes that when Bishop Conrad's two ships sailed from Constantinople to Tyre, they managed to avoid pirates, but at great risk: MGH, SS, 23: 118–119. As noted in chapter 22, n. 299, it is likely that Martin and Conrad of Halberstadt sailed in the same convoy from Acre to Venice. It is significant that the *GeH* does not mention pirates at all on this particular voyage. The anonymous author does, however, tell us that Bishop Conrad's ship experienced a frightful storm off Crete, which raged from Wednesday, April 6, to Easter, April 10: ibid., 119.

306. May 28, 1205.

307. Riant, *Guntheri*, 88, and Eduard Winkelmann, *Philipp von Schwaben und Otto IV, von Braunschweig*, 2 vols. (1873, 1878; rpt. Darmstadt: Wissenschaftliche Buchgesellschaft, 1968), 1: 358, n. 2, believed this was an allusion to the campaign of the bishop of Worms in the Marches of Italy.

308. Compare Sulpicius Severus, *Life of St. Martin*, chap. 5.

309. The Münster, chapter. 2, n. 27.

310. Luthold I von Rötelen (r. 1190–1213). Bishop Luthold had sworn the Cross in 1200 (chapter 2, n. 28), but there is no evidence that he ever fulfilled his crusade vow.

311. June 24, 1205.

312. Around 8:00 a.m.

313. *Nunc age*: the same words that begin poem 20. By this device, Gunther contrasts the different ends of Martin and Morciflo.

314. An ironic echo of the cohorts of pirates.

315. According to Riant, the monks of Pairis, believing Martin dead, had elected a new abbot. On February 8, 1205 King Philip of Swabia granted to Werner, venerable abbot of Pairis, and his community of broth-

ers imperial protection of the monastery's possessions: *Guntheri*, 91, where Riant quotes this charter. See also ibid., 88–89. J. F. Böhmer, ed., *Regesta Imperii*, V (1198–1272), 3. vols. (Innsbruck, 1881–1901) does not list the charter.

The only Abbot Werner whom Jenn, *Pairis*, mentions is a twelfth-century predecessor of Martin: 102, 157–158, 167. Pairis's necrology lists only one Abbot Werner (January 17), and the editor identifies him as the person who was abbot in 1187: Bernardin Buchinger, "Das Nekrolog der Cisterzienser-Abtei Pairis," ed. Joseph M. B. Clauss, *Mitteilungen der Gesellschaft für Erhaltung der geschichtlichen Denkmäler im Elsass* 2nd. ser. 22 (1908): 62, n. 14. Two extant manuscript calendars from Pairis, Colmar MS 104 and Colmar MS 300, also fail to list any Abbot Werner in their respective enumerations of Pairis's twelfth- and thirteenth-century abbots. If the monks of Pairis did elect a new abbot in 1204 or early 1205, Martin's return from the dead rendered that election void, and the interim abbot would not, therefore, subsequently be counted in the list of valid abbots.

316. Paul Riant has printed a letter of April 23, 1380 in which Cardinal Pileo da Prata, in the name of Pope Urban VI, guaranteed the grace of a year's indulgence to persons visiting the relics of Pairis on the Church's principal holy days or on other specified feasts: *Guntheri*, 89–90; *Exuviae*, 2: 166–167. The cardinal stated that the abbey had over sixty relics, including: the Sacred Blood in a golden monstrance; a golden tablet containing a piece of the True Cross; a large part of the head of John the Baptist; milk from the Blessed Virgin; and the members of Sts. James the Major and the Minor, St. Bartholomew, and many others. None of these relics is known to exist today. They seem to have been lost in the course of the political and military upheavals of the seventeenth and eighteenth centuries. According to Philippe Grandidier, by 1785 all that remained of these relics was the ampule of the Holy Blood and a fragment from the Virgin's sepulcher: Paul Riant, "Des Dépouilles religieuses enlevées à au XIIIe siècle, et des documents historiques nes leur transport en occident," *Mémoires de la Société Nationale des Antiquaires de France* Tôme 36, ser. 4., tôme 6 (1875): 194–195. Apparently these last two relics were confiscated when Pairis was suppressed during the Revolution.

317. The Baptist.

318. Riant, *Guntheri*, 90, believed that this and the following relics relating to the Holy Land were picked up by Martin in Syria-Palestine rather than Constantinople.

319. From the Holy Sepulcher.

320. On Holy Thursday night.

321. Orth, *Hystoria*, 176, and Riant, *Exuviae*, 1: 122, make it appear as

though these are two separate relics: a relic from the spot where the mother of God left earth and a relic from her tomb.

322. Philip of Swabia. Orth, *Hystoria*, 177, and Riant, *Exuviae*, 1: 123, supply *rege* (king), which all three MSS lack.

323. Henry II, count of Veringen and bishop of Strassburg (r. 1203–1223).

324. This entire passage echoes chapter 1.

325. *Ingenii memorem meruit Martinus honorem*: an echo of line 1 of poem 5. See the introduction, 44.

326. Here we follow the order of the poetic lines in M 146v-147r. C 47r, col. 2, records these last six lines in the order: 2, 4, 6, 1, 3, 5.

327. *Munere*. Here a verbal connection is made between Martin's service to God (*munus*) and the gifts (*munera*) he received for it.

328. Compare chapter 2.

329. Andrea, "*Historia*," 299–300, deals with the issue of the *HC* and Philip's imperial claims.

330. Andrea, ibid., 298, deals with Gunther's view of the legitimacy of the ruler of Constantinople's claim to the imperial title.

331. Probably a representation of Theos Pantokrator—God, Ruler of the world.

332. Compare chapter 7.

333. This imperial charter no longer exists. According to Riant, *Guntheri*, 91–92, it was catalogued in 1519. However, a later marginal note, in a seventeenth-century hand, indicated it was lost. Riant, *Exuviae*, 2: 97, also cites another lost imperial charter, in this case of 1209, in which Otto IV confirmed the earlier charter of his predecessor and foe.

334. *Tunc*. Possibly this indicates a postscript by a later hand. It can also be ascribed to Gunther's continued and consistent use of the historical past tense. See chapter 2 where he uses *tunc* when referring to the pope. Of course, both uses of *tunc* could be later interpolations.

Bibliography

Manuscript Sources

Gunther of Pairis. *De expugnatione Urbis Constantinopolitane, Unde, inter alias reliquias, magna pars sancte Crucis in Alemanniam est allata*. MS *lat*. 903, fols. 115r-148r. Munich: Bayerische Staatsbibliothek.

———. *Hystoria Constantinopolitana*. MS 321, fols. 1r-23r. Munich: Universitätsbibliothek.

———. [No title]. MS 248 [formerly 434], fols. 33v, col. 1–47v, col. 1 [formerly 35v–49v]. Colmar: Bibliothèque de la Ville.

Pairis Abbey. *Collectarium cum kalendario et obituario abbatum Paris*. MS 300, fols. 1r–7v. Colmar: Bibliothèque de la Ville.

———. *Martyrologe d'Usuard*. MS 104, fols. 1r–78r. Colmar: Bibliothèque de la Ville.

Printed Sources

Alberic of Trois-Fontaines. *Chronica*. Ed. P. Scheffer-Boichorst. MGH, SS, 23: 631–950.

Annales Colonienses Maximi. Ed. Karl Pertz. MGH, SS, 17: 723–847.

Annales Marbacenses. Ed. Roger Wilmans. MGH, SS, 17: 142–180.

Anonymous Canon of Langres. *Historia translationum reliquiarum S. Mamantis*. Ed. Paul Riant. *Exuviae*, 1: 22–34.

Anonymous of Soissons. *De terra Iherosolimitana, et quomodo ab urbe Constantinopolitana ad hanc ecclesiam allate sunt reliquie*. Ed. Alfred J. Andrea. "Holy War, Holy Relics, Holy Theft: The Anonymous of Soissons's *De terra Iherosolimitana*: An Analysis, Edition, and Translation," *Historical Reflections/Réflexions Historiques* 18 (1992): 157–163. Also edited by Paul Riant. *Exuviae*, 1: 3–9.

Arnold of Lübeck. *Chronica Slavorum*. Ed. J. M. Lappenberg. MGH, Script. rer. Germ., 14: 1–295.

Baldwin of Flanders. *Epistola*. PL 215: 447–54.

———. *Epistola*. Ed. W. Prevenier. *De Oorkonden der graven van Vlaanderen (1191–aanvang 1206)*. 3 vols. Brussels: Palais der Academien, 1964, 1971. 2: 583–591.

Bernard of Clairvaux. *Crusade Letter*. Ed. Jean Leclercq. "L'Encyclique de Saint Bernard en faveur de la croisade." *Revue Bénédictine* 81 (1971): 282–308.

———. *The Letters of St. Bernard of Clairvaux*. Trans. Bruno Scott James. Chicago: Regnery, 1953.

Bernard Silvestris. *Cosmographia*. Trans. with introduction and notes Winthrop Wetherbee. Records of Civilization: Sources and Studies, 89. New York: Columbia University Press, 1973.

Böhmer, J. F. See *Regesta Imperii*.

Boethius. *The Consolation of Philosophy*. Trans. Richard Green. Indianapolis: Bobbs-Merrill, 1962.

Boniface de Montferrat, Baldwin of Flanders, Louis of Blois, Hugh of Saint Pol et al., *Epistola*. RHGF, 18: 515–16.

Buchinger, Bernardin. *Epitome fastorum Luccellensium*. Porrentruy: Brunruti, apud J. H. Straubhaar, 1667.

———. "Das Nekrolog der Cisterzienser-Abtei Pairis." Ed. Joseph M. B. Clauss. *Mitteilungen der Gesellschaft für Erhaltung der geschichtlichen Denkmäler im Elsass* 2nd ser. 22 (1908): 55–103.

Burchard of Ursberg. *Chronicon*. Ed. O. Abel and L. Weiland. MGH, SS, 23: 337–83.

Catalogue général des manuscripts des bibliothèques publiques de France: 56, Colmar. Paris: Bibliothèque Nationale, 1969.

Chronicle of Novgorod. Trans. Jared Gordon. "Translation of the Novgorod Account of the Fourth Crusade." In "The Novgorod Account of the Fourth Crusade," *Byzantion* 43 (1973): 297–311. Also trans. Robert Michell and Nevill Forbes, *Chronicle of Novgorod (1016–1471)*. Camden Third Series 25, 1914; rpt. Hattiesburg, Miss.: Academic International, 1970. All citations are to the better Gordon translation.

Chrysoberges, Nicephorus. *Oration*. Trans. Charles M. Brand. In "A Byzantine Plan for the Fourth Crusade," *Speculum* 43 (1968): 462–475.

Clari, Robert de. *La Conquête de Constantinople*. Ed. Philippe Lauer. Paris: Champion, 1924. Trans. Edgar Holmes McNeal. *The Conquest of Constantinople*. New York: Norton, 1969.

Comnena, Anna. *Alexiad*. Trans. E. R. A. Sewter. Harmondsworth, England: Penguin, 1969.

De rebus Alsaticis ineuntis saeculi XIII. Ed. Philippe Jaffe. MGH, SS, 17: 232–37.

Devastatio Constantinopolitana. Ed. and trans. Alfred J. Andrea, "The *Devastatio Constantinopolitana*, A Special Perspective on the Fourth Crusade: An Analysis, New Edition, and Translation." *Historical Reflections/Réflexions Historiques* 19 (1993): 131–138. Also in *Chroniques Gréco-Romanes inédites ou peu connues*. Ed. Charles Hopf. Berlin: Weidmann, 1873. Pp. 86–92.

Ernoul et Bernard le Trésorier. *Chronique*. Ed. Louis de Mas Latrie. Paris: Renouard, 1871.

Dandolo, Andrea. *Chronica*. Ed. Ester Pastorello. RIS[2], Vol. 12, part 1. Bologna: Zanichelli, n.d.

L'Estoire de Eracles Empereur et la conqueste de la terre d'Outremer. RHC, Occ., 2: 1–481.

Gesta episcoporum Halberstadensium. Ed. Ludwig Weiland. MGH, SS, 23: 73–123. Trans. Alfred J. Andrea. "The Anonymous Chronicler of Halberstadt's Account of the Fourth Crusade: Popular Religiosity in the Early Thirteenth Century." *Historical Reflections/Réflexions Historiques* 22 (1996): 447–477.

Gesta Innocentii Papae III. Ed. David R. Gress-Wright. "The 'Gesta Innocentii III': Text, Introduction and Commentary." Diss. Bryn Mawr College, 1981; PL 214: xviii–ccxxviii.

Gunther of Pairis. *De oratione, jejunio et eleemosyna*. PL 212: 101–222.

———. *Hystoria Constantinopolitana: Untersuchung und kritische Ausgabe*. Ed. Peter Orth. Hildesheim and Zurich: Weidmann, 1994. Ed. Paul Riant. *Guntheri Alemanni, scholastici, monachi et prioris Parisiensis. De expugnatione urbis Constantinopolitane, unde, inter alias reliquias, magna pars sancte crucis in Alemanniam est allata; seu, Historia Constantinopolitana*. Geneva: I. G. Fick, 1875; Rpt. in *Exuviae sacrae Constantinopolitana*. 2 vols. Geneva: I. G. Fick, 1877. 1: 57–126.

———. *Ligurinus*. Ed. Erwin Assmann. MGH, Script. rer. Germ., 63: 151–495. An inferior edition is in PL 212: 327–476.

———. *Solimarius*. Ed. Wilhelm Wattenbach. "Le *Solymarius* de Günther de Pairis." *Archives de l'Orient Latin* 1 (1881): 551–561, Also in Assmann, *Ligurinus*, MGH, Script. rer. Germ. 63: 501–512.

Historia ducum Veneticorum, Supplementum. Ed. H. Simonsfeld. MGH, SS, 14: 72–97.

Historia peregrinorum, expeditio asiatica Friderici I. In *Quellen zur Geschichte des Kreuzzuges Kaiser Friedrichs I*. Ed. Anton Croust. MGH, SS, N.S. 5, pt. 2: lxxxi–xcv, 116–172. Berlin: Weidmann, 1928.

Hugh of St.-Pol. *Epistola*. RHGF, 18: 517–519. Also edited in *Annales Coloniensis Maximi*, MGH, SS, 17: 812–814.

Innocent III. *De sacro altaris mysterio libri sex*. PL 217: 763–915.

———. *Epistolae*. PL 214–17.

———. *Die Register Innocenz' III. 1. Pontifikatsjahr, 1198/1199*. Ed. Othmar Hageneder and Anton Haidacher. Graz: Böhlaus, 1964.

———. *Die Register Innocenz' III. 2. Pontifikatsjahr, 1199/1200*. Ed. Othmar Hageneder, Werner Maleczek, and Alfred A. Strnad. Rome and Vienna: Verlag der österreichischen Akademie der Wissenschaften, 1979.

———. *Die Register Innocenz' III. 5. Pontifikatsjahr, 1202/1203*. Ed. Othmar Hageneder and others. Vienna: Verlag der österreichischen Akademie der Wissenschaften, 1993.

———. *Die Register Innocenz' III. 6. Pontifikatsjahr, 1203/1204*. Ed. Othmar Hageneder and others. Vienna: Verlag der österreichischen Akademie der Wissenschaften, 1995.

Nicetas Choniates. *Historia*. Ed. J.A. Van Dieten. Corpus Fontium Historiae Byzantinae, 11, in 2 vols. Berlin: De Gruyter, 1975. Trans. Harry J. Magoulias. *O City of Byzantium, Annals of Niketas Choniates*. Detroit: Wayne State University Press, 1984.

Otto of Freising and Rahewin. *The Deeds of Frederick Barbarossa*. Trans. Charles C. Mierow. Records of Civilization: Sources and Studies 49. New York: Columbia University Press, 1953.

Otto of Freising. *The Two Cities*. Trans. C. C. Mierow. Records of Civilization: Sources and Studies, 9. 1928; rpt. New York: Octagon, 1966.

Otto of St Blasien. *Ad librum VII chronici Ottonis Frisingensis Episcopi continuatae historiae appendix*. Ed. Roger Wilmans. MGH, SS, 20: 302–337.

Pairis, Abbey of. *Commemorative List*. Ed. Joachim Wollasch. "Neue Quellen. . . ." Pp. 193–194.

———. *Necrology*. See Buchinger, Bernardin.

Ralph of Coggeshall. *Chronicon Anglicanum*. Ed. Joseph Stevenson. The Chronicles and Memorials of Great Britain and Ireland During the Middle Ages, 66. London: Longman, 1875.

Regesta Imperii, V (1198–1272). 3 vols. Ed. J. F. Böhmer. Innsbruck: 1881–1901.

Robert the Monk of Reims. *Historia Iherosolimitana*. RHC. H. Occ., 3: 717–882.

Roger de Hoveden. *Chronica*. Ed. William Stubbs. Chronicles and Memorials of Great Britain and Ireland During the Middle Ages, 51. London: Longman, 1868–1871. Vol. 4.

Rostang, Monk of Cluny. *Narratio exceptionis apud Cluniacum capitis beati Clementis, ex ore Dalmacii de Serciaco, militis, excepta*. Ed. Paul Riant. *Ex*, 1: 127–140.

Statuta Capitulorum Generalium Ordinis Cisterciensis ab anno 1116 ad annum 1786. Ed. Joseph Canivez. Louvain: Bureaux de la Revue, 1933. Tome 1.

Sulpicius Severus. *Writings*. Trans. Bernard M. Peebles. The Fathers of the Church 7. Washington, D. C.: Catholic University of America Press, 1949. Pp. 79–254.

Thomas of Spalato. *Historia Spalatina*. Ed. L. de Heinemann. MGH, SS, 29: 570–598.

Villehardouin, Geoffrey de. *La Conquête de Constantinople*. Ed. Edmond Faral. Les classiques de l'histoire de France au Moyen Age, 18, 19. 2nd rev. ed. Paris: Société d'Édition "Les Belles Lettres," 1961. 2 vols. Trans. M. R. B. Shaw. *The Conquest of Constantinople*. In *Chronicles of the Crusades*. Baltimore: Penguin, 1963.

Walch, Bernardin. *Chronicon*. Ed. Louis Stouff as *La Chronique de Lucelle du R.P. Bernardin Walch*. Collection d'études sur l'histoire du droit et des institutions de l'Alsace 14. Strasbourg: Heitz, 1950.

Literature

All works in the following select bibliography appear in at least two separate notes or relate directly to Gunther, the *HC*, or the Fourth Crusade.

Andrea, Alfred J. "Adam of Perseigne and the Fourth Crusade." *Cîteaux* 36 (1985): 21–37.

———. "The Anonymous Chronicler of Halberstadt's Account of the Fourth Crusade: Popular Religiosity in the Early Thirteenth Century." *Historical Reflections/Réflexions Historiques* 22 (1996): 447–477.

———. "Boethian Influence on Gunther of Paris's *Historia Constantinopolitana*." *Carmina Philosophiae* 1 (1992): 19–33.

———. "Cistercian Accounts of the Fourth Crusade: Were They Anti-Venetian?" *Analecta Cisterciensia* 41 (1985): 3–41.

———. "Conrad of Krosigk, Bishop of Halberstadt, Crusader, and Monk of Sittichenbach: His Ecclesiastical Career, 1184–1225." *Analecta Cisterciensia* 43 (1987): 11–91.

———. "The *Devastatio Constantinopolitana*, A Special Perspective on the Fourth Crusade: An Analysis, New Edition, and Translation." *Historical Reflections/Réflexions Historiques* 19 (1993): 107–149.

———. "The *Historia Constantinopolitana*: An Early Thirteenth-Century Cistercian Looks at Byzantium." *Analecta Cisterciensia* 36 (1980): 269–302.

Andrea, Alfred J. and Paul I. Rachlin. "Holy War, Holy Relics, Holy Theft: The Anonymous of Soissons's *De terra Iherosolimitana*: An Analysis, Edition, and Translation." *Historical Reflections/Réflexions Historiques* 18 (1992): 147–175.

Andrea, Alfred J. and Ilona Motsiff. "Pope Innocent III and the Diversion of the Fourth Crusade Army to Zara." *Byzantinoslavica* 33 (1972): 6–25.

Arbagi, Martin G. "Byzantium in Latin Eyes: 800–1204." Dissertation, Rutgers University, 1970.

Assmann, Erwin. "Bleibt der *Ligurinus* anonym?" *Deutsches Archiv für Erforschung des Mittelalters* 12 (1956): 453–472.

———, trans. Introduction and notes. *Die Geschichte der Eroberung von Konstantinopel*. By Gunther of Pairis. Die Geschichtsschreiber der deutschen Vorzeit, 3, 101. Cologne: Böhlau, 1956.

———, ed. Introduction and notes. *Ligurinus*. MGH, Script. rer. Germ. lxiii. Hanover: Hahn, 1987.

Bayer, Hans. "Gunther von Pairis und Gottfried von Strassburg." *Mittellateinisches Jahrbuch* 13 (1978): 140–183.

Brand, Charles M. *Byzantium Confronts the West, 1180–1204*. Cambridge, Mass.: Harvard University Press, 1968.

Brown, Elizabeth A.R. "The Cistercians in the Latin Empire of Constantinople and Greece, 1204–1276." *Traditio* 14 (1958): 63–120.

Brundage, James A. "A Transformed Angel (*X* 3.31.18): The Problem of the Crusading Monk." *Studies in Medieval Cistercian History Presented to Jeremiah F. O'Sullivan*. Ed. M. Basil Pennington. Cistercian Studies 13. Spencer, Mass.: Cistercian Publications, l97l. Pp. 55–62.

Chevre, André. *Lucelle: Histoire d'une ancienne abbaye cistercienne*. Délemont: Bibliothèque Jurassienne, 1973.

Cole, Penny J. *The Preaching of the Crusades to the Holy Land, 1095–1270*. Cambridge, Mass.: Medieval Academy of America, 1991.

Daly, William M. "Christian Fraternity, the Crusaders, and the Security of Constantinople, 1097–1204: The Precarious Survival of an Ideal." *Mediaeval Studies* 22 (1960): 43–91.

Ebels-Hoving, B. *Byzantium in Westerse Ogen, 1096–1204*. Assen, Netherlands: Van Gorcum, 1971.

Geary, Patrick J. *Furta Sacra: Thefts of Relics in the Central Middle Ages, 800–1100*. Princeton, N. J.: Princeton University Press, 1978.

Grandidier, Philippe A. *Alsatia sacra ou statistique ecclésiastique et religieuse de l'Alsace avant la Révolution avec des notes inédites de Schoepflin*. Nouvelles oeuvres inédites de Grandidier 3, 4. Ed. Augustin M. P. Ingold. Colmar: Huffel, 1899.

———. *Histoire de l'église et des évêques-princes de Strasbourg*. Oeuvres historiques inédites 3. Colmar: Georg, 1865.

———. *Vues pittoresques de l'Alsace*. Paris: 1785.

Hashagen, Justus. "Geschichtsschreibung im staufischen Elsass." *Elsass-Lothringisches Jahrbuch* 5 (1926): 33–50.

Janauschek, Leopold. *Originum Cisterciensium*. 1877; rpt. Ridgewood, N. J.: Gregg, 1964.

Jenn, Jean-Marie. "L'Abbaye cistercienne de Pairis en Alsace des origines à 1452." Dissertation. École des Chartes, 1968.

Knapp, Fritz Peter. "Gunther von Pairis." *Die deutsche Literatur des Mittelalters Verfasserlexicon*. Berlin: de Gruyter, 1978–. 3: 316–325.

Langosch, Karl. *Politische Dichtung um Friedrich Barbarossa*. Berlin: Schneider, 1943.

Leclercq, Jean. "Textes cisterciens à la Bibliothèque de Colmar." *Analecta Cisterciensia* 10 (1954): 308–314.

Madden, Thomas F. "The Fires of the Fourth Crusade in Constantinople, 1203–1204: A Damage Assessment." *Byzantinische Zeitschrift* 84/85 (1991/1992): 72–92.

———. "Outside and Inside the Fourth Crusade." *International History Review* 17 (1995): 726–743.

———. "Venice and Constantinople in 1171 and 1172: Enrico Dandolo's Attitudes Towards Byzantium." *Mediterranean Historical Review* 8 (1993): 166–185.

———. "Vows and Contracts in the Fourth Crusade: The Treaty of Zara and the Attack on Constantinople in 1204." *International History Review* 15 (1993): 441–468.

Maleczek, Walter. *Petrus Capuanus: Kardinal, Legat am Vierten Kreuzzug, Theologe (+1214)*. Vienna: Verlag der Österreichishen Akademie der Wissenschaften, 1988.

Manrique, Angel. *Cistercienses seu verius ecclesiastici annales a condito Cistercio*. Lyons: Anisson, 1649. Vol. 3.

McDonald, William C. *German Medieval Literary Patronage from Charlemagne to Maximilian I*. Amsterdamer Publikationen zur Sprache und Literatur 10. Amsterdam: Rodopi, 1973.

Müller, Wulf. *Die Siedlungs- und Flurnamen von Urbeis (Orbey) im Oberelsass*. Europäische Hochschulschriften 13, 15. Bern: Lang, 1973.

Mutterer, Maurice. "Un Document alsacien sur la quatrième croisade: La *Historia Constantinopolitana* de Gunther de Pairis." *Bulletin de la Société Industrielle de Mulhouse* 4 (1928): 433–450.

Nada Patrone, Anna Maria. *La quarta crociata e l'impero latino di Romània (1198–1261)*. Turin: Giappichelli, 1972.

Pannenborg, Albert. "Die Verse in der *Historia Constantinopolitana* und der Dichter des *Ligurinus*." *Forschungen zur deutschen Geschichte* 19 (1879): 611–624.

———. "Magister Guntherus und seine Schriften." *Forschungen zur deutschen Geschichte* 13 (1873): 225–331.

———. "Noch einmal Magister Guntherus." *Forschungen zur deutschen Geschichte* 14 (1874): 185–206.

———. "Über den *Ligurinus*." *Forschungen zur deutschen Geschichte* 11 (1871): 161–300.

———. *Der Verfasser des* Ligurinus, *Studien zu den Schriften des Magister Gunther*. Göttingen: Peppmuller, 1883.

Partner, Nancy F. *Serious Entertainments: The Writing of History in Twelfth-Century England*. Chicago: University of Chicago Press, 1977.

Prymak, Thomas M. "The Role of the Cistercian Order in the Third Crusade." M. A. Thesis, University of Manitoba, 1972.

Queller, Donald E. *The Fourth Crusade. The Conquest of Constantinople: 1201–1204*. Philadelphia: University of Pennsylvania Press, 1977.

Queller, Donald E., Thomas K. Compton, and Donald A. Campbell. "The Fourth Crusade: The Neglected Majority." *Speculum* 49 (1974): 441–465.

Queller, Donald E. and Gerald W. Day. "Some Arguments in Defense of the Venetians on the Fourth Crusade." *American Historical Review* 81 (1976): 717–737.

Queller, Donald E. and Irene B. Katele. "Attitudes towards the Venetians in the Fourth Crusade: The Western Sources." *International History Review* 4 (1982): 1–36.

Queller, Donald E. and Thomas F. Madden. *The Fourth Crusade. The Conquest of Constantinople: 1201–1204*. 2nd. ed. Philadelphia: University of Pennsylvania Press, 1996.

———."Some Further Arguments in Defense of the Venetians on the Fourth Crusade." *Byzantion* 62 (1992): 433–473.

Queller, Donald E. and Susan J. Stratton. "A Century of Controversy on the Fourth Crusade." *Studies in Medieval and Renaissance History* 6 (1969): 235–277.

Rathgeber, Jules. "L'Abbaye de Pairis dans le Val d'Orbey." *Revue d'Alsace* N.S., 3 (1874): 102–116,

Riant, Paul. "Des Dépouilles religieuses enlevées à Constantinople au XIIIe siècle, et des documents historiques nes leur transport en occident." *Mémoires de la Société Nationale des Antiquaires de France* Tôme 36, Ser. 4, tôme 6 (1875): 1–214.

———. Introduction and notes. *Exuviae sacrae Constantinopolitanae*. 2 vols. Geneva and Paris: Leroux, 1877–1878.

———. Introduction and notes. *Guntheri Alemanni . . . Historia Constantinopolitana*. By Gunther of Pairis.

Schmandt, Raymond H. "The Fourth Crusade and the Just War Theory." *Catholic Historical Review* 61 (1975): 191–221.

Stach, Walter. "Politische Dichtung im Zeitalter Friedrichs I. Der *Ligurinus* im Widerstreit mit Otto und Rahewin." *Neue Jahrbücher fur Deutsche Wissenschaft* 13 (1937): 385–410.

Stock, Brian. *Myth and Science in the Twelfth Century: A Study of Bernard Silvester*. Princeton, N. J.: Princeton University Press, 1972.

Swietek, Francis R. "Gunther of Pairis and the *Historia Constantinopolitana*." *Speculum* 53 (1978): 49–79.

Vautrey, Mgr. *Histoire des Évêques de Bâle*. Einsiedeln: Benziger, 1884. Vol. 1.

Wetherbee, Winthrop, trans. *The Cosmographia of Bernardus Silvestris*. Records of Civilization: Sources and Studies 89. New York: Columbia University Press, 1973.

Wetherbee, Winthrop. *Platonism and Poetry in the Twelfth Century: The Literary Influence of the School of Chartres*. Princeton, N. J.: Princeton University Press, 1972.

Index